D1201240

REDWOOD

WHERE MAIN STREET MEETS THE RIVER

BOOKS BY HODDING CARTER

LOWER MISSISSIPPI
THE WINDS OF FEAR
FLOOD CREST
SOUTHERN LEGACY
GULF COAST COUNTRY
(with Anthony Ragusin)
WHERE MAIN STREET MEETS THE RIVER

Where Main Street Meets the River

HODDING CARTER

NEW YORK
RINEHART & COMPANY, INC.
TORONTO

PUBLISHED SIMULTANEOUSLY IN CANADA BY
CLARKE, IRWIN & COMPANY, LTD., TORONTO

PRINTED IN THE UNITED STATES OF AMERICA

LIBRARY OF CONGRESS CATALOG CARD NUMBER: 53—6133

TO ALL THE BETTYS

With the explanation, in respect to my own,
that the repeated use of we *hereinafter is not*
editorial but only an expression of an
indivisibility of work and play and beliefs and love.

CONTENTS

WHERE MAIN STREET MEETS THE RIVER

1

First, Get Fired

The press lay in four broken, jigsaw pieces in a New Orleans junk dealer's warehouse. The junkman said that the pieces could be welded together and the press would then be as good as new and what did we expect for seventy-five dollars? Sidney Williams, who was to be foreman and half of the composing room, nodded dubious agreement. In an undertone he explained that such a press in good secondhand condition would cost anywhere from three hundred dollars up. It was an ancient job press, its bed measuring 14½ by 22 inches, which is the size of a tabloid newspaper page. He thought we could have this one patched.

I had to believe he was right, and the belief had to rest on faith alone, for on that April day in 1932 I scarcely knew a printing press from a linotype. Besides, Betty and I couldn't wait any longer. We had to prove to our families and ourselves and the man who had written the letter that the letter was wrong.

I still carried the letter in an inside coat pocket, although a month had gone by since I had received it. I had opened it on the steps of the Jackson, Mississippi, post office, and read the confirmation of dismissal for insubordination, which I had expected. But the writer, who was division manager of the Associated Press in New Orleans, had added another paragraph which hit me low in the stomach. I had some good qualities, he wrote, but I would never make a newspaperman, and I ought not to waste any time getting into another business. I had been a newspaperman all of three years, and with the

Associated Press six months when the letter came. Betty and I had been married five months.

In the same coat pocket I carried a checkbook. That day we looked at the press the checkbook showed a balance of $367.

Fourteen years later when he chose to use me as a whipping boy in his last campaign for the United States Senate, Theodore G. Bilbo used to say that the Associated Press had discharged me for stealing. Kent Cooper, the autocratic genius who directed the Associated Press, answered I had not, in fact, been discharged at all, only released for some more seasoning on daily newspapers. Bilbo was a congenital liar, Kent Cooper, a friendly interpreter of a long-ago letter of dismissal which he hadn't written. But Kent Cooper was also wrong. I had been fired, and my superior had added that I would never make a newspaperman.

His letter was the most helpful I ever received.

So I looked at the press, and nodded wisely, and gave the junkman a check for seventy-five dollars, and he and Sidney and I loaded the pieces on the farm truck I had borrowed from my father and set out for Hammond sixty miles to the north. Before we left New Orleans, we made three other stops. At the *Times Picayune*, Fred Forstall, who was the Picayune's production chief, loaded us down with an assortment of column rules, leads and slugs, advertising border, pounds upon pounds of material which Sidney had listed as vital. At the New Orleans *Item*, where I had found my first reporting job three years before at twelve fifty a week, we stopped again and carted off more loot. Then we drove to the headquarters of E. C. Palmer Company, a newsprint and printing equipment dealer, and spent about one hundred and fifty dollars more of our precious balance for some hand type and other odds and ends of essential minor equipment.

For the next few days I was carpenter, trader and head

converter of a little mimeographed, throwaway advertising sheet (of which I had not heard even a week earlier) into a tabloid daily.

My mother had told us about the throwaway when Betty and I had gone to my parents' house, angry and low in spirit after the ax had fallen. We had refugeed in Hammond instead of New Orleans because pride forbade a jobless husband to seek the shelter of his mother-in-law's roof.

So I had talked with the two young fellows who were publishing the throwaway, and we had come to an agreement to combine our talents. They had a mimeograph machine and a typewriter. I talked also to Sidney, who was a printer and, like myself and ten million other Americans, temporarily out of a job. All of us agreed that Hammond was eager for a tabloid daily newspaper, though just why we thought so I cannot remember. The town's population was only six thousand, and it was served by the long-established Hammond *Vindicator,* a weekly newspaper which, though considerably less than scrupulous in its politics, was readable and typographically excellent.

But since we wanted work, it was easy to persuade ourselves that Hammond needed a daily newspaper, and we set about producing one. We made a deal with the movie-theater manager to exchange advertising for a tiny office on the right side of the foyer. Sidney and I went to New Orleans and found the press, and after it was welded, it ran, protestingly and a little lopsidedly, at a speed of less than one thousand impressions an hour. Since its bed was large enough for only one page at a time, a thousand four-page papers required more than four hours to print, and we distributed two thousand papers from the beginning. That meant that the Hammond Daily Courier must be a morning newspaper, because we had to have all night to print it.

I brought in from my parents' home an old desk and a

kitchen table and two straight-backed chairs. We built what tables and racks we needed for the shop, which took up more than half of our twenty-foot by thirty-foot quarters. Since we didn't think we could afford a linotype, and didn't have money for a down payment anyway, we arranged to have our type set by the *Ponchatoula Enterprise*, a weekly newspaper in a smaller town five miles south of Hammond. That didn't work out. Such piece work was expensive and put too great a strain on the Ponchatoula plant which could set our type only in the late afternoon and night after which we would then have to transport the galleys of type back to Hammond, a precarious nightly operation which ended more than once with much of the type being hopelessly jumbled—pied, as the printers say, with embellishments. Within a month we had to buy a linotype after all, an ancient but well-reconditioned model, for a down payment of six hundred dollars and seemingly the rest of our lives to pay the twelve-hundred-dollar balance. We borrowed most of the down payment from a Hammond bank.

My father signed the note. And, since the *Daily Courier* could never have lasted had it not been for him—not because of the money he could procure for us, for it could not be much, but because he was Will Carter—this story in its beginning must also be his story and the story of Hammond, to which he came, not long out of Tulane University, in the first decade of the century, to settle on the land which he has never quitted.

Our family had been in that part of Louisiana long before Hammond was founded, and I am sure that some of our fellow citizens resented that which they sometimes mistook for arrogance, but which was nothing more than the assurance of belonging to a past that antedated the community's. There were older towns to the north and the east and the west of

Hammond, and below and close by was New Orleans; but Hammond, and Tangipahoa parish generally, had a frontier newness and a heterogeneous quality to its citizens that made the region unlike most of the South. Instead of cotton, its land was planted to strawberries and truck. There were no plantations, my father's three hundred odd acres being among the largest of the farms, and one of the few worked by tenants. The proportion of Negroes to white people was much less than the South's average. The white people of the town and the parish were not one-sidedly Southern in background, for the Illinois Central railroad, which was principally responsible for our growth, had joined with other land development agencies at the turn of the century to induce large numbers of farmers from the Middlewest—Yankees and some Germans and Scandinavians—to settle the country around Hammond. They were augmented later by a colony of Hungarians and by thousands of Sicilians who were brought in by other agencies, and who engaged happily and profitably in raising strawberries. Our parish lay just north of the predominantly French-speaking areas of South Louisiana, so we had our contingent of Cajuns and Creoles. Among us lived many New Orleanians, urban commuters and retired businessmen who preferred our pine forests and green, gently rolling countryside and small swift rivers and creeks to the subtropical beauty of their city. I am not sure that "cosmopolitan" is the right word for the little town, but, except for the toiling, mistrustful Sicilians whom the parish was cruelly slow to accept, no one was suspect because he was a Yankee or a Catholic or a Cajun or a squarehead. Actually, we were more inclined to be suspicious of the long-time rural Tangipahoans, for the parish had a deserved reputation for violent behavior and held too many families who had brought their feuds with them from Kentucky and Tennessee and near-by Mississippi.

My father has lived for fifty years now in that country, where his great-grandfather, a Louisiana supreme court justice, had once owned a fifty-thousand-acre hunting preserve and within it a home to which he could go with his family in the season of yellow fever. He and my mother, who is dead, and whose people had come to this region, which is called the Florida Parishes because they were once a part of Spanish West Florida, knew the parish when it was less settled than it is now, when its timberlands had not been cut away and there was good hunting anywhere a hunter sought it; I can remember, as a very small boy, how they would ride off together to hunt quail from horseback, and how there were not many weeks in the year when we didn't have game on the table. In those fifty years my father has become rich in everything but money. When there was bloodshed in the parish, which used to be often, he would be among the first whom the sheriff would summon as posseman to hunt the fugitive killer. I sat once in a barbershop, when two customers were discussing the merits of another citizen, and one of them said, clinching the argument in favor of the man, "He's as honest as Will Carter."

My father was ready with his fists, and even when he was past sixty and a member of the state legislature, he knocked down another legislator, a Long partisan, to whose remarks he had taken exception. In his time he has been police juror—a member of the parish governing board—postmaster, legislator, school-board member, director of banks and farm associations and production credit groups, one of three founders and regional trustees of Southeastern college in Hammond. He is a man whom most of his fellows like, a poker player and a fiddler and a hunter, and also a man whom some others were sometimes afraid of; I don't believe there were any decent folk who did not respect him. He and my mother had an almost idolatrous affection for my brother and sister and me, and they spoiled us and expected a great deal of us. They made our home in Hammond and, later, the home in the country, a place we wouldn't have to leave to look for fun; we had ponies and a tennis court, and a track and field area, and a completely outfitted gym above the big old carriage house; and every Friday night, after Scout meeting, my father would referee boxing matches in a lighted ring in the yard, in warm weather, and in an inside ring in the gym when it was cold. He was a powerful man, and once he saved all of us, mother and children, from drowning when we were all in swimming and my brother went down in the Tangipahoa river, and my mother pulled my sister and me along with her when she went after him. Not long ago, when he was past seventy and only recently on his feet after a major operation, his horse fell with him and pinned him down, but they both got up and he rode Silver home. I would like to write more about him.

That was the home and the town I had left when I was sixteen, the day after I had given the valedictory at my high-school graduation. The family went to Maine that summer, and I stayed there to attend college; except for vacations, I didn't come home for nearly ten years, not until I sought a haven with a new bride and no job and a letter that told me to try something else other than newspapering. And my father signed the note for six hundred dollars, and my mother fixed up a little two-room apartment at home for Betty and me, and the two of them set about dividing Hammond into the citizens who were for the *Daily Courier* and those who were against it. Whatever we have since accomplished goes back to our parents and the fierceness of their pride in us and their almost-serene conviction that we would make a go of that tiny four-page newspaper and whatever would follow it.

I am glad that it happened this way, and that our foremost debt is to Betty's mother and my mother and father. A man's first and overriding earthly loyalty is to his country, but that is an impersonal and complex concern, whereas the allegiance of the family to its individual members and the allegiance of the individual to the clan is a near and personal matter, and it is rooted especially deep in the soil of the South. I was raised to believe that whoever harmed my kinsman was also my enemy and whoever befriended him was friend of mine, and that the closer the relationship the greater the obligations and the privilege to stand near. I could not conceive of my father not making our small fight his own, nor can I imagine a time or a situation in which I would not do likewise for my sons or my brother or any relative by blood or marriage. Perhaps this is provincial, primitive, but I know of no firmer human foundation or anchor for even the most complex society than the family.

And this was especially true for two jobless young people who started their first newspaper almost in desperation, in a year of abysmal economic depression and in a place where the first American dictatorship burgeoned in fear and evil.

2

Brick and Some Others

Where Brick is now, I don't know. He would have been about the right age in 1942 for an infantry sergeant. When he came to us in Hammond out of the April night in 1932, like a cold and hungry and uncared-for lost puppy, he was about eighteen and licked. Maybe he did become a soldier, maybe he was killed, maybe his life has had since then not a sad ending nor an unending sadness, but instead something of the happiness and security that back in that April night he had long lost, if he had ever known them. That was the night Brick found us, and we discovered that he could and willingly would fold flat sheets of newsprint fast and painstakingly.

If you know anything about printing presses, large or small, you will know that it is a tedious and unusual task to print even a four-page tabloid daily newspaper on a slow-speed job press whose bed is just large enough to accommodate one tabloid-sized page. Not rolls, but flat sheets of newsprint must be used, of a size of two tabloid pages, so that, when folded, each sheet will form a four-page tabloid. These folded sheets must then be fed, one at a time, onto the bed of the job press, at a maximum speed of about 1,000 an hour; so that to print one newspaper, the sheet must be fed into the press four times by hand. Moreover, two foldings were necessary, which slowed things up. First the original blank sheets had to be folded in half, so that we could print page two and then turn over and print page three. Then, these printed sheets had to be folded so as to print page four and then page one. Our schedule called for printing page two first, since that was the editorial page and could be written fairly far ahead; next page three, the society and women's features page, because that also could be prepared early; the back or fourth page third, with a conglomerate of reports from correspondents and whatever other secondary news was available; and page one last of all, so that we could get in more important and late news right up to presstime. That presstime, in the beginning, was anywhere from two in the morning, if we were lucky, to six and seven, if things were going on as abnormally usual.

The very first night Betty and I found that folding these sheets was the most unromantic side of newspaper publishing. Nobody wanted to do it. Everybody took a try at it, and it wasn't easy to make the corners of the folded sheet come out squared with each other. If you think otherwise, try sometimes to fold by hand two thousand sheets of newsprint twice in an evening, after a fairly strenuous twelve hours of work.

It was on the second night that Brick came in out of the dark, unobtrusively sat on the floor and began working on the first folding. I thought Sidney had cajoled some acquaintance to help; Sidney must have thought that Betty or I had employed him. He just sat there, folding away, creasing the fold with a short strip of lead column rule, which we hadn't thought to do. His hair was overlong, his shirt and trousers hung dirtily and too loosely on his body, and he had a doggedly jutting jaw in a tired, thin face.

We finished the first folding about eleven o'clock and took a break and crossed the street to the Gem Café for coffee. Brick came along. Maybe somebody asked him. We ordered coffee all around, and then I happened to look at Brick, who sat a seat apart from us and was himself looking with a frighteningly hopeless intensity at a customer who was putting away a platter of ham and eggs. As I watched, the boy's lips moved as if he were trying to taste something or capture a forgotten taste, and his eyes closed and he swayed a little. I knew then that coffee wasn't what he needed, and with my own stomach taut and queasy, I moved over to him and asked in an undertone, "How about something to go with that coffee?" He looked at me and started to shake his head negatively; his eyes moistened and he whispered, "Mister, I ain't eaten since yesterday morning," and I thought again that he would faint. But he didn't and after he had eaten, wolfishly, a stew and milk and some pie, we loitered behind the others, and he told me almost all that I ever knew about him. He was the son of an Arkansas tenant farmer, and he had gone through a year of high school. After that, an occasional job in town—and then his father had been flooded out in the big 1927 overflows and everything had closed down and he had gone on the road. Two nights before he had dropped off a slow freight, slept in an outbuilding on the edge of town, and had started looking for work. He hadn't found any. He had come into our tiny office because there were people in it, busy at something, and he had figured maybe he could help out a quarter's worth or so.

Brick slept that night on a pile of paper, on the bottom shelf of the stock cabinet Sidney and I had built, not knowing then that we were making them just the right length and width for a hungry boy who would come in out of the dark. The next morning we brought him a huge breakfast on a covered plate and a thermos of coffee. We brought him also a bundle of clean shirts and socks and underwear and a pair of trousers that I had outgrown, and a canvas army folding cot that had been gathering dust in the family attic. We had no job for him, we explained, nor would we likely have one for many months if ever; but if he would like to sleep in the office and fold papers at night, we would bring him his meals, and he could look around for work or do what he wanted in the daytime, and we would try to keep him in pocket change.

Brick stayed with us more than a year. After we moved to a larger building, he had better quarters, a little partitioned-off corner in the shop, and a lavatory. He kept himself amazingly clean. I found more clothes, including an almost-new suit—it was lucky for him that I kept gaining weight under the fifteen hour shift instead of losing—and he served as handyman, janitor and apprentice, and made a few dollars a week and began to learn printing. Then, one day, he collected a few dollars over the counter and didn't tell us about it, and when we found out I asked him why he had done it, and told him I was disappointed, but to forget it. He cried, and left me a note the next morning that began "this is very embarison to me and I am sorry" and ended up with "goodby, Brick." He must have taken a freight out of town.

He was just one waif, and luckier than most of the youngsters whom we could see in the box cars and flatcars of the Illinois Central freight trains that trembled north and south through Hammond. Luckier in more ways than one, for our two policemen weren't easy on kids whom they caught dropping off a freight at night. It was simpler to keep them moving than to bother with them, and the best way to let them know they weren't wanted was to face them in the direction they were to go, rap them smartly over the head with a billy and growl "get going."

Sometimes we were feeding more strays than just Brick. One day we heard that a whole family had been found camping in a shut-down box factory, stranded with their Model-T Ford, and unable to find enough work picking berries to make a living; one of them had just had a baby. They numbered two middle-aged parents, their married daughter and her husband, and two younger children; and surely John Steinbeck must somewhere have seen them before he wrote of the Okies of the West. A doctor had come, and the Red Cross was helping. We published a story under a two-column head, "The Madonna of the Box Factory"; and Hammond adopted the family for the time being with that spontaneous small-town generosity that I have witnessed hundreds of times; and the family was better off than in many a month. Then my Dad, who like the rest of the farmers was losing everything on his strawberries, too, but who was in a better position to lose, said that he would let them live on our place as tenants, and furnish them until the next year. They stayed on for ten years, maybe more, and they are farming for themselves now; the last I heard, the boxcar baby herself was getting ready for marriage to a boy with a home and a farm of his own, which makes a nice ending.

But there weren't so many nice endings. Had we waited another month to begin our newspaper, we would not have gone into newspaper publishing at all. Only an idiot would have. For some reason, the depression had scarcely affected the strawberry crop prices in 1931. The crop had been bountiful, the prices good. But by mid-May of 1932, we all knew that disaster had struck the strawberry belt. A crate of berries was not bringing what the crates themselves cost, even though the box-factory workers who turned them out were not averaging eight dollars a week. We had no other industry in a little city whose prosperity depended upon what the fruit and truck and dairy farmers of Tangipahoa parish received for their produce.

That spring and summer, farmers in our parish and elsewhere in Louisiana and the South and all through the nation began to stand in line for Red Cross flour, and sometimes to riot and break into foodstores; but only infrequently did they kill themselves, as did other and better-off Americans in the cities, though once on the outskirts of Hammond, a highway policeman came across a Tennessee farm couple, in their old car, horribly dead from carbon monoxide poisoning; and beside their swollen bodies, all toil ended, was a note, evidently scribbled in pencil just before they pushed the tubing from the exhaust through the floorboard: *"It isn't no use, we have lost our farm, and we have just two dollars, and we're going to put this last gas to good use . . ."*

That summer and fall, the clamor of national politics seemed far away and unrelated to poverty and despair, except that men hated the word "Republican" and the name "Hoover," since it is as easy as it is unjust to simplify the causes of calamity. But after Chicago, something hopeful stirred, at first lazily, in the air, because a man named Roosevelt was speaking brave words and making strong promises, and even we responded who misdoubted him because Huey Long's contested delegation had been so largely responsible for his nomination, and said when we Democrats come in, things will be different.

But that spring and summer and fall and early winter were no different from each other, save as to the weather, in our beaten little town. Actually, we on the *Daily Courier* were too busy and too harassed and too young to take time out for bewailing our lot. I wrote optimistic editorials about the future, alternately with intemperate, angry denunciations of Long and, so I thought, worldly, wise editorials about the state of the nation and the world and the new menace of a man named Hitler, and how unfair it was that a Hammond girl hadn't been selected Miss Louisiana. And the Red Cross continued to help the farmers as much as they could, and soup kitchens began opening up everywhere, and the banks took land they didn't want, and the owners of the *Daily Courier* learned how to barter.

I almost disbelieve today what I know we practiced then as a matter of course and survival. We swapped movie advertising for office space. We swapped what must have been crude letterheads and other printing for a motor which powered the one press that printed the letterheads and the newspaper and anything else that was not too big for the press bed. We framed the first dollar we took in the first day. It was paid for some sheets of colored cardboard. We hung the dollar over my desk. The next day it was stolen. We announced proudly in the second day's edition that we had received our first commercial printing order. We never collected for it. A strawberry broker, a Midwesterner with a bad temper and no manners, gave us our second printing order. It wasn't ready the following day when he called, and he began cursing in the office, so I caught him by the collar and pushed him out, and we never got paid for that one either.

And when we were paid, it was only infrequently in coin of the realm. We swapped advertising for groceries, for drugs, for what clothing we needed, including a blue sailor-type dress concerning which Betty wrote rapturously to her mother: "It's very practical and really a bargain at ninety-eight cents." We needed cash only to pay Sidney and Wallace and Bill the minimum they required in addition to what necessities they themselves could swap out with advertisers. We swapped circulation for anything edible, and used farm produce in turn as a medium of local exchange. We swapped advertising of Dr. Miles's patent remedies for minor printing equipment. An enterprising Missourian opened up a small cannery, taking his pay in kind, and selling or hoping to sell the tithed canned goods to the public. Since he needed labels for his cans, and an irreducible minimum of advertising, we effected a deal for dozens of cans of assorted foodstuffs, of which I best remember pears, string beans, chili, Hungarian goulash, tomatoes and peas, which filled our shelves and left us in a quandary when the labels, being of inferior sticking quality, peeled off so that we never knew what we'd be eating until we opened a can. We swapped for gasoline, and eventually for automobiles, and in time some national advertisers, who came later, even offered such swaps as razor blades, of which we took fifty thousand and gave them away for Christmas for years. The chain stores were our principal cash customers, and we loved them, for their dollars meant newsprint, which was C.O.D., and printing supplies. Every day Betty would take to the streets, making the rounds of the merchants in competition with Mildred Campbell, the pretty, brunette daughter of the weekly *Vindicator's* publisher, and in the afternoons we'd tally her sales under swap and cash categories. We had one tremendous advantage in those dismal first months. We didn't have to worry about eating or a place to sleep, because we were living in the country with my parents, and they wouldn't have thought of our paying anything. They were also busy in the paper's behalf, my mother, sick and only two years from death, making us believe that ours was the finest newspaper in all America, inevitably successful, and my dad, counting his friends and his enemies on the basis of their support or non-support of the *Daily Courier*.

It was a wondrous, heart-warming, heartbreaking, impossible year, that year of 1932. But by swap and sweat, before its end we had moved into a pretty cottage in town, and were on our own again. The stove we used was an oil-burning discard from Tate and Cable Young, whose Episcopal parishioners had presented them with a new gas stove; and our icebox was new but not electric, purchased in response to a special offer from the Hammond Ice and Coal Company, which for five dollars a month not only sold the icebox but kept it supplied with ice for the twenty months of time payments. But there was honeysuckle and wisteria across our porch, and an open fireplace in each room, and in the fragrant yard bloomed crape myrtle and jasmine, and our living room was bright and perhaps even a little important looking, what with the Napoleon desk on which we had squandered all of one hundred and fifty dollars of wedding present-money that we later wished we had held on to. And only a few miles away was Chappapela Creek, cold and swift and green, with a sandy beach, where two newspaper publishers could forget for a while each afternoon everything but the fun they were having.

Not even 1932 could really be bad, not when our friends were just as poor and just as young and just as defiant of pessimism as we were. In November, somewhat suspiciously, we all voted for the New Yorker, Roosevelt, and later we heard him say words which Americans must always believe. "The only thing we have to fear is fear itself," he said, and I remember that Betty and I talked about those words and said to each other that they were true. Weren't we approaching the end of our first year as publishers, and had we not only kept our heads above water but bought some more equipment including a press that was bigger and faster, a flat-bed that could take full sheets and eliminate hand folding? Had we not been able to borrow six hundred dollars from the bank for a down payment on a linotype which we were paying back, without too much difficulty, at fifty dollars a month? And, miracle of miracles, had not those distant workers of magic, our national advertising representatives, already obtained several national schedules for us and promises of cigarette advertising to come? And, did we not have on deposit a balance that had begun to remain constant at several hundred dollars? Now, the Democrats were bound to make things even better.

And then, almost the knockout punch. On March 6, 1933, which was a Monday, the new President of the United States closed the nation's banks, which for the most part indubitably would have been shortly closed by panic and runs anyway. Most of our banks in Tangipahoa parish were shaky, the one in which we kept our little deposits no less so than the others, though no one knew just how bad they were except a few, including the president of another of our banks, who tactfully withdrew fifty thousand dollars from his bank just before it closed. We editorially criticized him, but that only served to cut us off from whatever advertising he controlled, and he kept his fifty thousand, and I suspect he still has it.

Anyway, on Monday I somehow had a five-dollar bill in my pocket, and that was all. We knew by then that we wouldn't be getting much on the dollar when the banks did open again. We had no credit with any supply house, nor did we yet deserve any. And by Saturday there was the matter of a payroll, about one hundred dollars not counting anything for ourselves, and one hundred dollars was no small matter then; and ahead lay rent and the need for more newsprint and the other irreducible demands that only actual money could answer, and there wasn't any money, and our world was suddenly going to the dogs. So Betty and I shrugged and summoned up smiles, saying that this was probably the end, though inside we just didn't believe it, and why not drive to New Orleans for the weekend, spend the five dollars on fun, and start worrying again Monday? We told the men that there wasn't any cash, and asked them what would they like in grocery tradeouts. When they had named their imperative needs, and we had written out orders on the merchants who advertised with us and owed us, we drove on Friday afternoon to the nearest filling station which advertised, filled up on credit, and started for near-by New Orleans, not too happy about what we'd be facing on Monday.

It was dusk when we reached the outskirts of New Orleans. We took a short cut from the highway to Carrollton Avenue, as we always did, and on the way drove past some buildings that we hadn't thought much about before. They were two of the big gambling casinos that bordered New Orleans, just over the parish lines, and we were passing the second one when I thought to myself: one dice table, one five-dollar bill, one chance in five or ten or a hundred, and why not? I said to Betty, this five dollars won't make us and it won't break us, so let's come back to Old Southport after dinner at your mother's and see what I can do. I wasn't too confident, because rolling dice never has been my game; but after dinner we drove back to Old Southport, and sure enough, everyone else in New Orleans with any cash at all had the same idea. There were two kinds of dice tables at Southport, the poor folks' tables where a bettor could play for as little as a quarter, and the big tables where a dollar was the scorned minimum and the house would gladly cover bets all the way to a thousand dollars, and, I suppose, ten times that amount. I wanted to get it over with as soon as possible, and the two-bit table couldn't do us any good anyway, so I told Betty to go watch the roulette wheel because if she watched me, I knew she'd make me play as safe as dice can be played, which isn't very safe. After I squeezed my way to a place at one of the big tables, I tossed my five-dollar bill at the croupier and got five blue chips and a pitying look. I gave a leer that meant you-don't-know-it-bud-but-there's-a-lot-more-where-this-came-from, and, studying the next player, who was fat and seemingly indifferent to what fate had in store, I put two chips on the line. He won and I let the winnings ride, and he won again and again and again; and so did I when it came my roll; and to shorten a story that has a happy if unmoral ending, Betty and I walked out of Old Southport an hour later with almost four hundred dollars in crisp bills, and both of us so delighted that I wasn't even upset about the last hundred that I'd bet and then rolled snake-eyes.

We hadn't had four hundred dollars cash when we started the *Daily Courier*, so we knew there wouldn't be any trouble keeping it going with four hundred. Once again we were sure of ourselves and the world. And to make the evening completely perfect, Betty had her Idea just after we left Old Southport.

The four hundred, she said, would keep us in newsprint, a few reams at a time, and give us whatever other cash we would need until the banks opened and life settled down to the usual unusual again. But why not systematize, at least during the banking crisis, the haphazard swapping that we carried on with advertisers? Why not issue script this very next week, she asked, good with each of our advertisers who wanted it that way, up to the amount of money they owed us for advertising? The advertisers ought to like it, because they could square their accounts in goods, on which they would be making a retail profit. Our printers wouldn't mind taking most of their pay in script if we gave it to them at a discount and made up as much of the rest as we thought advisable from the four hundred dollars in my pocket.

By the time we'd returned to her mother's home, we had our script issue planned even to the wording and art work. Each bill would be labeled "Daily Courier Co-operative Script," and on it would be a picture of President Roosevelt with the slogan Betty thought up: "We bank on him." We would have some cheery little message on the other side, and the name of each participating merchant would appear on script up to the amount he owed us.

That was the turning point in the life of the *Daily Courier*. When our banks finally reopened, paying from five to twenty per cent on the dollar, we were in fairly good shape. Our merchants had squared most of their accounts, we were only a little behind in our payroll, we still had some Southport cash left. And while I am as much against organized gambling and sin in general as is Senator Estes Kefauver, I am glad that he didn't invade Louisiana twenty years earlier.

Most of us think in terms of anniversaries, and usually in multiples of five. During this spring and summer of 1952, as I write of events of twenty years ago, consequential only to ourselves, we have observed three anniversaries.

One is the twenty-fifth anniversary of the great Mississippi River flood of 1927, which left Greenville and so much of the lower valley in watery ruin and drove Brick's tenant father from yet another profitless farm. The second is our twentieth anniversary, Betty's and mine, of that night in the depths of the great depression when we labored so bewilderedly and our mouse of a paper nearly died a-borning. And the third is the first anniversary of the reopening of the Greenville Air Base, where young Americans and some of the chosen young of free Europe are once again learning to do battle in the skies. Each of these anniversaries is meaningful, and all are related to each other and to themselves and to that half-forgotten boy who crawled sleepless and hungry into the light of our newspaper office long ago.

Anniversary of flood. . . .

One distinction sets that flood of 1927 apart, aside from its magnitude, from other floods that have followed in the twenty-five years since the levees burst above Greenville. In 1927 there was no federal aid for the stricken, and the Congress of the United States had not yet admitted that the nation should be collectively responsible for flood control. Not until the lower Mississippi valley lay beneath the flood waters which poured upon it from two thirds of the United States, did America finally recognize the moral right and the economic necessity for collective action against natural catastrophe. And so, out of an angry river's pillaging has come a national sense of responsibility for the victims of nature.

Anniversary of a tiny newspaper born in the worst days of depression.

Out of the broken heads, the tired, blistered feet, the bread lines, the homeless boys and girls, and the hopelessness of that spring of 1932, which was this nation's peacetime worst —a time when boys named Brick could and did go hungry and starve or steal and often sweat in a stinking jail—have come the programs for collective action against economic disaster. Bank-deposit guarantees, so that the small people will not see their scant all vanish while only a few lucky ones like me roll sevens in a gambling casino and keep going. Wage and hour laws . . . social security . . . unemployment benefits . . . child-labor restrictions . . . and so on and on, so that I could smile in 1948, when as a fellow reporter at the Republican convention, I met Norman Thomas and heard him say, only half jestingly, that both parties had stolen all his Socialist thunder, since every plank in his berated platform of 1924 had either become part of the law of the land or was being espoused that summer by both major parties.

Anniversary of an airfield's reopening. . . .

As part of our Greenville celebration, the Base's six hundred cadets marched in review before the visiting generals and the applauding townspeople. And of the six hundred, more than one hundred were Belgians, Danes, Norwegians, French, Netherlanders, the lads of the nations of the Atlantic Pact, young foreigners marching in a Mississippi cotton town. Again collective action, and this time for the security of free men. Out of the hideousness of war, and the worse threat of a new dark age of Communism, has come the collective purposefulness of the Atlantic Pact and the yet imperfect NATO and the persistent, troubled dream of the United Nations.

And all this in twenty years, in the twenty years since Brick sidled in out of the April night, Brick whose tenant father had been ruined by nature's flood, who had himself been bruised perhaps beyond repair by economic disaster, and who, for all I know, may have fought and fallen in that war from which, if we have learned anything, we have learned that free men can survive and conquer only by marching together.

3

Tangipahoa Was Bloody

One afternoon, not long before our first son was born, Betty made a date with a friend to go to the movies that night. The same afternoon a vengeful man unwittingly set a date with death, and it was only because a stray bullet missed Betty by an inch or two that she did not join this stranger in his appointment, though he would have been most apologetic, had he lived, to learn that one of the bullets which he fired had come so close to her.

But it is better to start at the beginning so that you will understand something about the "parish"—Louisianian for "county"—named Tangipahoa, which everybody then called (and sometimes proudly) Bloody Tangipahoa, a place where sudden and violent death bore a familiar visage. Our newspaper had the distinction of chronicling more homicides and fewer resultant convictions in our parish during our four years in Hammond than were recorded by the newspapers in New Orleans with more than ten times our parish population.

About a year and a half before we came to Hammond to publish the *Courier*, a young and popular dentist, then unmarried, had been lured one night to the adjoining rural parish, known boastfully as the Free State of Livingston, there to be tarred and feathered by a band of brothers who afterward dumped him on Hammond's main street with the order to leave town by the next day. The brothers, led by the oldest, a brawler with a local reputation as a dangerous man when drinking, had mistreated their victim because they suspected him of more than professional attentions to the oldest brother's wife. None of his friends, I among them, believed a word of it.

Dr. Newsom, the dentist, was courageous. He took to wearing a gun under his coat, let it be known that he wasn't moving, and began criminal and civil-court action against the brothers. Our town and parish were with him, but the tarring and feathering case was tried in Livingston parish, since that was where the offense was committed. Livingston parish was loyal to its own, and the brothers, who never denied the crime, and were, in fact, pleased with themselves, went scot-free after pleading the unwritten law. But the dentist was persistent, and in a subsequent civil trial in district court won a verdict granting him civil damages. The Starnses were not rednecks or poor whites, but substantial farm owners and longtime settlers, and their father, himself a proud and hot-tempered old man, owned a thriving furniture business in Hammond.

We had been publishing the *Courier* about a year when the dentist won his civil suit. We printed the account in detail, on the front page, with a background story of the tarring and feathering, and I wrote an accompanying editorial applauding the justice of the civil verdict. As far as I was concerned, and as far as any newspaperman would be concerned, it was simply the obvious and routine treatment of a good story.

The Starns family thought otherwise. The day the story

and editorial appeared, the father telephoned me and said he wanted to see me because neither he nor his family liked what I had written. He was at his store. I told him I'd be right over. I was a little nervous when I went in because several members of the family were present, and the old man asked me why I had to print anything at all about the case. I started to explain, but he didn't want to listen. Instead he said, "The Starnses have been living in these parts a long time, and we don't like what you wrote. Understand? We don't like it."

I was frightened, but I was also angry and young. I answered, trying my best to sound like a feuding Tangipahoan, "I'm sorry you don't like it. But my folks have been around here just as long as you all have, and there are just about as many of us as of you," which was an overoptimistic calculation. I walked away as slowly as I could, wondering whether there was another pot of tar cooking in the back yard. But nothing happened, and I heard later that the old man was amused at me when he thought things over. He also continued to advertise now and then.

But if the Starnses were forgiving toward me, they still hated the young dentist whom they hadn't forced to leave town and who had even won a damage suit against them. Nothing happened for another year and a half although stories circulated from time to time that the Starnses were still planning to run the dentist out of town or kill him. He kept wearing a gun in a shoulder holster.

Then came the afternoon when Betty and her friend planned to see a movie, and Ike Starns and his father drank themselves to a decision that it was time for a showdown with the dentist. The two of them drove into Hammond, found him in the Central Drug Store, and told him that they'd be back at seven that night, and if he wasn't out of town they'd kill him. Several people in the drugstore heard them, and heard the dentist answer that he'd still be here when they came back.

Sedgie didn't tell the police, but someone else did. Hammond's police force consisted of a city manager, who was ex-officio chief of police, but who had been a businessman and knew nothing about guns or law-enforcement tactics; a night marshal and a day officer. Just before seven o'clock, this force deployed in the vicinity of the drugstore which stood on a corner of the principal street. They tried to make the dentist take cover, but he wouldn't. Instead he waited next to the drugstore in the stair doorway of the building he owned and in which, on the second floor, he had his dental offices. Bert Hyde, our lone reporter, had heard that trouble was brewing, and with some other curious and foolhardy souls, he was loitering in front of the drugstore. I didn't know anything about the incident, having been busy at home, and when the Starnses came back, I had just returned to the office, a half-block from the drugstore on a side street. I had left Betty and her friend at a parking place convenient to the theater and only a few feet from the drugstore.

The two of them had just reached the drugstore when the Starnses—father, son and mother—drove up. Ike Starns stopped the automobile in the middle of the street just in front of the drugstore. The son wrestled free of his mother—who had forced herself into the car as the pair left home, trying to dissuade them—and jumped out, shooting, as the policemen closed in. The elder Starns had climbed out of the right side of the car with a buckshot-loaded shotgun, but before he could level it, one policeman and the city manager reached him and grappled with him. The night marshal and Ike Starns fired at each other at almost point-blank range, but Ike's last shot missed, as had the first five which he had directed at the dentist. The policeman didn't miss.

I heard the shots and ran from the office toward the drugstore. In the street, almost in front of me, two officers were clubbing the father into submission. The third was gingerly approaching the dead Ike Starns, who was lying on his back by the curbstone with his empty pistol clutched in a stiffening hand. The dentist stood in his doorway. He had not drawn his gun. And across the street from me, peering from the side wall of the drugstore, was my city-bred, pregnant and unperturbed wife. I ran across the street, stopping first to look more closely at Ike Starns. The officer said, "I think he's dead, but you'd better be careful." But he was dead, and I ran toward Betty, calling angrily, "What are you looking at him for?"

Betty said, "I thought we ought to have an eyewitness story," and then, "one of those bullets just missed my tummy." She pointed to a hole in the drugstore show window. "I was over there." She felt all right, she assured me, and off she and her friend went.

The street and sidewalks began filling up again. I walked over to the dentist to get his story, and the officer who had killed Ike Starns came up and said, "Doc, I never killed a man before"—he had been a well-liked barber before he turned police officer—"I need a drink, bad." Sedgie asked me, "How about you?" I nodded and the three of us went upstairs to his offices where we each had a drink. I looked down on the street below where Ike Starns's body lay in the gutter awaiting the perfunctory verdict of a coroner's jury. People milled around the body, and other people were acting as self-appointed traffic directors, trying to unsnarl the traffic. Sedgie and the policeman gave me their accounts of what had happened, and I shook hands with them and told Sedgie he was what I would call a man, and walked downstairs and back to the office to telephone the story to the *Times-Picayune* in New Orleans in time for their bulldog edition. I was the *T-P's* correspondent. Betty was in the office, having changed her mind about going to a movie, as I thought she would, and halfway through her own story, she began to cry. She said, "There's too much of this going on." I patted her and said, "Bloody Tangipahoa," and took her home. Elsie, our cook, predicted that the imminent Hodding Third—we *knew* the baby would be a boy—would likely have a pistol-shaped birthmark, but when he came, he didn't. Betty said it was lucky her time wasn't up the week of the gunfight, because she'd have been bigger by two inches anyway, and little Hodding would have been hit.

Betty's comment that too much of that sort of thing went on in Tangipahoa parish was an understatement. Tangipahoa was still a violent country twenty years ago, its gunreadiness a hereditary compound of old feuds among the Kentucky and Tennessee families which had settled along the river bottoms, political enmities, racial conflicts and the tempers of a rural people who for generations had been their own policemen and personal avengers of insult. Undeniably, the people of the deep South, the rural South, are more inclined to violent retaliation than are our Northern brothers, and more disinclined to punish a killer unless he also steals when he kills. My own parish had a special reputation for bloodletting, not an enviable one, but well-earned.

In the four years we lived in Hammond I saw two white men shot to death on the streets, and I came upon three others within minutes after they were slain. One of these men, a Greek secondhand dealer in anything he could dispose of, had sold me only the day before several unopened boxes of books for forty dollars—we were running a lending library and bookshop for a while in the *Courier* office—and I had not paid him that next night when a young married man shot him to death, without warning, in front of his store. Again, the unwritten law and no indictment. Another man, an ex-convict and a member of one of the old feud families, was killed by a Hammond policeman as he sat in his automobile after creating a disturbance in the Negro section. I was in a car just behind them, for Bert and I had heard that there would be trouble, and we could see the orange spurts of the .45. This was the first time I had smelled the hot, sweet stench of the new and violently dead; and years afterwards in Africa, when I smelled again that odor, not of the one dead but of the many, I thought first of the dark, mean side street in Hammond, Louisiana, and of a backwoods badman slumped over a steering wheel with his bloody khaki shirt torn by six pistol slugs.

The policeman was a member of a family with whom the disturber's people had feuded, but he couldn't be discharged for this and other examples of overzealousness because Long had put every local police officer under "civil service" which made them loyal and untouchable. A year or so later this policeman survived a foolish, grimly laughable gesture of his own when he handed his pistol to a drinking companion whom he had gun-whipped, and dared him to shoot. His friend shot him through the stomach, but he recovered, quit his police job and settled down to farming again with four or five notches in his gun and, I hope, a prayer in his heart.

We started out as friends. He had accompanied us, guns on his hips, when my father, some friends and I went to a Long meeting at which Gerald L. K. Smith had promised to tell how I'd been run out of Mississippi like a hound-dog. Gerald didn't tell that story, in spite of the state police and plainclothesmen around him because my father and his friends and maybe I myself meant business. During that tense meeting, which was held outdoors in conjunction with an

Italian-American religious fiesta, someone shot off a fire-cracker. Gerald, who had reason to be afraid, spread-eagled his arms and shouted, "They crucified Jesus Christ and now they're killing me." That broke the spell and nobody was hurt, and nobody's reputation either, which was what we had come to protect.

When this policeman switched to Long—which he had to do to keep his job—and began using his pistol and his power promiscuously, I wrote an unfavorable editorial about him. I was told afterwards that he decided to teach me a lesson, though I doubt that he would have shot me, only beaten me with his gun or billy. Anyway, he started for our office. He was dissuaded by a young Italian, a Long man, friendly to us, who was a state highway patrolman. He talked the chief out of bothering me, as he expressed it. A few days later I went into a barroom-grocery two doors from the *Courier* office to buy cigarettes. The chief was drinking at the bar and he beckoned to me. I went over and he asked me if I knew the right way to handle a gun when I wanted to hit a man without killing him. I said no. He said, "Don't never hold it by the barrel, hold it by the butt and make a sidewise slap with it." As he gave the instructions, he pulled out one of his two revolvers and raised it in demonstration. He brought the pistol down slowly toward my head, grinning at me, and just barely touched my forehead with the side of the butt. "That's the way," he said. "It's a good thing to know," I said, and that was that.

We always kept a pistol in the office, and in our automobile when we went out nights, for in one way or another the *Courier* angered a lot of people, and now and then I would get anonymous threatening letters or telephone calls from deluded people to whom Huey Long was a saint and his Share the Wealth clubs the Lord's chosen instrument for the distribution of manna in the twentieth century. Twice our baby was threatened with kidnaping. But only once did I have to make an individual show of force, and that wasn't because of political differences, but only because we printed a story that we had been warned not to print.

It wasn't much of a story. A young Hammond man I had known almost all my life, who had a robbery term behind him, had knifed a grocery-store manager at a public dance. The next morning we began getting the story. A little later in the day, another of the town's characters, also a former short-term convict, whom I remembered from grammar school, came into the office. We had always been friendly, a fact of which he reminded me. He said, "Jake don't want a story about that cutting in the paper. He says that if it goes in there'll be another cutting in town."

I pulled open my desk drawer and took out the .38. I said, "Ed, you tell Jake that his story is going to be in tomorrow's paper. If he walks through that door or gets within ten feet of me, I'll use this gun." Ed said he'd tell him, and he must have, because the story appeared and Jake didn't.

I'm not sure that I'm proud of that incident. Never before had I threatened to kill anyone. Today, I suppose, I would notify the police. But the police in Hammond were something else again, and what was pertinent then was a man's personal reaction to attempted intimidation. I do know that if the knifer had come into my office, or approached me on the street for the week or so I packed a gun, I would have shot him. I'm glad I had only to threaten.

A few years later, after we had moved to Mississippi, I chanced to meet him at a filling station near New Orleans where we had stopped for gas on a Sugar Bowl visit. He must have been a passenger on the bus that had also stopped, and he recognized me and came over, but all he said was that he never had believed I had treated him right about the cutting story. We talked mostly of nothing until the bus driver summoned his passengers.

Betty and I grew sick of killings. Once I was made foreman of a jury which tried a middle-aged man who had killed an innocent man and maimed two others when he shot into a group of young fellows who had been teasing him. He was charged only with manslaughter, an offense for which a man can be convicted or freed in Louisiana by a nine to three vote; and the jury by just that vote turned him loose on the first ballot after an elderly farmer opined that "Joe wouldn't have been much of a man if he hadn't fired on them boys."

Later, when there had been five or six killings in the parish in less than a month, I irritated our Chamber of Commerce with a front page editorial, a mock letter to the Winchester people. In it I suggested Hammond as the most logical of all sites for a small-arms-and-ammunition factory, because we could guarantee that our local population alone would use up all the shot and shell they could turn out.

We were afraid many times. But the one time when Betty and I believed we were in complete and mortal danger, we were actually as safe as if we had been in the headquarters of the Salvation Army.

We were alone in the office one noontime, the two of us, when a young, husky, wild-eyed man, dressed in khaki and laced boots, and wearing a thick, red beard, stalked into the office and asked for the editor. I identified myself from the interior side of the counter against which he leaned.

"You are, are you?" he roared. "Then you're the fellow who killed me." At that he thrust a hand down his shirt front.

"Here's the gun you killed me with." He pulled out what may have been just an ordinary .45, though it looked like a howitzer. With his other hand he tugged at his shirt, pulled it back from his throat, and said, "Look, here, right here is where the bullet went in. Do you see the hole?"

I managed to say "N-o-o, I don't," remembering to press my hands hard on the counter so that they wouldn't seem to tremble, and remembering too not to lower them, for that might give him a chance to say later that I had reached for a weapon. He looked like a maniac, and there wasn't anything to do about a maniac but pray, because he was too close for us to run. Betty began in a falsetto, soothingly, "My husband, of course, my husband didn't kill——" and the redbeard threw back his head and began laughing.

"Of course he didn't," he said. "But your paper killed me. Look here." From a shirt pocket he dragged a column torn from the *Courier* and handed it to me. I read, and remembered the story. A trapper in Pass Manchac, sixteen miles south, had shot another trapper through the heart with a .45 as the man came at him in a pirogue with rifle blazing. The postmaster at the Pass, who was our correspondent, had telephoned the story a few days before.

"You got your names mixed," the redbeard said. "You got me as the dead man and gave the skunk I killed the credit for doing the killing. The grand jury just met and didn't indict me—it was self-defense, mister—and I just came up to get a correction. Just thought I'd scare you a little. One shot. I got him right through the heart with this baby here." He fondled his pistol.

"Swell," I said. "Swell. I'm mighty glad you came clean. We'll get that correction in tomorrow."

We did. I think it's worth reprinting, in its front-page entirety:

CORRECTION ON A KILLING

The *Daily Courier* takes pleasure in announcing that it killed the wrong man in a story from Pass Manchac last Thursday in which it was reported that Joe Doe shot and killed Richard Roe when the latter began shooting at him with a rifle.

We are happy to say that it was Mr. Doe who was killed and Mr. Roe who did the killing, with one remarkable shot with a .45 at about sixty feet, hitting his assailant right in the heart. We congratulate Mr. Roe on his marksmanship and hope that he will not be called upon to demonstrate it again.

I thought about that story many summers later when I read in the Camden (Maine) *Herald* a card of thanks from up in the North country. It said:

We wish to thank the forest rangers, our good friends and neighbors and all the others who so kindly assisted us when our dear mother was shot for a bear.

It would seem that deadly mistakes, journalistic and otherwise, can happen anywhere.

Tangipahoa parish isn't like that any more. Civilization is overtaking the river-bottom frontiers: movies, radios, paved roads, near cities, prosperity and time are assuaging the blood grievances. The policemen wear uniforms now and go to police academies and sometimes to the FBI school in Washington; and there are better equalizers than the gun. . . .

In the late spring of 1952, I went to Hammond for a glad event. Little Southeastern College had asked me to give the Commencement address; and so, on a June morning I stood in cap and gown on an arboreal stage on the pine-thick campus where once I had ridden my pony and camped and fished. Nearly thirty years before, my father, who was then a school-board member, together with another board member and the principal of the high school, had founded Southeastern as Hammond Junior College. Its first classrooms, for the original enrollment of nineteen students, were some unused rooms in the then new Hammond high-school building. Through the years the college had grown to a four-year state college with more than a thousand students.

What I said was not memorable. What was eventful to me was the roll call of the graduates. Among them were Sicilian Americans, whose fathers and grandfathers had brought to our country the memory and the reality of the vendetta and the Mafia's vengeance. Among them too were the old Scot-Irish and English names, the names of the feudists who had carried their blood-anger with them from the Appalachians and the Smokies, the names of the tall men who in my father's young manhood and even in my own boyhood had shot each other off their horses, laid in wait by the forest footpaths, and carried their hates through the bloodstained generations. I must have recognized at least twenty such names among those graduates, the children of feudists and fighters and Old World refugees now passing before me in cap and gown, extending their hands for their diplomas and smiling and saying "thank you."

Afterwards, at the noontime reception, when the lines of parents, so many of them the river-bottom people, had passed, I fell into conversation with one of the graduates whose forebears in bloody Tangipahoa had held the ready rifle as their one true friend. I asked him what he was going to do now. He said: "I want to go on to graduate work in sociology. We've still got a lot to do in old Tangipahoa parish." A lot to do, he said, and I know he was right. But so much had been done, even in his short lifetime; so much that I, remembering, feel old and a relic.

4

So Bert and Alsia Got Married

Bert Hyde was a rawboned, hefty, six-foot-one home-town boy, and still growing at nineteen when he became in the summer of 1932 the entire reportorial staff of the *Daily Courier,* with side lines of duty which included what bookkeeping we needed and occasional selling of advertising and a little press feeding now and then. He was, at the time, in his senior year in Hammond High School, and he was the oldest student in his class, for he had quit school at intervals to help support his widowed mother and a younger sister. He had worked in drugstores, in garages, in butchershops, and as a grocer's deliveryman, in which capacity he came to know the insides of the kitchens and, more helpful to his reportorial career, the kitchen gossip in just about every home in Hammond.

Bert backed into reporting during those first desperate months when we were finding it difficult to fill even four tabloid pages with news stories and advertisements. Betty was trying to sell all the advertising and write the social items. I was reporting, writing editorials, making up the paper and taking my turn feeding the press. We employed two full-time printers and one part-time helper. Bert's first contributions came in unsigned, under a heading "The Low Down," and they were breezy, and occasionally questionable paragraphs, which we culled only a little and put into the paper without the least regard for that dictum of journalism which says properly that a newspaper must not accept anonymous communications. At the time "The Low Down" started coming in I had been reduced to writing letters to the editor and denouncing or praising the thoughts of the illusory citizen who signed himself "De Profundis" or "Patriot" or "Disillusioned Democrat."

We had published "The Low Down" almost daily for more than two weeks before Bert identified himself as its author. He did it out of the side of the mouth, as we stood near each other at the soda counter of the Central Drug Store. I hardly recognized him for I had not seen him for years, not since he was eleven or twelve years old, five years my junior and an occasional student in a lower Sunday school class. He asked, "What do you think of that 'Low Down'?" and I answered that it was all right, and he snorted and said, "I wrote it, and I'm looking for a job when school's out next month."

Right then we made a bargain. Bert would continue to write "The Low Down," already our most popular and controversial attraction. He would work afternoons after school until graduation, I would undertake to teach him the fundamentals of journalism, complete with textbook and trial assignments, and he would be paid five dollars a week. Bert says that he was paid the five dollars all right, every Friday, but that I would always borrow most of it back by Monday to make the weekly mailing charge deposit at the post office. He was a born reporter, brassy, inquisitive, eager to learn, and on the surface the most exuberant of extroverts, with a smattering of knowledge about a great many things, a distaste for mental discipline in any form, and a rare feeling for right words, wrong situations and drama. He learned fast, and I learned from him, and also fast, many home-town facts and rumors which I had either never known, or in nearly nine years of absence had forgotten.

Bert grew taller and heavier and more threadbare on his five dollars a week and the *Daily Courier* grew in stature, circulation and wisdom but not in bank account. We kept up our two-man journalism school, became close friends, and in moments of optimistic delirium debated whether the two-hundred-and-fifty-dollar-a-month income which Bert said he'd settle on for the rest of his life was more realistic than the four hundred dollars which I insisted was the least I'd make a lifetime bargain with anyone for. By the end of the year, he was making fifteen dollars a week, and Betty and I, theoretically, were drawing $120 a month together. As often as not, he had more cash than we. Nobody complained. We were making a go of the impossible.

Then, one winter morning two years later Bert told us that he and Alsia were planning to get married, and the four of us had better start figuring out something.

If he was determined to marry, neither Betty nor I could have thought of anyone who was finer than Alsia, nor could we have picked out another bride of whom some of the narrower citizenry of Hammond would have been more skeptical. She was a blonde young widow. She came from New Orleans. She was a professional dancer, who commuted from the wicked city twice a week to conduct her dancing school in Hammond, and while there stayed, unchaperoned, overnight at a hotel. That was twenty years ago, and our opinion of Alsia hasn't changed, but the skeptics' opinions did, and quickly, as we knew they would. She had a most wonderful name which became a battle chant; Alsia Alizina Louisiana Cecilia Corbera Higgins Hyde.

There wasn't much question but what they could make ends meet once they were married. Alsia did well, for the times, with her dancing school, but there was Bert's masculine pride in respect to salary, his scarce wardrobe, their lack of furniture, and the need for a reasonably priced place to stay.

We talked things over and solved the salary problem first. In a burst of wild generosity, I told him that we'd raise his salary from $15 to $18 a week, and complimentarily observed that this would put him in a class with experienced reporters on the New Orleans *Item,* which was true enough. In the next day or so, Bert and Betty came up with another idea. We hadn't been able to sell any advertising in Baton Rouge, the state capital, just forty-four miles away, despite our contention that our two thousand or so subscribers only needed the lure of a few full-page ads in the *Daily Courier* to flock to Baton Rouge's frequent clearance sales. We decided that Bert should try to sell advertising to Baton Rouge furniture stores on a trade-out basis and that any furniture he could acquire that way would be his and Alsia's as a wedding present from the *Courier.* We estimated, hopefully, that he could get maybe a hundred dollars' worth of furniture in trade, and, the market being what it was, that would mean anyhow a bed, a table, a chair or two and a chest of drawers. We thought too that such advertising might stimulate our own reluctant Hammond dealers to follow suit.

Two or three days later Bert was offered a plan which would make him the best-dressed groom Hammond had seen since the beginning of the depression. Remember that his column, "The Low Down," was our most closely read feature, especially by the high-school and college students to whom he principally catered. No one knew this better than did Pres Stedman, the manager of the new J. C. Penney Company, one of our few steady advertising—and steady pay—accounts. Pres was and is a smart merchandiser. He had just put in a young men's department, and he wanted it to go over.

I really don't know whether Pres or Bert had the idea first. I do remember how Bert looked, his big arms dangling from his outgrown jacket and his ankles a good two inches below his trouser cuffs, when he approached me with the proposal. He knew better, he said, than even to bring the matter up, because he knew I was absolutely opposed to letting advertising creep into any news column, and I was right, yes, I certainly was, but anyhow, he and Pres had been talking—here Bert almost began drooling as he described a tantalizingly forbidden vision—and Pres had said that if Bert would devote one day's "Low Down" to some wisecracking comment on the young-men's department at Penney's, he would be given a new suit, a half-dozen shirts, a pair of shoes, a couple of ties and appropriate socks, all from the most up-to-date toggery in the Florida parishes. "But," Bert finished up lamely, "I told him what our policy on advertising is . . ."

I don't think Bert really doubted what I would say. Never before had we made a deal with an advertiser to give him unwarranted space in the news columns, nor did we ever do it again. But there stood Bert, too well-fed for his clothes. So I said, "Lay it on as thick as he wants. You've got yourself a trousseau."

That column provided Bert with both the proper appearance and the confidence to tackle Baton Rouge. He drove over one day, dressed like a bright Penney model, and made the rounds of the furniture dealers. We could hear him shouting a half-block away when he returned late in the afternoon.

"Furniture, we got it!" he roared as he sailed through the *Courier*'s front door. "Bedroom suites—living-room suites—radio—dinette—refrigerator—man, oh man, oh man, you're looking at the best-dressed, best-furnitured bridegroom in the Florida parishes!"

When he had calmed down, he told us that he had simply related the true story to each Baton Rouge furniture dealer upon whom he called. He was a country boy trying to furnish a home for his wife to be, he had told them, and besides getting the benefit of the best advertising medium they ever had, they'd be giving him a nice wedding present. Altogether he rounded up a little more than five hundred dollars' worth of furniture accounts, and five hundred dollars' worth of furniture in 1934 was enough to set any couple up in light housekeeping.

So now, Bert had a weekly salary that equaled what many a depression-time big-city reporter was getting—all of eighteen dollars—a wardrobe, and enough furniture to hold open house when the time came. All he and Alsia needed was a place to stay.

From that need developed the biggest deal of all, one that was to make me a sizable property owner, and combine in one two-story brick building a daily newspaper plant, a dancing school and an efficiency apartment for newlyweds, at an investment of only ten dollars in cash and at what actually ended up as free house rent for the newlyweds.

In those depressed days, the nation's building and loan companies and homestead associations were also having hard times. They had been forced to repossess much property for which they could not find new buyers. Their stock was frequently selling far below par, and they were trying desperately to get themselves in more liquid shape. There was in Hammond one such association, honestly run and once prosperous, as it now is again, but in 1934 it was loaded down with repossessed property and its outstanding stock was down from the original one hundred dollars a share to thirty dollars.

We needed bigger quarters for the *Daily Courier.* The tiny space in the theater foyer had been inadequate from the beginning. The next location to which we had moved was larger but the rent was too high for what we were getting—I believe it was all of fifty dollars a month—and we could not persuade our landlord to make any repairs.

So, one afternoon during the time we were scheming how to get Bert and Alsia married, I talked to the president of the homestead association, whom I had known since my childhood, about the possibility of renting from him a better building than we occupied. I did not have the slightest idea that I would emerge from that conference a potential property owner. But in less than an hour we had come to terms on a deal which I still find fantastic. The association had repossessed a two-story brick building on Hammond's main street, less than ten years old and in good repair. A movie theater had occupied the first floor. The rear two-thirds of the second floor had been the headquarters of some fraternal organization, which had moved to a meeting hall of its own. The front one-third was cut up into four or five offices.

I was a good credit risk, said the real estate man. What he really meant was that times were so bad that they'd take a chance on anybody. The association, he said, would sell me the building for ten thousand dollars—it couldn't be built for forty thousand today—and not ten thousand dollars in cash, but ten thousand in stock in the homestead association itself, which could be bought on the open market for three thousand. Moreover—hold your breath!—the association would be glad to lend me the three thousand with which to buy the ten thousand dollars' worth of stock which it would then accept as full payment for the building. And how to repay the loan? By long-term payments of principal and interest, at, say forty dollars a month.

I felt dizzy. Was that all there was to it? Yes, that was all except for a small legal fee which I would have to pay to the lawyer of my choice. Usually ten dollars. And all we would have to pay was forty dollars a month? Yes, that was all.

Right then I knew exactly where Bert and Alsia would live, where Alsia would teach dancing, and how much their rent would be. Alsia was paying forty dollars for a studio alone. Here was a package deal. We would convert the upstairs offices into an apartment, and what would make a better and more convenient dance studio than the meeting hall where fraternally mysterious rites were once performed? On the first floor we would install the newspaper plant. We might even put in a firehouse pole, so Bert could slip down it to work.

I bought the building. We did our moving—dismantling the flatbed press, stripping the two linotypes and carefully loading the rest of the equipment on a borrowed truck—all in one weekend, so that we didn't lose a day of publication, though we almost lost a linotype when the wheels of the dolly on which we were trundling it across town jammed between an Illinois Central track rail and the bordering asphalt just before the arrival of the Panama Limited, and were freed only by volunteer pushers. And then we went into the apartment remodeling business. A painting contractor owed us money which he couldn't pay, and he was more or less willing to square up with labor and paint. Bert and I turned jackleg carpenters, tearing down some partitions and walls and putting up others. There already was a bathroom attached to one office. In less than two weeks, apartment and studio were ready.

Only the stag supper, wedding and honeymoon remained to be attended to, as far as Bert and I were concerned, although there were some women's doings, like kitchen showers, in which we had no interest. The honeymoon arrangements were easy. Our red Chevrolet, obtained on an advertising swap, was an ideal vehicle for honeymooners. The Gulf Coast was just the place for a bride and groom to go, especially since the *Courier* held due bills from a Gulf Coast hotel which exchanged rooms for newspaper advertising. The stag supper was a cinch. Down at the trapper and fishermen's settlement at Pass Manchac, which connected Lake Pontchartrain and Lake Maurepas, Bill Williams operated a seafood shack. Bill was a brother-in-law of Wallace Mills, our pressman, and he had been delighted sometime earlier by a "Low Down" paragraph extolling his bill of fare. For fifty cents, Bill gave a customer all the boiled shrimp, boiled crabs, fried fish, fried oysters, fried froglegs, sliced tomatoes and coffee he could hold; not all of one dish or another, but all anyone could eat of all of these. But we could get a better bargain than that. In appreciation of Bert's one comment, Bill never bothered to charge us for food, only for the drinks that we might order. Naturally Bill's place was our favorite dining-out spot. It was certainly just the place for Bert's stag dinner.

And so Bert and Alsia were married. I was best man. They came back to a newly painted little apartment, fully furnished by courtesy of the Baton Rouge furniture dealers. Alsia could step out of the back hall door into her studio. Bert was a minute away from his desk downstairs. In the nighttime waits between page proofs Bert and Alsia and Betty and I had a gay little kitchen or living room in which to relax with sandwiches and beer, and spin our dreams. Every night, at eight, we turned on Alsia's radio for a newscast from which we carefully took notes and then amplified them into bulletins for the *Daily Courier*. We could not afford to subscribe to a news service. We headed the column of world news bulletins "AR News Reports." The "AR" meant Alsia's Radio but no one knew that but us.

When Betty and I go back to Hammond, we almost always get together with Bert and Alsia, who have their own home now and two children, a boy and a girl, and a dance studio of their own. They had joined us in Greenville not long after we left, and Bert was our managing editor for three years. He went from Greenville to New Orleans and was as good a reporter as the States ever had before he left newspaper work for the automobile business, which is more lucrative for him, I guess, but I am sorry he did it. Alsia has her dancing school, and so has her daughter by her first marriage, who is married now and the mother of a little girl who dances too; and one spring, the three of them were on television together—the dancing grandmother, the dancing mother and the dancing daughter—when they attended a convention of dancing teachers in Chicago.

We like to talk when we get together about yesterday and today, about our children and the way Hammond and Greenville and the world are changing. And, unfailingly, we talk also of how we managed that marriage. We don't grow rhapsodic about our ingenuity or the lighter side of the depression, which people generally remember, if they remember it at all, for its shadows of despair and surrender. We just recall how we furnished a home and bought a building and obtained Bert's wedding wardrobe and had a festive stag supper and provided a wedding honeymoon, all of it, I am certain, for less than forty dollars in cash.

5

Huey Long's American Empire

Bolivar Kemp, Jr. lived in Amite, which was Tangipahoa parish's seat, twenty miles north of Hammond, and when we were high-school students we competed for a couple of years in oratory at the state high-school rally. He declaimed *Spartacus to the Gladiators* both times, and I retaliated with *Regulus to the Carthaginians*, and he won, and once became state declamation champion. Bolivar's mother was an informed, hospitable and relaxed lady whom we called Miss Lallie, and who liked on summer mornings to recline in a front-porch swing in a kimono while she conducted her neighborhood salons. She was a lifelong close friend of my father's family, and the summer in Amite, when I first met Betty, who was a college schoolmate of Peeps Kemp, we often joined the crowd of young and old guests on the Kemps' gallery. The elder Bolivar Kemp was the congressman from our Sixth District of Louisiana, and in my own undergraduate days I had spent a couple of weeks tacking Kemp campaign posters all over Tangipahoa parish. I am setting this down to underscore the closeness of a friendship that was to be broken, as a great deal else in Louisiana—from banks and businesses to heads and promises

—was broken by a brilliant, vulgar, insatiable, creative man who gave the United States its first home-grown dictatorship and whose name was Huey Pierce Long.

Congressman Kemp came up for re-election in 1932 soon after we started the *Courier*, and at a time when Louisianians were still wrongly convinced that Long could be halted and that his personal domination of the state had gone as far as a legislature or citizenry would permit. We hadn't seen anything yet. Mr. Kemp was a good congressman, who had not identified himself with the Long faction or with any other; but this time, thought a great many citizens of the Sixth District, the chips were down, and a candidate ought to say which side of Long's fence he stood on. Mr. Kemp declined to give an opinion on Longism, but his ability and popularity were such that he was re-elected, although our Sixth District, which included Baton Rouge, the state capital, had never surrendered to Long or any of his avowed candidates.

Betty and I had reluctantly supported Mr. Kemp's opponent, after trying to persuade him—two youngsters against a successful, middle-aged lawyer and politician—to come out against Huey. Understandably, the Kemps thought we were traitors to old ties, and it hurt them. Then, early in his following term, Mr. Kemp died. Under the law, the governor, a miserable puppet of Long's named O. K. Allen, was required to call a special Democratic primary election at which a successor would be chosen by the voters of the district. As always, the primary victor would be the new congressman since there was never any Republican opposition in a general election.

But Long didn't want a primary election, because he was not sure a Long candidate for Congress could carry the Sixth District, which had been hostile to him since first he entered politics. With the classic direction that characterized his political thievery, he simply decided not to have a primary election at all. Instead, he ordered his state Democratic Executive Committee to declare the congressman's popular widow, Miss Lallie, as the Democratic nominee without benefit of any contest. As the party's nominee her name would go on the special general-election ballot without opposition. Long must have figured that sympathy for the widow and the esteem in which she was universally held would nullify any opposition to his maneuver. But this time he guessed wrong, and in so doing received ultimately the only major setback in his career as Louisiana's dictator.

In our town lived a principal foe of Long, an implacable old man, who had once been governor of Louisiana, and whose often highhanded behavior in his earlier political life had given Long a target which he used over and over again. Former Governor Sanders, Ol' J.Y., we called him, had once in an elevator physically attacked Long, little more than half his age, and had the satisfaction of seeing Huey break and run when the elevator reached the ground floor. Theirs was a deep personal hatred. Ol' J.Y. had a son, Little J.Y., an able Baton Rouge lawyer, who had announced that he would be a candidate for the vacant congressional seat. Only, said Long, there wouldn't be any contest.

This was not the first time that Huey had abolished self-government in Louisiana, and he would take far more extreme action later. The Sixth District's sense of outrage was spontaneous and violent. I wrote an editorial which proclaimed that the time had come for shotgun government in the Sixth District. It would not be the last time the *Courier* spoke for the extra-legal action which then seemed the only resort in a state where legality was a tool to build a coffin for self-government. Nat Tycer, a judge whose district embraced four parishes of the congressional district's twelve, ruled that Long's stratagem was illegal. In an accompanying statement, he commented that it was a poor judge who couldn't enforce his own ruling, and called for volunteer special deputies who could prevent any balloting in his four parishes. That was the signal for what was up to that time the nearest thing to anarchy which Long's tactics created in Louisiana.

As election day approached, bands of men, and I was among them, broke into the courthouses and publicly burned the special election ballots, and other election paraphernalia which had been sent into our district from the state capital. In handbills, in newspaper statements and on the radio Long warned that the penalty for interfering with an election was a heavy fine and up to five years in jail. We burned more ballots. In the *Courier* office we built a magnificent effigy of Long and a gallows to go with it, together with crudely appropriate signs, and burned the effigy at noon on Hammond's main street, previously having taken photographs of our handiwork and rushed them to the New Orleans afternoon newspapers so that the event would get the fullest publicity. Long threatened to call out the militia. In the other eight parishes of the congressional district anti-Long citizens began a more pacific campaign to persuade the voters to boycott the election. Our own judicial district was in complete rebellion.

A few days before the special general election day, Judge Tycer began swearing in his deputies by the hundreds. But when we began assembling throughout the district on election eve, the hundreds had dwindled to handfuls, though Long didn't know it. Ol' J.Y. had lent me a beautifully chased sawed-off shotgun, complete with leg holster, a present to him from a Mexican general when he was serving a long-ago term as congressman. I also had a .38 pistol. According to plan, the special deputies split into groups of eight or ten men, and began patrolling their respective parishes about midnight. Before our group left, Betty served coffee and sandwiches to some of my fellow deputies and four or five newspapermen who had come up from New Orleans for the show. She must have been as frightened as I was, but she pretended not to be; and I never loved her as much as when, as we were leaving our house, she said, almost casually, "Honey, you've forgotten your shotgun," which I had. She kissed me good-bye and went inside where she telephoned her mother in New Orleans and had a good long-distance cry.

Throughout the night, we patrolling deputies heard rumor after rumor. *National Guardsmen are on their way up from New Orleans. State police are running in fresh truckloads of ballots from Baton Rouge.* One squad hastened south to the highway bridge at Pass Manchac, to take possession of the drawbridge in case the troops were heading north from New Orleans. Others of us lay in ditches near the East Baton Rouge parish line, waiting for the state policemen and their ballots. There was some shooting that night, but no one was killed, and no one voted in our judicial district. I arranged a news picture showing some chickens and pigs near a backwoods election booth, shortly after dawn, and then we went home. Elsewhere in the congressional district, voting was so light as to be almost nonexistent.

A few weeks later, we anti-Long forces held our own rump election, polling a far greater vote for Little J.Y. than Miss Lallie had received.

As we hoped, the United States House of Representatives refused to seat either Miss Lallie, whom Long's state party committee had certified, or Little J.Y., whom we had sent up to contest the seat; and Long was forced to hold a special primary. He chose the state commissioner of agriculture, a long-time office holder who was liked by members of all political factions, as the administration's candidate; but the Sixth District, giddy with the success of its ballot-burning, special-deputy revolution, sent Little J.Y. to Congress, where he finished out that term and went back, unopposed, to another, before he was buried in the Long landslide that followed Huey's assassination in the fall of 1935. Not for several years were we forgiven by our old friends, the Kemps; but we weren't fighting Miss Lallie at all.

Reading what I have just written, I am disturbed at the recollection of how casually, even lovingly, we embraced the belief that ultimately a resort to violence must be our defense against the sordid, bribed rape of Louisiana. I am made uneasy in retrospect, even though I know that armed rebellion against tyranny propelled our nation, and many another, to enduring or transient freedom. This is probably because hindsight reveals the grays between the blacks and whites that divided our political landscapes. The compulsion to take up the shotgun, the readiness to applaud even the assassin is understandable still, for we were the inheritors of a tradition of direct action that goes back a long way, even to the Magna Carta.

Deep down went the roots of Longism, which were the roots of tyranny by any name—fascism, communism, totalitarianism—and they found nourishment in the same soil that has soaked up the blood of freedom's martyrs; for while it is the way of some to espouse political liberty as the antidote to economic blight and political corruption, there are others who too readily accept the strong man who promises the filled stomach and vengeance, bread and circuses and a top place for the bottom rail.

That was Louisiana's way during the years just prior to and during Long's despotism. More than any other state Louisiana can look back upon a one-sided past of civic corruption and, worse, civic indifference to corruption. As Jonathan Daniels has described my native state, Louisiana is a Caribbean republic. Governed indifferently or worse by Frenchman, Spaniard, and American, this abundantly diverse land never fulfilled its promise to the many, only to the successive few. Huey Long was the revolutionary, preaching a sharing of plenty, punishment for the monopolist, the triumph of rural virtue over metropolitan evil, restitution for ancient wrongs. In plain, angry, everyday language that Cajun and redneck and poorwhite and despairing white-collar folk of the depression could understand, he promised and produced free school books, free bridges, good roads, free hospitalization, practically state medicine, bigger and physically better schools, humiliation for the city bosses and the big corporations, winning athletic teams, the biggest university bands and longest swimming pools and the best-paid college faculties in the South. He had as targets the political and economic ducks which were not only sitting but anchored in a bayou of special privilege. He spoke for objectives that we, the young men and women of Louisiana, had dreamed of in our dreaming days; but his voice was the voice of the soul's destroyer, and, for some of us, the price he asked and got was far too high for anything he could offer.

Too high for some of us, but not for a majority. In Louisiana's defense, or at least in explanation, remember not only that the locale was one of the most backward and exploited of the states, a region of poverty and accustomed political debauchery and marked illiteracy, but also that the time of Long's ascendancy coincided with a prolonged and acute national depression. Place and hour and regional past alike were with him, as they have been with most of those whose civic immorality has met with popular endorsement, even approval, because it was cloaked in beneficence.

I can be relatively philosophic now. More than fifteen years have passed; the Long brother who was a cheap facsimile has been dismissed from the Louisiana scene, and the son who is in the United States Senate is not the father. I could not philosophize then, being young and partisan, a good hater and believing, as I still do, in certain absolutes. Often during the four years that Betty and I kept the little *Courier* going, I felt soiled. This is true. I could almost see the sootiness on my soul when an old family friend—a good man, I had thought, but one who had three children to educate—went over to Long for a sinecure that meant three hundred and fifty dollars a month which was then a princely ransom in Tangipahoa parish; when, in the land where my forebears had been decent, successful citizens, an anonymous letter warned me not to fill a speaking engagement at a hapless settlement with the unbelievable name of Punkin Center, though I did, with a pistol and an armed companion, and suffered only some hissing and boos; when our hard-put newspaper was subjected to boycott, and a plate-glass window was broken, and the assured jackals finally began to offer us more and more lucrative, but never more tempting inducements to get into line; when the anonymous threats by letter and telephone grew; when my father, as selfless a man as I have known, was removed as a trustee of the little college in Hammond which he had helped to found, only because he was independent and indignant and my father; when, as I shall relate later, almost everything in Louisiana, except a handful of newspapers, were Huey Long's, his by legislation which abolished community authority over teachers, policemen, city councils, school boards; when even supervision over the ballot's sanctity was taken away and there remained only the despairing resort to force.

We felt dirtied sometimes, Betty and I, yet we also felt free, because we never gave in. But the shadow of Huey Long blotted out for us most of the considerations to which our contemporaries elsewhere were paying heed. A famous baby was kidnaped; a world war was threatened in China; a man named Hitler was making trouble in Germany and a man named Roosevelt was (with the Carters' indifferent blessing) elected President of the United States; a new concept of national responsibility in time of stress was a-borning.

But for us the only issue was Longism. We hit at Long in every way we knew how or could discover, above the belt, below the belt, with the belt off, any way at all. Objectively, there were more than a few social measures he proposed with which we would have agreed. But always the sleek blackguards hovered around him; always the economic thumbscrew and rack awaited the dissenter; always the Kingfish of Louisiana stamped malignantly upon the protestant.

We did what we could, but it was not much. For four years hardly a day passed without a critical editorial in the *Courier*. But what good were editorials in a tiny daily, whose peak circulation was only four thousand? I wrote articles about Longism for any magazine or newspaper which would accept them, for the New Orleans newspapers and a few others outside the South. I remember the week that the late *Literary Digest* described me as one of the most articulate of the editors who were opposing Long. At that time Betty and I were reduced to a four-dollar-a-week food budget, and we celebrated our recognition by adding chopped up wieners that night to a dish of which I had long since tired, a casserole cookery concoction made up of canned tomatoes, cheese, onion and a young wife's optimism.

I have been re-reading some of those editorials. After each one, I have asked Betty, who has looked them over with me, why I wasn't shot or at the least manhandled. They were brutally personal, no matter whether the target was a neighbor down the street or a Long goon who had just been commissioned a state-highway patrolman because of the vote he could command and the fear he could engender. Little of what I wrote was good journalism, but I still think that most of it was good citizenship, even when we described a police appointee as jail bait, and derided an announced officer of Long's Share Our Wealth society as a one-time hog thief, which he was.

Maybe in those days we were looking for trouble. One of my Hammond friends, who is still living as I write this, is Arthur Jones. He was a railroad man, and is someone whom I would like at any time to have close to me in a tight place. Arthur and I once campaigned together, and we both lost—he was running for a state senatorship and I for representative—but in a small way we helped win a skirmish which I will never forget. That was in 1934 when Long tried to frighten New Orleans into electing his candidate for mayor. He threatened to use the National Guard as he did before and afterward. His henchmen were ready to stuff the boxes. The New Orleans police, poor devils, didn't know what to do because there was no way of knowing which way the city's machine, the Old Regulars would jump. The Old Regulars, with whom I sided only because they were opposing Long, sent out an S O S to the outlying parishes, and particularly to Tangipahoa because of its tough reputation, for volunteer deputies. Arthur and I were among the group, and we stood together, our backs against a French Quarter wall, while the ballots were being counted inside the polling booth. In the streets and on the sidewalks around us, precinct hoodlums jeered and cursed and laughed. But the booth wasn't stormed, and the ballots were counted more or less honestly, all over New Orleans; and the anti-Long people elected the Old Regular candidate for mayor. Not long afterward Long beat the city machine and the city itself to their knees, so that the victory, like all the others, was fleeting.

Nevertheless, we took heart from the most transient triumph, and from the resistance of our small ever-shrinking core. A new aristocracy was being fashioned in Louisiana, having neither pride of origin nor honor among its attributes. Its members had in common shamelessness and love of any dollar. Their leaders were the inner circle around Long, men —and a woman or two—who were after big stakes and got them. Some of them later went to jail for terms that were as short as the memories of those who subsequently accepted them; a few committed suicide. Most of them simply cashed in. On the outer fringes slunk the jackals, holders of state jobs, small contractors, "double dippers"—lesser favorites who were on two or three state payrolls—and a pitiable and ever-changing medley of hopeful little traitors, offering the votes of a few families or of a backwoods community or their own services as political gutter-sweepers in return for any kind of reward.

If these had been all, Long could not have become or remained America's first absolute ruler. He and his court and their immediate lackeys stood on the offered backs of the believers. After Huey's assassination, some enterprising Cajun ballad-maker wrote a patois lament for the dead leader with such verses as these:

> *O they say he was a crook*
> *But he gave us free schoolbook*
> *Tell me why is it that they kill Huey Long?*
> *Now he's dead and in his grave*
> *But we riding on his pave'*
> *Tell me why is it that they kill Huey Long?*

The concrete ribbons bound Louisiana together. The city and country school children, Cajun and redneck, well-to-do and poor, studied the free school books. New free bridges spanned the sleepy rivers, a skyscraper charity hospital and a skyscraper capitol split the Louisiana skies. They were there for all to see, nor did a majority of Louisianians think the price was too high. All Louisianians heard, and a multitude believed, the gaudy doctrine of Huey's Share Our Wealth movement, which promised land and income and an allocation of life's good things to the people. They listened and they believed, not only in Louisiana, but in Arkansas and in Mississippi and wherever the spokesmen and disciples of a soulless Utopia carried the grinning messiah's message.

The objecting minority had believed well before the spring and summer of 1935 that Long had done all that needed to be done or that even he would want to do to make Louisiana his. But in that nightmarish year, which ended almost inevitably in his murder, we found out that self-government could be made completely to disappear in a state of the American union.

The story of how Huey ruled Louisiana from Washington, through puppets in the governor's chair, in the legislature and in the state supreme court has been told in sickening detail. Before 1935 Huey had taken over, sometimes violently, every state board, every state-controlled officeholder, a majority of the legislature, bragging that he could buy the members like sacks of potatoes. He made the banks and the politicians of New Orleans knuckle under. The National Guard had become his private police.

His weekly newspaper, the *Progress* (which was printed in Mississippi and financed by forced levies on the employees' salaries), tossed, as Harnett Kane sums up its content, "allegations of loathsome disease, insanity, Negro blood, financial-criminal activities and assorted social indecencies" at any opponent or other victim of the Louisiana Kingfish. Beatings of newspapermen and other objecting citizens by Long's body-guards had become commonplace. Long's state policemen more than once abducted citizens whose testimony in one affair or another might be embarrassing; and when they were freed the citizens usually had learned to keep their mouths shut. Long had gone to Washington as United States Senator in 1932 with Louisiana securely his, and he made headlines there. He had broken with Roosevelt, but not even the New Deal's opposition could loosen his hold, and in the nation he was becoming an alarmingly appealing figure.

He experienced some setbacks however: our district's congressional rebellion, the victory of the Old Regular candidate for mayor of New Orleans, and a series of lesser misadventures including a nonpolitical beating in a Long Island club at the hands of a man whom he had drunkenly and primitively offended in the lavatory. Then he got even, using the legislature and the supreme court as his clubs. By summer's end, of 1935, no man could stand successfully against him. To line up the people, he had offered a debt moratorium law, tax exemption up to two thousand dollars for homeowners, abolition of the poll tax and reduction of the automobile-license fee—all welcome measures. To end any chance of further opposition, he literally abolished self-government. State-appointed election supervisors were given charge of all ballot boxes, with power to name all voting commissioners and as many special deputies as they wanted, at local expense. The attorney-general could replace any district attorney in any case and at any time. No court could enjoin Long, or his governor, from calling out the National Guard, and the governor won the power to increase a secret, ununiformed police force to any size he—or rather Huey—wished. The governor was granted the right also to reprieve any convicted man, even in contempt cases. A state tax commission was empowered to raise or lower taxes anywhere in the state. An illegally secured four to three majority on the supreme court gave Huey judicial backing in any measure he desired. A so-called civil-service board was created, with power over police chiefs and fire chiefs, and this substitution for local government was extended until every local school employee from principals and teachers on down could be removed by the state. Where the parish governing bodies, the police juries, opposed him, Long enlarged them by enough appointees to produce a majority. And so on and so on, law after law, special session after special session. . . .

We still tried to fight back. Late in 1934, angry men in Baton Rouge and elsewhere in our district organized a Square Deal Association, drilled under arms, planned hotheaded, impossible revolt. I belonged. In January the Baton Rouge Square Dealers temporarily seized the courthouse, and so martial law was declared. The next day, other Square Dealers converged upon the Baton Rouge Airport. I was to have gone, but my mother was dying. The fellow Tangipahoan with whom I had planned to go was George Alessi, a likable, physically powerful Italian-American. George was riddled with buckshot as he ran to escape the National Guardsmen who surrounded the field. Somehow George lived, but the Square Dealers surrendered and the organization died.

The following summer perhaps sixty Louisianians met in the DeSoto Hotel in New Orleans to plan a state campaign to select our candidates for state office, and to curse hopelessly against enslavement. Long had dictaphones planted in our meeting rooms. It is very probable that more than one of the men gathered in the DeSoto said there that the only way to get rid of Long was to kill him. Many Louisianians were saying the same thing. On the floor of the United States Senate Long dramatically accused us of plotting his murder and intimated that the Roosevelt administration was a co-plotter. He was speaking to the nation, because he was planning to seek the presidency on his Share Our Wealth program—confiscation and redistribution of much of America's personal and corporate wealth, so that every family would get a six-thousand-dollar house, a twenty-five-hundred-dollar income, old-age pensions, free education through college, a radio, automobile and refrigerator. Everything but political and economic freedom. Many people liked that kind of platform in 1935. Many still do. Give to me and gut the other fellow. . . . Huey had the votes, the voters, the election machinery, the police, the entire state treasury, the courts, the city, county and state employees, even the local taxing power. Everything. Americans ought to reread the story of Long in Louisiana.

And in that summer of 1935 he set about to get the handful of smaller newspapers which, like most of the few larger newspapers, had held out against him. His device was a new state public printing law, and our *Courier* was the only newspaper against which it was actually employed. The law set forth that any selection of a newspaper as the official journal of a city, a school board, a parish or other political subdivision must be approved by a state printing board, forthwith created, composed of the Attorney General, the Secretary of State and, as I remember, the Supervisor of Public Accounts. In those depressed days, public printing—the publishing of tax lists, official proceedings, sheriff's sales and sundry legal notices—could often be for a small newspaper the margin between life and death. The *Courier* was the official journal for Hammond, the parish and one or two other bodies. Our politically amoral contemporary, the Hammond *Vindicator,* had cheerfully gone over to Long when the vise closed, and the official printing was to be its earthly reward. The State Printing Board advised the several political bodies involved that the *Courier* was not approved. No reason. No legal justification; in Louisiana Huey's laws superseded justice.

We employed a brilliant New Orleans lawyer, Eberhard Deutsch, who had successfully represented the state's larger dailies in their fight against a "two cents a lie" special tax on advertising, which Long had levied as punishment. Eb Deutsch sought to prove that our contract with the police jury had not been breached but instead had been impaired. The distinction, if upheld, would permit us to seek remedy in federal court. We knew that there could be no remedy in the Louisiana State Supreme Court, to which the case would otherwise ultimately go, for Long's creatures were in the majority. We won in federal district court against the state's battery of lawyers. We were reversed in the Court of Appeals, and the United States Supreme Court upheld the reversal, agreeing that our contract had not been impaired and that redress for a breach of contract must be sought in our state courts. We had lost several thousand dollars, but what was important and frightening was that Louisiana's little newspapers could see the handwriting.

But before the final decision was handed down, we had other and more absorbing matters to keep us busy. That fall Huey Long, who had lived in fear of death for more than a year, and understandably, was assassinated by a young surgeon whose act, I am sure, was not prompted by politics but by a sense of profound family wrong. If I were to say now, or if I had written then, that Long's death distressed me, I'd be lying. As an abstract political or moral principle, assassination cannot be defended. But if ever a tyrant invited death, Huey Long did.

That same fall, I sought election to the state House of Representatives. I did so reluctantly, having made the decision the previous summer, and only because somebody had to. I knew I couldn't win. I didn't want to win, for Betty and I had by then set our hearts on the invitation from Will Percy and David Cohn and Billy Wynn and their friends to sell the *Courier* and come to Greenville, Mississippi, to start a new newspaper. Besides, I am no campaigner. My opponent was a state officer, maybe president, of the Share Our Wealth society, a former box-factory worker who had gone through the third or fourth grade and who later served a term in a federal penitentiary for invading and destroying government property during a milk-price war. He was a "double-dipper," an idol of the Share Our Wealth following, an ignorant but not overly malicious man. He beat me that January election day in 1936 by about a five to three margin, and he would have defeated me, I am sure, even if the votes had been honestly counted everywhere. I made scores of talks, which impressed no one, not even Betty who was more amused than carried away; and I also made many good friends in that campaign.

The thieves and opportunists who succeeded to the control of Long's organization swept the state, and thereafter planned to bring harmony to Louisiana so that the state could be robbed in peace. They succeeded fairly well until, a year after we went to Mississippi, their house of stacked cards fell about them, not because Louisianians were yet sickened, but because they ran afoul of the federal government and also because they were not sufficiently adroit in their thieving. In the wake of their collapse, Louisiana self-consciously washed its public face if not its soul. In 1940 my father won, one-sidedly, the legislative post I had gingerly sought in 1936, and Louisiana temporarily succumbed to a decent political impulse all along the front.

But by then Betty and I were Mississippians, and trying to tone down our editorial comment to meet the customs and requirements of a state that had only a Bilbo instead of the

Longs. For we had sold the *Courier* in the spring of 1936—four years after its founding—and our successors were three newspapermen who had worked for Long's weekly, the *Progress.* If they beat down the price, knowing how much we wanted to leave, the sum was more than thirty times our capital when we started; enough to establish us in Greenville, where the air smelled clean and we didn't feel ashamed of our state. I'm grateful to them. No newspaperman, not somehow identified with the Long dynasty, would have dared to take over. From the purchasers I exacted an agreement to change the *Courier*'s name. I wrote a farewell editorial to the home town that had largely been friendly and loyal.

Then, in my last few minutes in the office of the newspaper which Betty and I had founded, I told my successors, John Klorer, Tom Gillen and George French, a story which I still think made an appropriate farewell to Long's Louisiana. It concerned a Negro preacher whose congregation had decided to dispense with his services, and who was preaching his final sermon.

"I won't tell you hardhearted people 'good-bye' because that's too sad," the preacher said. "And I won't tell you 'au revoir' because none of you is smart enough to understand what that means. But when I walk down the aisle for the last time, I want you to take notice of the piece of mistletoe that's pinned on my coattail."

6

Gentleman Unafraid

When Will Percy's father, who had been United States Senator, planter and corporation lawyer, died back in 1929, no one thought that Will would take over the sprawling plantation with its one hundred and fifty families. Will was not in the planter mold. Like his father, a lawyer by training, he was a poet by inclination and paid more attention to his poetry than to his clients.

But when Will turned planter, he surprised everyone. First he told his managers that they were to operate on the Golden Rule, which was the most improbable order ever given in cotton-raising history. "If a plantation of rich Delta soil can't be run that way, it ought to go broke and I hope we do. But I want you to prove to the world that we *can* operate that way." Whereupon, he went traveling, and the Golden Rule went to work. Now, ten years after his death, it still works on Trail Lake, just as the memory of Will Percy in his home town still makes that rule have especial meaning.

He didn't know a thing about farming. In the springtime, instead of commenting on the weather or the condition of the land, he'd stand in a field and say that he liked the aroma of the freshly ploughed earth. When a manager or tenant pointed out a rich stand of cotton, Will would stray off to the cabin yard to look at the flowers he encouraged the tenant wives to plant. He refused to have anything to do with all-out agricultural mechanization because, he said, "We've got to think of the human side. The tenants have their homes and their roots here, and I'm not going to pull them up." He never did. And few of Trail Lake's one hundred and fifty families have ever left. Will Percy supplemented the meager state salaries paid the Negro teachers on Trail Lake. He matched each dollar raised by plantation congregations to rebuild their churches. He set up endowment plans for his managers and helped them acquire land of their own. Trail Lake thrived.

His treatment of Trail Lake's tenants was a target of caustic comment by some of his fellow planters who predicted that the great plantation could not survive such behavior. In those days, every plantation had a commissary where the Negroes were virtually forced to trade, and often landowners made exorbitant profits by overcharging their tenants for supplies and "furnish" during the year. Will instructed his managers to make all charges to tenants at cost, and to charge no interest on the "furnish" though the accounts were carried for a year at a time.

He did not approve the "meal, meat and molasses" diet of the average tenant, all bought at the commissaries, and induced the people of Trail Lake to vary their diet through home gardens. He sold them cows, pigs and chickens on credit and at cost. He gave cash prizes for the best gardens, and once tried a communal garden in which the tenants would each work so many hours for a share of the produce, but the plan failed because the workers spent more time accusing each of shirking than they did hoeing. More successful was his employment of a canning specialist each summer to teach the Negroes how to put up the vegetables.

Another unheard of venture was the screening of every tenant house as a safeguard against malaria which was then prevalent throughout the Delta. This program was not immediately successful, for a good many of the tenants, unused to screens on doors and windows, tore out the screens on the kitchen windows to throw out the dishwater, and cut a hole in the back doors to let the pet dogs and cats come in and out. But there are no holes in Trail Lake's screened windows and doors today.

Will's concern for the tenant's health made him a pioneer in venereal-disease control long before the establishment of state health department venereal clinics. A doctor was employed periodically to give the tenants a Wassermann test, and once a week all the positives were taken by bus to the doctor's office for shots, the whole expense being borne by the plantation.

David Cohn, who was born and raised in Greenville, says that Will represented the last stand of noblesse oblige. If that is so, then noblesse oblige means doing things you don't always want to do and don't really have to, and doing them because you consider it not only your inherited but your moral obligation to your fellows. That definition fits Will Percy, who was poet, planter, lawyer, soldier, naturalist, and believer in old-fashioned absolutes. To list those absolutes—truth, duty, charity, justice, honor—is to risk the accusation of stuffiness. But Will translated them into everyday behavior which was at the opposite pole from stuffiness.

I first met him in December, 1935, in the great hall of his home in Greenville, where Betty and I had come, at his invitation and Dave's suggestion, to explore the possibility of a new newspaper for Greenville. I saw him last in the selfsame hall in December 1940, when, after four years as his fellow citizen, I was going on active duty with the Mississippi National Guard and had come to tell him good-bye. I knew of his first fifty years only second hand. But in those final five years I learned how the outmoded values and a rare valor lived in a man who was displaced in time and whom we remember as a timeless spirit.

Will Percy was born to the manor, a feudal, patrician manor. His Percy grandfather had been a Confederate colonel and the leader of the river people in the drear time of Reconstruction. His father was the last United States Senator from Mississippi to be elected by the state legislature, and was defeated in the state's first popular election by James K. Vardaman, the earliest of Mississippi's notable demagogues.

Most of the Percys were outdoor, forceful men. But Will was not a robust child. He preferred to the hunting camp his books and music lessons and the verse he began to write in childhood. Musician and poet and lover of trees and flowers, he was Orpheus in a small town, perplexing to his father and suspect to his fellow river folk. Instead of attending state institutions, he was tutored at home and went away to college, first to lovely, secluded Sewanee on its Tennessee mountaintop and then to distant Harvard. After he returned home to practice the law he never really liked, except when he could defend an underdog, he broke away often to travel. He never learned to drive a car, or to master any contraptions of the machine age. In a town where a hat was considered as necessary as a pair of pants, he wore a soft cap or went bareheaded. He played the piano instead of poker, shunned baseball games and took only an occasional drink. Young William Alexander Percy was a strange fish in the little cotton town that expected something quite different of the Percys.

I imagine that it was the poetry which baffled people most.

It was the outpouring of an often melancholy, indomitable fighter, actively identifying himself with small-town and world-wide struggle against wrong. It was poetry in which he saw beauty and nobility foredoomed but no less worth fighting for.

But Greenville discovered early that its strange young fish of a poet had other and more applauded and endearing qualities. First proof came when, during a savage campaign, his father's political enemies dared the Percys to appear in a hostile town. Young Will armed himself with an unfamiliar pistol. So did a handful of kinsmen. They went to the town, and his father was heard without molestation.

Later in the campaign, at a backwoods speaking, Will was told that the crowd of unfriendly hill farmers intended to pelt his father with rotten eggs. He went hunting for the hidden hampers of eggs, found them, and stood guard over them. They were not used.

Will was in Paris in the summer of 1914, when Germany—he called her "the mad dog of the world"—broke loose. He joined and worked with the Commission for Relief in Belgium, under Herbert Hoover, and remained with the organization until the United States entered the war. Then he came home and enlisted. Will had no business being in anybody's army. No present-day draft board would accept him, for his only strength was spiritual.

But somehow he got into officers' training school, a member of a "pewee squad." Miraculously, he made the grade. Part of the miracle was the devotion of his fellow Pewees, who sometimes literally dragged and carried him through the tail end of a day's march and nursed him along when he was, as he put it, "three-fourths corpse and too far gone to pray for resurrection or dissolution." The three-fourths corpse made it to France and battlefield service, and returned home unscathed in body, with decorations and a captaincy.

Not long afterwards he was fighting in a different kind of war. Across the nation burned the fires of bigotry. The Ku Klux Klan began to count its members by the tens of thousands and its victims by the hundreds. The hate organizers came to Greenville. They were publicly denounced by the Percys, father and son, but their poison spread. Will's father became head of the Protestant Anti-Klan committee and of all the anti-Klan forces in the South. The Klan hated him more than any other of their opponents. As the threats against the Percys increased—an attempt was even made to kidnap the Senator—Will Percy went to the local Cyclops.

"I said 'I want to let you know one thing,'" Will recalled afterwards. 'If anything happens to my father or to any of our friends, you will be killed. We won't hunt the guilty party. So far as we are concerned, the guilty party will be you.'"

The Percys and their friends broke the back of the Klan in Greenville and the county. The Klan was dead in the Delta, but the wounds remained raw a long time. Will was approached fifteen years later by a one-time Klansman, who asked why Will had never forgiven him.

"Forgiveness is easy," Will said. "I really like you. The trouble is I've got your number, and people's numbers don't change."

In 1927 an ancient enemy struck. The Mississippi River went on its worst rampage. The levee broke just above Greenville, and the little city was submerged beneath flood waters from three to ten feet deep.

The mayor appointed Will chairman of the local flood-relief committee of the Red Cross. As such he was charged with supervising the rescue and care of sixty thousand people and thirty thousand head of stock in the surrounding area.

The surplus white population was evacuated. The Negro plantation refugees were housed in tents on the levee. The National Guard maintained order, the national Red Cross sent funds and personnel, the nation contributed generously to relief, and Greenville began almost to enjoy being drowned out.

The flood didn't end in June as was usual with high water. The co-operation began to slack off. The Red Cross had an unwritten rule that those who received its food should unload it from the food barges without charge. As the waters slowly began to recede, it became more and more difficult to get unloading crews from the levee-encamped Negroes, who received almost all of the Red Cross provisions. As a last resort, the city officials decided to use the police to round up unloading gangs. A green policeman shot and killed a Negro who refused to come along. Will learned that the Negroes blamed him, as Red Cross director, for the killing and that Greenville feared an uprising of the angry, restless refugees. He requested a meeting of the Negroes in one of the churches that by now was free of water. A large crowd of Negroes attended the meeting and Will confronted the resentful gathering alone.

First he recounted the killing of the Negro by the policeman, and told of his and the white community's regret.

"I look in your faces and see anger and hatred," he then said. "You think I am the murderer. The murderer should be punished. I will tell you who he is . . .

"For months we Delta people have been suffering together, black and white alike. God did not distinguish between us. He struck us all to our knees. During all this time you did nothing for yourselves or us. You were asked to do only one little thing. The Red Cross asked you to unload the food it was giving you, the food without which you would have starved. And you refused. Because of your sinful, shameful laziness, because you refused to work in your own behalf unless you were paid, one of your race has been killed. You think you want avenging justice, but that is the last thing in the world you want. I am not the murderer. That foolish young policeman is not the murderer. The murderer is you. Your hands are dripping with blood. Look into each other's faces and see the shame and the fear God has set on them. Down on your knees, and beg God not to punish you as you deserve."

As Will Percy and the refugee Negroes prayed together, the crisis passed.

Until 1935 I had known Will only by reputation. In December of that year Betty and I set out for Greenville. On a muddy detour, in a heavy rain, we skidded into a ditch; and when we finally rang the doorbell of the big, oak-shaded house, we were three hours late for seven o'clock dinner, wet and cold, and worried at our inauspicious start.

The door opened, and Will Percy stood framed against the softly lighted interior. "You poor children," he said. "Don't say anything until you get warm."

We saw a small, frail and beautiful man, whose eyes were blue-gray and smiling. His face was young, and he had thick, silvered hair, and a sad, sensitive mouth above a fighter's jaw.

Looking us over, he began to chuckle. "You've got Delta mud on you," he said. "Now we'll never get rid of you."

He held out his hand to us. It was always to be a helping hand; because of it, and because of the friends who joined him in matching our funds to start a new newspaper, that newspaper won out. It is mine now. The Delta mud stuck.

When we came to Greenville Will Percy's life was quiet for his small store of physical strength was diminishing. He was often ill in bed; but it seemed that the nearer life approached its end the more he shared it with anyone he thought he could help.

So it was that coming to the house whose doors were never locked, I would almost always have to wait upon someone else who was already in the high-ceilinged study or in the walled garden. The callers were of all kinds, having in common only their need for some aspect of Will Percy. I sat in the study one night while a young, despairing ex-convict, released only that day from the state penal farm, ate from a heaped-up tray while Will schemed how he could again fit into a free society. A week later the boy was working in Memphis. Waiting outside the study that night was a South African authority on racial sociology who had come to the Delta, not so much to probe the South's irritated wounds as to seek counsel on his country's problems in human relations, which dwarfed our own.

Day in, day out, people came to Will's house. Some were angry folk from the East, who usually went away with less anger and more understanding. Some were writers and artists and musicians of reputation; and others were talented or untalented unknowns who hoped that Will could set them right on their creative path. He listened to and sometimes criticized their writing; heard them play, and sometimes played their songs. I know two successful writers who will tell you today that they would not have gone on had they each not spent an afternoon with him.

But a majority of the visitors were those who had little or nothing to offer and much to ask; broken and hungry and spiritually crippled folk, most of whom received what they sought —money or advice or comfort or encouragement or recognition. The procession never ended. Will Percy sent penniless youngsters to college, helped jobless men find work, set up ambitious people in small businesses. It was a giving of self at which I still marvel. Of course, some took advantage of him, but they were the true cheats, for no one else would. Many of his fellow Greenvillians said that he was soft-headed and easily fooled. I don't think many fooled him. Even when he knew what the worst were like, he helped anyway.

We don't know how he managed to do as much and see as many people as he did in those latter pain-ridden years; and I didn't understand until the last time I saw him why he wanted to busy himself with what many would term inconsequential affairs. He was concerned about every aspect of community life. He adopted and raised to productive manhood the three orphaned sons of a Percy first cousin. He found time to write, after he had given up his law practice, his haunting biography, "Lanterns on the Levee." Will attended regularly what is probably the only non-singing Rotary Club in America; he laughed his fellow members out of perfunctory song, and prodded them into making the club instead an unorthodox forum for community problems. He served on civic and charitable boards, and though he never sought elective office, he took sides vigorously in city and county politics. He conferred with an endless procession of ladies from the garden clubs, for he knew flowers and shrubs and trees, describing them in the words of poet and naturalist and making his brick-walled, tile-lined garden a springtime mecca and a year-round envy.

Once, when the cotton South sought desperately for new and wider uses for its depression-surplus product, some hopeful Southern stylist suggested that many thousands of bales of cotton could be used up if only the ladies would wear cotton stockings. The idea took hold, at least in theory, among Southern men. Southern women, taking one look at cotton-stockinged femininity, held distinctly aloof. But in Greenville, Will bought dozens and dozens of pairs of cotton stockings and distributed them to the wives and daughters and sweethearts of all his friends. It is a rare tribute to his leadership and persuasiveness alike that the comely maids and matrons of Greenville went about self-consciously in bunchy cotton stockings for months after their Dixie sisters had refused to sacrifice their calves on cotton's altar.

In those years my newspaper never lacked an editorial target. Neither Will nor any of the other men who were then stockholders ever tried to direct the editorial policy. But if we overlooked a possible issue, Will was quick to point it out. In 1937, a Negro was horribly slain by a Mississippi mob. A quarter of a century before, Will and a few friends had prevented the last lynching attempt in our own county. The morning after this lynching, which was committed far from the Delta, Will phoned me. He was raging angry.

"I've just looked at your editorial page," he said. "Isn't a lynching worth commenting upon?"

"Look on the front page," I told him. "That's where I put my editorials when I'm really mad."

In his own outrage, he had not even scanned the first page before turning to the inside to see what I had to say about the murder.

And for me, the newcomer, he was unerring in separating the sheep from the goats. Once I commented favorably upon a man whom I had just met.

"But he's one of the rabbit people," Will answered. The rabbit people, he explained, were those able-bodied men who fled the high water in 1927 when they could have been useful.

Not until the last night I talked with him did Will Percy put into words for me the reason he dealt so fully and selflessly in the affairs of a small city and the ordinary folk who populated it. I have told the story before, many times, but it can never be repeated too often. On that night of discovery, as I came, self-conscious in uniform, to say good-bye, we talked unhappily about the darkening world. In that December of 1940, all Europe had fallen and only England stood. Will's sadness was the greater because, a sick man well past fifty, he had been turned down by the American, the Canadian and the Free French forces when he had tried to enlist.

After a while, I asked him what any of us could do to remake whatever we could save.

"You can't do anything on the grand scale," he said. "But when this comes to an end, you can work again for your own people in your own town. It isn't national leaders we need so much as men of good will in each of the little towns of America. So try to keep Greenville a decent place by being a correct citizen yourself. The total of all the Greenvilles will make the kind of country we want or don't want."

That was his reason for devoting himself to his town, and many times since then I have recited to myself and to others this credo of William Alexander Percy, poet and lover of mankind, whose reservoir of good will and charity and honor overflowed the confines of our little city. I know of no greater need than that which he filled.

He brought me to his town and he made me forever glad that he did.

7

Whose Skeleton Was That?

Often I am asked how new daily newspapers survive against established competition inasmuch as their mortality rate these days is statistically ninety-eight out of a hundred. I think we know the answer.

Besides luck, five indispensable elements are needed to keep a new newspaper going and, in the end, to enable it to take over an established competitor in a community not large enough for two newspapers. The competitor must be tired, or inept, or disinterested, or too easygoing or too sure of himself, or all of these. The new newspaper must differ strikingly from the old one, and in such a way as to wean away readers whether or not it makes friends. The staff of the upstart newspaper must be young, zealous, idealistic and loyal, with round-the-clock energy and a love of fighting. The new paper must have a nucleus of astute and respected supporters who are citizens of the town, and who can and will remove the taint of newness from the interloper. And obviously, it must be reasonably well financed, though no amount of money can of itself put a new newspaper across.

We enjoyed all of these elements in Greenville.

The old *Democrat-Times,* the newspaper which we engaged in mortal combat for a year and ten months, and outlasted, was more inoffensive than any newspaper has any right to be. Its editor, a gentle kindly man, had considerable talent as a musician and liked to travel, but he had neither talent nor any great liking for the post he had inherited. Ernest Smith's father had bequeathed three quarters of the newspaper's stock to his second wife, the editor's stepmother, and only one sixteenth to each of his four children; and that division was no small factor in our own victory.

Ernest, a good man, had nothing much to gain from fighting back, even had he wanted to fight; and like many lifelong citizens of a growing community, he didn't realize that Greenville was changing from an amiable small town to a city with new problems and wider interests. The only real fighter on his staff was a reporter named Charles Kerg, three hundred and twelve pounds of single-minded devotion, who had begun his newspaper career as a nine-year-old carrier, progressing therefrom to office boy and part-time pressman. Finally he served, at one and the same time, as the telegraph editor, sports editor and only reporter on a daily newspaper in a growing little city which, in 1936, could count nearly twenty thousand citizens who deserved a more complete paper. When we eventually purchased the *Democrat-Times,* Charlie was afraid that because of his aggressive resistance to our *Delta Star,* we might not want him; but I would not have traded him for the Memphis *Commercial Appeal*'s city room; and he is now the staff's veteran, a civic encyclopedia, forty of whose forty-nine years have been devoted to one newspaper and its successor.

Ernest Smith had said often that he did not believe a newspaper should hurt the feelings of anyone if it could possibly be helped, and he meant it for that was his nature; but this delicacy was a principal reason why Will Percy and David Cohn were able to persuade their friends to join them in helping finance a new newspaper. Little good is accomplished without controversy, and no civic evil is ever defeated without publicity. The only critical editorial I ever read in the old *Democrat-Times* was one which suggested that parents advise their small boys not to throw peanut shells from the movie balcony upon the patrons below. In the first year of competition the *Democrat-Times* fought us principally by listing in a front-page box an ever-increasing number of subscribers, while in actuality they were losing them. When the owners finally got around to employing additional and combative staff members, it was too late.

Before we came to Greenville, in 1936, the *Democrat* had printed local news only when it was brought in or when overworked Charlie Kerg could get around to gathering it, which was sometimes considerably after it happened. Things changed somewhat after our arrival, for the *Democrat* could not afford to let us print first, the next morning, a story that had developed before their afternoon deadline. So it was that this bulletin on a citizen's passing appeared as undoubtedly prepared and brought in by someone who loved fine writing no less than he cherished the deceased:

> The gentle spirit of Miss ——— was wafted heavenward at two o'clock this afternoon (more tomorrow).

The truth was that, to our own good fortune, the publishers of the old *Democrat-Times* were not nearly as interested in the newspaper as in the commercial printing plant which they operated as a profitable adjunct. The *Democrat*'s advertising rates were ridiculously low even for the depressed times. The circulation was not audited or collected for regularly or even solicited, for it was easier to announce that the paper had so many subscribers, since nobody would bother to check, and nobody did until we came along. Instead of buying a full news service from the Associated Press or the United Press, the *Democrat* subscribed only to a brief bulletin summation of the day's outstanding events which was telephoned from Jackson at noon; so that it was not unusual for a story from London or Washington or New York or Rome to have more words in the headlines than in the text itself.

All of which made our infant *Delta Star* look very good indeed; and especially did the *Democrat's* policy of keeping out unpleasant local news make our own policy of printing all the local news we could get, regardless of anyone's feelings, appear excitingly Hearstian to Greenville. Some Grenvillians, I knew, didn't like it, but they subscribed to the *Delta Star* all the same, and when we finally took over the *Democrat-Times,* its circulation had shrunk to less than half of our own.

I am not telling this in derision of a defeated competitor, but in amazement at the survival ability of even the weakest newspapers against aggressive and determined competition. The *Democrat* should have given up sometime during the first year, for it was losing circulation and money too; but the Smiths hung on, and we had as hard a time financially as did they, and maybe a harder time, until Billy Wynn, an astute man and one of our principal stockholders, negotiated the purchase of one winded old newspaper by an equally winded new one. The good will built up through the years, the personal friendships and loyalties that go deep in our smaller communities, the reluctance of advertisers to use an untested medium, and habit most of all—these are the assets upon which any established newspaper, no matter how poorly operated, can depend. And additionally, the *Democrat* relied mistakenly on its policy of not hurting anyone's feelings. The trouble was that our competitors kept their friends, but their friends took our newspaper to find out what was going on.

We probably won the fight two months after we began publication. The *Democrat* never revealed the identity of any white offender found guilty in city court of misdemeanors, reporting only that "A white man was fined twenty-five dollars for assault with a dangerous weapon." The *Delta Star* did publish such names from the start; but during the first several weeks of publication no one of consequence was haled before the city judge, and so there was no outcry from anyone else of consequence, it being the custom of Greenvillians no less than of other folks elsewhere to be undisturbed by change if it is titillating or personally beneficial or, negatively, harmless to oneself or one's kind. I doubt that one among a hundred of them even mused upon the unfairness of conferring protective anonymity upon one group of offenders and withholding it from another, simply on the basis of skin color.

Late one night a prominent and well-connected and prosperous citizen had a few nips too many and thereafter took a quick turn around town in his automobile. What happened then could have happened to many of us. In no time at all he fetched up against a lamppost and was arrested and escorted to the city pokey. Greenville's police and city court had a reputation then—and deserve it to this day—for impartial law enforcement. The leading citizen was booked for drunken driving and locked up overnight; his trial was set for the next afternoon.

Most of the town heard about the mischance the next morning as soon as did we on the *Delta Star*. Wagers were made as to whether we would dare to print this man's name in the court news. To make sure that we wouldn't, a number of influential people telephoned us out of friendship for the defendant and his family and urged us to leave out his name. If we had, I doubt that we would have lasted very long; nor could we, in good conscience, deviate from a policy because of a man's prominence or wealth or friends or the advertising he might control. His name went in and his advertising came out; but not often since then has anyone asked us to omit names from unfavorable news stories. I regretted and still regret that we had to shame that man and his fine family; but it is a universal human failing in such cases to blame the newspaper for printing the story and not hold a grudge against the law or the offender or the arresting officer. We made enemies with that story, but we also made friends and converts and, more consequentially, we established ourselves as a newspaper which was neither beholden to nor influenced by anyone in town, not even our stockholders.

It is of no use to detail all the difficult aspects of establishing a sizable daily newspaper, from the renting of an empty building to the purchasing of secondhand equipment and furniture and the rounding up of a mechanical, news and advertising force. Nothing works out in actuality as does the plan on paper.

I personally had to clean out our rented building, unoccupied since the 1927 flood, for it was caked with the silt left by the overflow; and one unhappy dawn, as I, barefoot and in undershirt, was hosing gooey mud out of the front door and into the street, I blew the mess all over an early rising businessman. He didn't know or recognize me and when I later met him, I didn't remind him of the tongue lashing he gave me.

We bought some impossible equipment at bargain prices from conscienceless firms, and we had trouble assembling even the workable secondhand machinery we had brought together from all over the country. We ate and worked and slept with trouble.

In the beginning Betty tried to sell all the advertising alone, and my brother John attempted in those first few months to take care of the circulation department as well as our one-man engraving shop. We had no trouble finding a society editor and a one-man-and-one-woman news staff. But the *Delta Star's* percentage of sober, able and permanent printers was abysmally low, nor do I wonder, remembering the impossibly long hours, sometimes twenty at a stretch, during which we wrestled with frozen linotypes and a press that tore the paper to shreds. This mechanical turmoil continued from early November, when we began publication, until Christmas and afterwards, and the turnover of printers and linotype operators was unending. Among the loyal, rugged survivors of the first two months was one cocky little New Yorker, who had spent much time as a newspaper strikebreaker and, as it turned out, as much time in serious drinking. He was a dogged, profane, skillful man who could do anything in a newspaper shop, and it was our fault that he also fell by the wayside.

Before we left on Christmas Eve morning with the sugar-plum vision of two days' vacation, I distributed to each printer, as holiday largesse, a pint of whisky, part of a case rustled by Bob Brown, the male news staff, from a friendly deputy sheriff in dry Mississippi. We planned to go to press by noon that day with the morrow's Christmas Day morning newspaper, a pre-date filled mostly with greeting advertisements. There would be no paper the day after Christmas—I think it was Saturday, the day we normally skipped publication anyway—so that the staff would also have nearly two days of rest. Shortly before noon Betty and my brother and I set out for Hammond and New Orleans, and before we reached Greenville's city limits, the caps were off the bottles back in the *Delta Star's* shop. That was costly because in an hour the boys were taking turns firing each other and throwing empty bottles against the walls; and about that time, a new and important advertiser, to whom Betty had sold a half-page post-Christmas-sale ad—his first appearance in the newspaper—turned up to get a proof. Instead he got one of the closest calls of his quiet life, for our strikebreaking printer let fly with an empty bottle which just missed the man's head, and told him to get the hell out and let some hard-working printers enjoy Christmas. So he did, and he was lost to us for a long time, too.

I don't know why I didn't turn prohibitionist then or soon afterwards. A riverman, who had been accustomed to having his fling on odd weekends, landing in jail and paying his fine on Monday mornings, with few the wiser and generally only himself the sadder, found his name in the court-news column one Tuesday. He came to the *Delta Star* sober and angry and told me that it wasn't to happen again. When it did happen again, he waited until his next drunken spell and then telephoned me to say that he was in a small café, about three doors down the street from us, and that if I cared to join him, he'd be proud to blow the top of my head off. I can't yet explain the impulse that moved me, but I pretended not to understand and asked him to hold the line a minute. Then I beckoned to Bob Brown, and we walked quickly to the café where the bemused frolicker was still holding on to the receiver. Bob grabbed one arm and I took the other and we began explaining to him that there wasn't anything personal about his newsworthiness. About that time the police arrived, for the proprietor's wife had heard the customer's message to me and had wisely dispatched her husband to the station, less than a block away; but Bob and I told the officer that nothing much had been going on and that our friend wasn't making any trouble; so that night he slept in his own bed and he never bothered us again, even though he did provide a minor paragraph every now and then for some time.

If the easygoing ways of the *Democrat* were one necessary factor in our eventual victory in Greenville, and our own print-it-all policy another, a vital third was the assembling of news and business staffs which quickly and wondrously were annealed into a pugnacious, enterprising and fanatically loyal team. The average age the first year was twenty-four, and I at twenty-nine was just next to the oldest. They were eager, spoiling for a fight, and most of them had either very limited newspaper experience or no experience at all. I wish I could tell of them all. Rodney Defenbaugh of Kentucky—who came to be advertising manager after Betty had worn herself out trying to do, and doing, the hardest job on the paper with only indifferent help or none at all—went on later to the ownership of his own little daily. John Gibson, then nineteen years old and the ailing circulation manager's assistant, stayed with us and is now general manager and a minority stockholder. Don Wetherbee, a Greenville boy, and a tennis-playing Phi Beta Kappa just out of the University of North Carolina, was with us for three years and was editor during my first year in the army; then he went to medical school and became a doctor, which is what he wanted to be all along. And there was Virginia Callahan, a breathless cub, and Lou Crump and Shelby Foote, and my brother, who at one time or another held every kind of job on the paper except in the shop, and Electa Atcher, who began as a columnist-bookkeeper.

And especially there was Bob Brown. His letter of application, which arrived about a week after we had put out the first issue and were beginning to wonder why, read: "Young.

Alert. Aggressive. Experienced. Ninety bucks." I telephoned him, confirmed my hopeful suspicion that the ninety bucks salary was for a month, not a week, and told him that unless he could get to Greenville from Hattiesburg in twenty-four hours, he needn't come, because I'd be dead and the *Star* fallen.

Bob arrived at midnight that same night, all of twenty-two, with deceptively sleepy eyes, a slow-breaking grin and the biggest bagful of untried tricks that ever bewildered another newspaper. Just before we won out, Bob went on to the Associated Press, then to the New Orleans *Times-Picayune*, to Washington, to a radio stint in New York, and finally to the executive editorship on the Columbus *Ledger-Enquirer* in Georgia, with a year out later as a Nieman fellow. I'm thankful for his two years with us. Bob haunted the police court and fire stations, the courthouse and the hotels. He slept maybe six hours a night, and the rest of the time he gathered news during and after hours. Some fortunate reporters have the ability to dig up and to write readable stories and write them fast. Bob was one of them, a newsman who could and almost every day did gather and write from twenty-five to thirty-five stories, ranging from one paragraph in city briefs to exclusive tales which he developed himself. To goad our competitor he suggested that beneath each local story that we printed ahead of the *Democrat-Times*, we run in very small type the line "You Read It in the Star," which we did, and in no time at all people were complimenting us on having so many firsts. Once Bob wrote a paragraph in his column—I grieve to say it was "Things Done Brown"—which nearly caused the American Legion to boycott us because he questioned the intelligence of the state commander who, in his banquet address at the annual state convention in Greenville, had forgotten to include our newborn newspaper in his acknowledgments of gratitude for publicity.

Whenever Charlie Kerg got a ticket for overtime parking, which was often, Bob would add a tabulative sentence: "This is Mr. Kerg's fourth such offense this month." On the serious side, he was forever coming up with stories which our public bodies, like most public bodies, didn't want printed, not because the politicians were dishonest but because they were not accustomed to reportorial questioning or editorial challenge. As offset, he wrote story after story on community personalities, from the newest cop to the oldest courthouse worker. And he wrote a most memorable series, entitled "The Case of the Mysterious Skeleton."

The skeleton was ploughed up by a levee building crew, and Bob made it locally famous. For a week after the disinterment, he hung around the courthouse much longer than usual, going through newspaper files and court records, and talking to deputies and old-timers. He supplemented this activity with overlong visits to the police station. And then we began his series, which each day delved into the possibility that these bones were the remains of a different Washington countian, man or woman, white or black, who sometime within the memory of man had disappeared and had never been heard of since. Bob quoted pleased elder citizens in each case; and on the next day, the previous day's surmise would be discarded in favor of another unfortunate. The skeleton series made good spring reading and so maddened the *Democrat-Times* that Charlie went about denouncing the whole affair as a fraud, which it almost was.

Not all of Bob's stories were as successful. One weekend a citizen disappeared with several hundred dollars of his own money in his pockets. Bob, who was the best foul-play scenter in the state, immediately smelled murder for profit, and wrote for the Sunday paper a detailed speculative story, as to where, when and how the victim could have been waylaid, murdered and robbed. For Monday, he had a personal interview with a somewhat dubious wife. It began simply: "I interviewed Mrs. Zilch today. 'I am afraid,' she said." Bob may also have been a little afraid a day or so later when the husband turned up in Natchez, bereft of his bank roll, and the irate wife took part of her wrath out on us for making her look so silly, which hadn't been Bob's purpose at all. His only ambition all the time he was with us was to make the *Democrat-Times* look silly and us look good, and he was generally successful.

This is only the lighter side of a versatile newspaperman's activity. Bob had what were then relatively unusual beliefs about social inequalities and their cures. He and I conspired to print for the first time in a Mississippi newspaper the taboo words "syphilis" and "gonorrhea," in a campaign for free treatment of their victims. An older citizen came in to protest vigorously the use of those sordid words in a household publication. Bob told him earnestly that we were doing it in the public weal, and that before we finished we hoped to have syphilis in the minds of every citizen in the county.

Our staff never believed that we could be whipped, nor knew that we almost were. But despite the favorable factors, the Greenville story could have been considerably different had it not been for Will Percy and the kind of men he rallied as stockholders. In another book, but too briefly, I have acknowledged these men who were strangers and became our friends; and the story in any case is happy enough to merit retelling.

The arrangement Will and I agreed upon required Betty and me to put up half of the sum which I thought would be enough to equip a newspaper and get it on its feet. He and the men whom he proposed to gather as fellow stockholders would put up the other half. I would have editorial and managerial control, but the stockholders would sit with us as a board of directors and advise on business matters. When and if I was able to purchase their stock, I could do so. The original stockholders, in addition to Will and Dave were William T. Wynn, a Greenville lawyer who is, unobtrusively, a dominant financial and political figure in the South; Edmund Taylor, a major wholesaler, who has always given away so much of his money and his time that I don't know how he had any for us; Colonel Alexander FitzHugh of Vicksburg, a Jeffersonian Virginian; Joe Virden, a young lumber dealer and a leader among the Catholics of Greenville; J.Q. and Joe Strange, who held the Coca-Cola franchise and would do anything Will asked them; Mrs. Paul Gamble, a surgeon's wife, and, of all things in Mississippi in 1936, a Republican; Frank England, the Ford dealer, who was usually the chairman of every civic fund-raising drive. They differed among themselves in all manner of ways, but they were alike in their community standing and integrity and in their faithful observance of our verbal agreement that I alone could make the editorial decisions.

The amount of money I figured would be enough was too small, and it seems today in retrospect impossibly inadequate. The machinery, poor as some of it was, cost more than I had figured and soon we had to buy more equipment too. Cotton was lower than even our advertising rate, which had to match the *Democrat*'s giveaway advertising price structure, and the merchants only infrequently increased their budgets, preferring instead to split them, so that each newspaper received only half rations of advertising at rates no more than half of what they should have been. Our circulation grew and grew and in the end was the principal factor responsible for victory; but distribution was costly, and whenever we announced a new figure, the *Democrat* simply added to its stated circulation. We were chronically short of cash but Will and Billy and Edmund and the rest came through time after time, one with an additional thousand dollars, another with two thousand, all with something, while Betty and I tried to hold up our financial end by borrowing from the banks and on my life insurance and, once, in desperation, selling a fine old wardrobe we had recklessly bought.

At least once a month the directors would hold ludicrously long-faced sessions in which Betty and Rodney and I would report that we were in bad straits but that they ought to see the other fellow; and it was apparent from checking the *Democrat's* lineage that our opponents were being hurt at least as much as were we.

We came to set great store on proper business management, believing, or professing to believe, that a good general manager could make ends meet at twenty-five cents a column inch, and agreeing with solemn unanimity that I was no business manager and should be relieved; and so I was, first by one and then another; Rodney and then Don, and for a short while my own overworked wife; and while these changes didn't seem to affect the balance sheets they did give us something to look forward to until the next dejected meeting.

Those directors stayed with us until the happy end, which was skillfully brought about by Billy Wynn after some unorthodox detective work had convinced us that the *Democrat-Times* would soon be willing to quit or sell. Thinking back now, I know that it wasn't so much the directors' money—though that was imperative—as their identification with the *Delta Star* that really counted, for they took from us the curse of strangeness. The first week we were in Greenville, Will gave a champagne supper for an assortment of Greenvillians of all ages whom he thought we would like—we came across that supper list not long ago, and it was a marvel to see how right he was in nearly every instance—and the other directors joined in, each in his own way, in their homes and in the homes of friends on whom we would call together, so that in a very little time we had an inner assurance of belonging.

The end of the fight came suddenly. John Gibson and I were convinced that the *Democrat-Times* was making inaccurate circulation claims, and that our own audited circulation was in reality much larger than theirs. The trick was to prove it. The *Democrat-Times'* press, a relatively slow, eight-page duplex, was located in the front of its building, just behind a large plate-glass window, and a passer-by could count the printed newspapers as they came from it. But we could hardly stand on the sidewalk in front of the press and count the papers, nor could we set anyone else to counting from such a conspicuous vantage point. We went to the owner of a building across the street, in which two upstairs front offices were vacant, and rented those offices for a week. During that week we, and a friendly notary public, watched with binoculars, counting aloud as the *Democrat* came off the press. We did this four times, and then drew up a notarized affidavit that the circulation as carefully counted was not much more than half of what our competitors claimed. Then we sent a copy of the affidavit to the *Democrat,* with the notification that unless their circulation statements were immediately amended, we were prepared to inform the post office that they were false.

The measure was harsh, but so was the provocation; and such provocation continues to exist wherever daily or weekly newspapers present false claims in the annual statements of ownership and circulation required by the post office from every publication using the mails for any part of its distribution. The abuse of the mailing privilege—through the making of unsupported and often invalid circulation statements as against the audited figures supplied by most dailies and the better-run weeklies—is a continuing newspaper scandal which the American press itself should remedy from within. But in this instance, we turned the abuse to good advantage.

We didn't hear from the *Democrat* directly, but the word got around, as it always does in small places, that something was about to happen. Certainly the *Democrat* people must have been getting discouraged. They had been losing circulation, lineage and money for a year. While they had many allies, against them stood some of Greenville's most irreproachable and powerful citizens. And our *Delta Star* was the better paper. Meanwhile, we had talked matters over with the directors, and especially with Billy Wynn, whom we all recognized as our best negotiator. Billy went to the Smiths and, after no more than a month of parleying, he succeeded in arranging the purchase of the *Democrat* for a price which, if it was too much for what was left of the *Democrat*, was still not as much as we would have paid to get it. Billy knew we were overpaying and his own reason for doing so was a splendid one, even if I wasn't so sure of that at the time. After all, he said, the Smiths were Greenvillians too, and the family had a right to a fair price. They got it.

All that seems a long time ago. The veterans of the conflict are more than a little grizzled, but most of the time they and the transient young newcomers behave as if we must still beat the competition to the story. Last spring the *Delta Democrat-Times* won three first places, two second places and a third place in the Mississippi Press Association's six competitions for Mississippi dailies; and we have a dozen more trophies which staff members have won singly or together. I'm glad of this because whenever a monopoly acts too much like a monopoly it is likely not to be a monopoly much longer; and while I am predisposed against newspaper monopolies elsewhere, I am all for the one in Greenville.

8

A Lady Known as Lou

The best way to tell about Lou is to start in the middle or even further on, for that's her own way and she has been accustomed to having it for all of the sixteen years since she became the first staff member of our a-borning newspaper in Greenville and, more important personally, our oldest and dearest friend in a land where old friendships count for a great deal.

Lou is one of that consecrated, sometimes maligned sisterhood known in an earlier day as "society editors," but in a world of expanding feminine activity are titled "women's page editors." Lou uses the job and the rank alike as a sort of Trojan horse with which to breach any wall in Greenville.

Her full name, which on occasion she can give with some hauteur, is Louise Eskrigge Crump. She is handsome in a rangy English way. When we first met, she was a grassy young widow whom Dave Cohn called the Widder Smith, and who, Will Percy said, would shortly be running the town, including us, if we selected her for the post for which he had so strongly recommended her.

But that is no way to start in the middle. Maybe the story of Lou and the Arrogant Agent will do. . . .

One day, shortly before noon, about a year after the end of World War Two, a tall, brusque, youngish man came into our newspaper office and thrust a penciled classified ad at little Emily, who was eighteen or so, and new at the job of tending counter. He told her that the advertisement must appear in that day's paper. Emily answered that he would have to wait until the next day since the classified deadline was four o'clock the afternoon before insertion, and that today's first edition would be going to press in about half an hour.

The stranger slammed his fist on the counter and told Emily she didn't understand. The ad had to go in today, or else there'd be trouble. It had to do with the loss of his set of office keys. He was John X—there's no use giving his name now—he was an Internal Revenue Agent, and if Emily and the newspaper knew what was good for them they'd stop the presses. That was in the days when folks had a great deal of respect for the Internal Revenue Department, more than they came to have later. Emily quailed and said she'd see. She took the ad to Jimmy Gatens, who was advertising manager, and repeated the man's threat.

Jimmy Gatens didn't like it, but he figured a soft answer was the best way to turn away wrath, so he went to the counter and began explaining about deadlines. He didn't get far. Agent X pounded the counter again and harder, lifted his voice to a roar and told Gatens and the office in general that the newspaper was heading into some real trouble if that ad didn't get in. Jimmy, who also has a temper, turned away and left him.

About that time Lou and Jimmy Alsop went into action. Jimmy, God rest him, had joined the paper soon after the end of the war—just as we had planned five years before back at Camp Blanding—as soon as he could get back from the Pacific with his three healed wounds and the jungle-weary heart that was to kill him two years later. Jimmy and Lou had both heard Agent X—everybody had—because in the sprawling first floor of the *Delta Democrat-Times,* there are no partitions between the news, business and circulation departments, and everybody has a fine time listening to what is going on everywhere else, which is better for morale than for efficiency.

So they came up to the belligerent Agent X, and Jimmy asked in his deceptively soft voice, "What's the trouble, friend?" Agent X started all over again, if possible even more loudly. Jimmy interrupted with a question which must have shaken him.

"Do you want to be thrown out on your ear?" he asked as one big and angry man to another.

In the angry hush, Lou went into action.

"You're in a lady's presence," she said in her best Father-came-from-England accent and manner. "You have no business, moreover, to disgrace your position this way. And I can tell you that you're a fortunate man that our publisher is out of the office. Now go quietly before—before"—she nodded at Jimmy—"our Mr. Alsop has to use force."

The big agent looked at Louise and at Jimmy, and I know which one he was more in awe of. He spat over his shoulder, "Somebody will pay for this," and out he went.

I had been covering a meeting and when I came in, about

fifteen minutes after the invasion, work had not been resumed in the front office of the Delta's largest daily. When Lou and Emily and the two Jimmies told me what had happened I blew up too. I said, "We'll give him his ad. We'll give it to him on the front page."

They looked disappointed. I banged out a short box for the front page. In it I reported that Agent X—giving his name—had lost his keys and that Agent X had thoroughly cowed the staff of the *Democrat-Times,* so that we were breaking all deadline and position restrictions with this front-page announcement. In short, the *Delta Democrat-Times* was herewith offering a five-dollar reward to whoever would throw Agent X's keys in the river after finding them.

The story made both editions. Everybody in the office thought it was fine. Agent X never reappeared. But, two days later, a quiet, middle-aged man came into the office. He identified himself as the agent in charge of the whole district, and he had journeyed from New Orleans to investigate the incident behind the news clipping which someone—perhaps Agent X—had thoughtfully sent him. I wondered whether the story had violated any law relative to encouragement of the destruction of federal property. But the quiet visitor went on to say that his office was distressed by what was apparently inexcusable behavior on the part of Agent X, and was there anyone in the office who could give him an eyewitness account?

Was there! At her desk, Lou was watching us with the intensity of a mother bear scenting threat to her cave. I beckoned to her and after presenting the visitor to her, and identifying him, I asked if she could tell him just what had taken place between Agent X and the embattled staff of the DDT.

Lou is the only person I know who can look haughtily down her nose with one eye while the other twinkles conspiratorially. When I saw that look, I knew what was coming. Not that she deviated from the truth; but she told the truth with overtones of aggrieved womanhood, stressing her loss of faith in the Bureau of Internal Revenue and a sense of outrage at an unfair attack upon the freedom of the press. The very decent investigator began to look about helplessly for the door. When she had finished, he turned to me.

"I don't think we'll have to ask further," he said. "I know that our whole department wants to join me in apologies. And I don't think anyone will be bothered much longer by Agent X." We found out later than Agent X was let out the next week. We learned too that he had used his position as a means of trying to frighten other people before he had sought to get his classified into the *Democrat-Times*, so we didn't feel sorry for him.

So much for a beginning in the middle. The beginning at the beginning, ten years before, was an augury of the kind of society editor I was acquiring.

That job, I had told Will Percy, was perhaps the most important one to fill for a newspaper whose editor was a newcomer and whose prospective readers, as in all small cities, were more interested in each other's business than in earth-shaking editorials or the latest confidential report from Washington. The society editor had to know everybody; she had to be somebody herself and have the ability to make everyone else feel like somebody, for towns such as ours do not have and should never have a restricted list from which social items are drawn. She would have to be someone whom we would like and who would like us, because, if the staff didn't get along it would never weather the long, hard hours that went into launching a competitive newspaper. We knew from our four years in Louisiana.

So Will mused and giggled, and said, "Louise Eskrigge Smith"—she was still the Widder Smith, courted by Brodie Crump whom she would marry the next year—"that is, if you can show her that it's a cause. Lou has to have causes." Will, who delighted in the tender absurdities, giggled again. "Only thing, she'll be running you all and the paper and the town too."

So the next day Betty and I got together with Lou. We drove to the top of the levee on the Greenville water front. At the beginning Lou put on what Dave describes as "dignity wid dawg," because she was unsure of what we were like and what the job was like. We talked of this and that for a while and then I began to tell her what was required of a society editor. I didn't get far. Lou's eyes fixed on a tin can that lay to the side of the sloping concrete ramp on which we were parked.

"Tin cans, tin cans," she mused dramatically. "That's the very first thing we must get started. Everyone must punch holes in tin cans."

Betty and I looked at each other covertly. She had seemed so right, she knew everyone, she was interested in the job. Could she be a little odd? Tin cans had nothing to do, as far as we knew, with society columns. But Lou, as we were to discover later, was not one to concentrate on such restricted topics as society.

"What about tin cans?" I asked. "Why punch holes in them?"

It was to be the first of her many triumphant encounters with an editor blind to the finer things of life.

"Why, malaria," she said. "Mosquitoes breed in tin cans. We have to get everyone to punch holes in tin cans before they are thrown away so they can't fill with water. That's one of the very first things we'll campaign for."

And so it was. So, too, it was that Lou became society editor of the paper, from which vantage point she would thenceforth direct tin-can punching and a myriad of other civic enterprises that at their outset sometimes left me quaking and more often moved at her compassion and the nimbleness with which she skipped from civic need to civic enterprise.

Like the adoption of the orphanage. . . .

One fall, about five years ago, Lou came into my office. She had that look. She said, "We're going to do the most wonderful thing this Christmas." I said, "Lou, the most wonderful thing for this paper to do at Christmas is to sell a lot of Christmas advertising."

She said, "Be quiet, Nutsie, and listen." She started calling me Nutsie the first month of the old *Delta Star*, when everything was going wrong, and I had yelled in anguish one dreadful afternoon, "I'm going nuts! I'm going nuts!" and Lou had shouted back, "Don't yell so loud, Nutsie."

I listened. She said, "We're going to have Greenville adopt an orphanage for three days at Christmas time. Some people can take two children or three into their homes. Some can take just one, some won't be able to take any, but they can contribute. There's a Methodist orphanage in Jackson, with three hundred children, and I think you and Betty ought to take two . . ."

The project was that of Beta Sigma Phi, an organization of younger women whose Greenville chapter Lou herself had fostered. Now she turned all her energy to the fairy-godmother job of moving the orphanage.

Never will I—nor anyone in Greenville who participated in the Christmastime orphan adoption—forget those three days. The townspeople, under Lou's and the organization's canny screening, snapped up those three hundred orphans, gave the reception party for them at the country club, and on Christmas morning watched with tear-wet eyes as three hundred little waifs enjoyed, in homes that had children and homes that did not, a family Christmas. The town would have adopted them again and again, but the orphanage directors decided, and perhaps wisely, that the emotional strain upon the children themselves was too great—perhaps a little too much like showing them a glimpse of Heaven and then taking them away.

Some years before the beginning of her career as a newspaper woman, at the depth of the depression, Lou was one of a small group of women which started a local club patterned in part after the Junior League. This group, the Junior Auxiliary, became sponsors of the underprivileged children of Greenville, providing medical care and groceries for the sick, milk for the undernourished, and clothing for those who needed it. No small-town, socially self-conscious imitation of its archetype, the Junior Auxiliary in Greenville has built a day nursery, complete with equipped playground, and hires a full-time supervisor for the twenty and more children of underprivileged families and working mothers; it distributes three hundred dollars' worth of milk and medicines a month, and is active in every community drive. In 1936, Lou, the newspaperwoman, could see even more clearly the amount of energy being wasted in the smaller cities, energy too often turned only to bridge, mah-jongg or canasta when work with children was at hand needing to be done. She and some friends decided to organize this energy. They founded the National Association of Junior Auxiliaries, which now has twenty-two chapters in six Southern states. At the "national's" tenth birthday convention Lou was given the birthday cake to cut in recognition of her mothering of the infant organization.

Lou—with a strong assist from her banjo-playing farmer

husband, who has a photostatic memory—operates through their joint column an unofficial clearinghouse for the relief of any living thing in need—from canaries who require a home, or dogs that are lost, to a child who should be adopted —and was—and families who have been burned out and who want any kind of clothing suitable for one-year-olds, two-year-olds and up. Lou's column, "Delta Scene," appears three times a week and alternates with Brodie's nostalgic, vividly recollected "Mostly Old Stuff." Once Lou got six wheel chairs from one paragraph about a crippled little boy. Brodie topped her not long afterward by getting a truckload of clothing and furniture for a tenant family which had lost everything—just as the Crumps themselves had lost everything when their lovely old plantation house had burned to the ground soon after Brodie's father died. Medicines, blood donations, toys, whatever is needed off the beaten track of the welfare workers, have become Lou's and Brodie's responsibility; and along with it, as a matter of course, the publicity chairmanships for almost every formal welfare drive in town.

Lou is directly and almost solely responsible for the Newcomers Club, an organization of young married women newly moved to our rapidly growing town; it provides a way of knowing each other and becoming known; and a new garden club, also for the younger women to whom the swollen lists of the established clubs were closed in our flower-loving river community. Whenever the organizer for any national women's group comes to town she comes first to Lou. And she's right to do it.

It's fifteen years now since Lou first sat down, with fingers unaccustomed to a typewriter and with a spelling system all her own, to report the social doings of our little Mississippi city. There is no way of telling the social errors she has covered up, the delicate decisions made about birth announcements, the advice she has given to brides and grooms, the schools and colleges she has helped select for the children of puzzled parents. Let an ancient relic of an old Greenville family pass away and it is Louise and Brodie who will supply the sidelights that are best left out of the obituary, like: "Oh, yes, she was Cousin Amanda's great-aunt, Brodie, the one who was in that scandal with the deacon forty years ago." It is Brodie's reserved privilege to write the proper editorial about a deceased citizen, often with another private one, never to be printed, describing for our howling staff's benefit just what the other side of the all-too-human old-so-and-so really was like.

In those fifteen years, Lou has seen a lot of us come and go —to war, to new jobs, sometimes to pot. Her own Richard, now a six-foot-five giant, is in uniform; and during the war it was Lou who channeled the stories about Deltans in service, led in opening a recreation center for the cadets at Greenville's airfield, and told for those young, homesick men overseas the chatty little tales of home town and home people that were too inconsequential to make the regular news columns, yet so much more meaningful than any story in them.

She has an undiminished pride in performance. Not a week goes by but what she places her Sunday front society page beside the creations of her sisters on the Memphis and New Orleans and Jackson dailies. And not a week but what, after the inspection, the Eskrigge English eye runs scornfully down her nose and the Eskrigge voice takes on its most modulated English tone as she comments that there's simply no comparison. And most times there isn't, because Lou has an artist's feeling for gay, balanced and imaginative picture layouts.

Small city newspapers being what they are, Lou has extracurricular duties. Once a week she is food-page editor. As such, she tired long ago of the impersonal recipes and household hints. She invented a family, which she pretended was real, and presented menus, dishes and shopping lists in dialogue under the standing title, "Life with the Joneses." Once a week, she is also church editor, in which post she is chiefly occupied with cutting down the lengthy notices prepared by our clergymen, seeing to it that all denominations get the same space, and pacifying ministers who accuse her of playing favorites, including one whom she scolded once to his face for acting like a clerical hog.

There is one other little extracurricular duty in which she takes delight. Lou is the official mother confessor of the office, the patcher-upper of the small jealousies, quarrels and politicking that mark every enterprise in which two or more are gathered together. Her technique with the younger members of the staff is to become melodramatic, almost to the point of tears, and recall the old days when we were all so busy—a sort of there-were-giants-in-the-land approach—that we had no time or inclination to fall out. With the veterans she just talks tough. And in no time at all the aggrieved principals and Lou are having coffee at Al's Café Number 2, that incredible hangout of the *Democrat-Times,* which observes the amenities of segregation by having its many Negro and white patrons sit at opposite counters, which face each other, in the slightly partitioned room.

Yet all the while Lou had been nursing a secret grief, which needs be a secret no longer. For some reason or another, our little newspaper has consistently attracted reporters to whom journalism was second to the writing of magazine articles, short stories or novels. Shelby Foote left us for war and the subsequent writing career, back home in Greenville, which already has produced five novels, two of especially high merit. Ben Wasson, editor of Mississippi's only full book page, has published one novel and still turns out magazine pieces. Tom Karsell, who is in Korea now as a recalled reserve captain, was beginning to sell to the magazines before he left, and David Brown, who is just back from Korea after a year and a half as Army combat correspondent, is writing his first book. So is Bob Tims, who writes editorials. And George Stroud's by-line is coming to be known in the national farm magazines as well as it already is on our Farm Page. I can't criticize them for paying more attention to their creative brain children than to their jobs on the paper, because they answer that I do the same thing.

Only Lou hadn't tried to write a book, and I think it bothered her. So, she came in to see me one day, about two years ago, and with a couple of preliminary dramatic flourishes of voice and manner, announced she was about to write a novel. I pretended not to have heard her, and she pretended in turn to be furious.

Then I said, "You'll never finish it; you won't stick at it. So forget it," figuring it would make her mad enough to start that day. It did. In the early spring of 1952, Lou finished *Helen Templeton's Daughter*, a voodoo, Delta-cotton and love novel published in August. I never thought she really would finish it, and I'm not sure that she thought so either, but there it is, and a good yarn, too, and she has another in the making. The women's-page department isn't suffering either, for Lou has earned, and the paper has grown to require, an assistant in that most imperative of a newspaper's departments.

But last spring, just after the book was finished, the assistant carried the load alone for two long and anxious months. Probably because she wanted to complete her book, come high water or low cotton, Lou had delayed undergoing an operation for an obstruction in her throat. She almost delayed too long, for when she finally went to the hospital, the surgeons were afraid that they could not operate successfully. I don't think any society editor in all the history of newspapers ever had as many or as different people praying for her as did Lou Crump when word got around Greenville that it might be touch and go. Her room was a florist's shop at Eastertime, there were bottles of old bourbon hidden behind bedpans; there were cakes and candies, which she could not drink or eat herself, but which were hauled out many times daily for visitors.

I even wrote an editorial, though I explained later to Lou that it was only to forestall Brodie from writing a too-prejudiced obituary in advance. In it I told the surgeons and nurses of King's Daughters hospital in Greenville that they had a very special fellow practitioner as a patient. She was Lou Crump, doctor of humanities, and they'd damn well better make sure that she got out again.

They did and she did, and when she reads this she'll be as surprised as I was sixteen years ago when she told me we had to punch holes in tin cans. And in passing, I am certain that there are Lous and Bettys and Davids and Charlies and Johns and Toms and Georges and Bobs on other and larger papers who are just as devoted and hopeful and ambitious and united as is my own news staff of irreverent prima donnas led by a prima-prima donna who calls me Nutsie. But maybe the difference is that because our paper is small I know what I have, and am humbled and happy in the knowledge.

9

The A.M. of *PM*

One night back in 1937 I read in *Editor & Publisher*, which is the newspaperman's *Variety*, a story about a new kind of fellowship which Harvard University had just announced. It was the Nieman Fellowship for newspapermen created by President Conant on the sagacious assumption that there were better ways to spend money in behalf of higher newspaper standards than to found still another journalism school.

The widow of Lucius Nieman, who had been a remarkable Milwaukee publisher, had left to Harvard some two million dollars in her husband's memory, with no strings attached except that it be used to invigorate the newspaper profession. President Conant's decision was to set up fellowships which would bring to Harvard younger newspapermen with at least five years' experience for a year of study, writing, self-searching and informal weekly meetings with the nation's best journalists; a sort of breath-catching sabbatical which no ordinary younger newspaperman had ever found time or money to enjoy.

The Nieman grants were generous. Each recipient would receive at least as much as he was earning from his newspaper work, up to a ceiling which then seemed fabulous indeed, although later, I am happy to note, it was sometimes invoked. If his salary were so low as to make living in Cambridge a hardship, as was true of more than a few and especially those from the South, the Fellow would receive a cost-of-living increase. Academically, a Nieman Fellow could do whatever he wanted, except that he could not work for a degree. If he wished only to write or read and not take courses, that was up to him. If he wanted to attend classes, as almost every Fellow did, all Harvard schools and departments were open to him. Each week, and sometimes more often, the Foundation would informally entertain at dinner an editor, correspondent, columnist or reporter whom the Fellows would choose because they admired, disliked or were skeptical about him. There was a preliminary warm-up hour before the steaks, and a lengthy give-and-take discussion afterwards. For his own protection, the recipient must have gained the permission of his employer to apply and the promise of his old or a better job when the academic year was up. A curator would direct the Foundation and co-ordinate the Fellows' work. The fund was large enough to assure fellowships each year to from twelve to fifteen applicants who would be selected on the basis of their letters of application reviewing their careers and an accompanying statement of their reasons for wanting the fellowship and what they would study, together with examples of their newspaper or creative writing and, of course, a list of references.

I couldn't apply the next spring because we hadn't won the Greenville fight. I read later a summary of the Foundation's first year and wrote for application blanks. In the late spring of 1939, Harvard notified me that I had been selected as one of the twelve Nieman Fellows for the academic year of 1939–40.

Technically, I still have one semester as a Nieman Fellow coming to me. We couldn't go to Harvard that September of 1939 because our second child was scheduled for late October, and our doctor said no, but right after Christmas we bundled up five-year-old Hodding, put our brand-new son, Philip, in a basket and struck out for fair Harvard. Archibald MacLeish, who was the first curator of the Foundation, told me that we could come for the second half of the 1939–40 year and the first half of the next, but I never got around to the second shift.

The crowded semester at Harvard was the most satisfying time of my life as a newspaperman; and directly or indirectly, it led to most of the agreeable happenings of the next ten years. After long scanning of horizons over the grindstone's edge, Betty and I had time to look around and to read and to discover and rediscover the collective mind of man; and to meet and debate and disagree and agree with other newspapermen of different and wider experience. We began work on a first book. We learned to slow our day-to-day tempo and to fill the days with something more than just the effort to survive economically until the next day. We explored Boston and adjacent New England, and found time to browse in museums and go to the theater and listen to live music; we were stimulated and sometimes antagonized by bright, professorial minds. But most of all, I think, I liked the weekly dinners at which the Nieman Fellows picked the minds of men and women who, for one reason or another, stood on the journalistic summit.

One of these was Ralph Ingersoll who came to us with the most provocative idea of all. Because he wanted to found a new kind of newspaper, he was turning aside from a career which had taken him in fifteen years from a cub reporter's job on Hearst's New York *American* to the managing editorship of the *New Yorker* and later of *Fortune,* the general managership of all of the Luce Publications and finally to the Olympian post of publisher of *Time.*

Chance put me next to Ingersoll during the pre-dinner highball session and we argued through dinner and afterwards. The next morning I told Betty ashamedly that I'd made a fool of myself by telling Ingersoll that his plan for a newspaper which would carry no advertising just couldn't work. He had said, I recalled, that I ought to come to New York and help make it work, and then we had gone on to other aspects of the unborn newspaper which would be called *PM.*

Ingersoll gave us a magnetic, provocative preview of *PM.* Most of us had our own criticisms of newspaper publishing methods and that night we believed Ralph Ingersoll's *PM* would soon be answering all of them. Since *PM* would not accept advertising, this newspaper of tomorrow would be as free as the un-trade winds, whereas its earthbound contemporaries were fettered by advertising and advertisers. This was the point over which Ingersoll and I had differed that night. I had no prior experience which would make me assume that advertisers could or would often seek to dominate a publisher who was willing to stand up to them, and I doubted that many advertisers were interested in trying. Besides, I believed and still believe that a newspaper without advertising would have much less reader interest than a newspaper which carried advertising. But everything else sounded too good to be true. *PM* would be "against people who pushed other people around." It would be completely departmentalized. Out the window would go the abused who-what-when-where formula for writing news stories; out all other stereotypes, all hackneyed phrases, all that spelled impersonal dullness and useless convention and superficial treatment. *PM* would be personal, and it would insist on the why; it would dig for the reason and expose for the reader whatever lay beneath the casual surface. It would tell the shopper what was what, where the bargains were, and what were bargains. *PM* would be a beautiful newspaper. More like a daily magazine in appearance, its high-grade paper would be printed partly in color with quick-drying ink; it would tell as much of the story in pictures as possible, for the very name, *PM*, would mean picture magazine as well as indicating that it was an afternoon newspaper. Its tabloid-sized paper would be stapled. It would be the journalistic dreamboat.

Many more newspapermen than the twelve Nieman Fellows were persuaded that spring by brilliant, erratic, eloquent Ralph Ingersoll, who believed so completely in himself, that his formula would happily revolutionize America's newspaper techniques. The biggest initial mistake Ingersoll made, aside from his belief that an independent daily newspaper could make its way from circulation income alone, was to oversell *PM* in advance, not only to newspapermen, who chronically dream of perfect newspapers owned by irreproachably unbusinesslike publishers and staffed by themselves, but to the public from which its readership would come. No newspaper could possibly be as good as *PM* proclaimed before publication that it would be.

Long after Ingersoll's visit, *PM* dominated the Nieman conversations. Only three of the twelve of us expressed no wish to be on *PM*'s staff; and I was one of the three principally because I couldn't imagine being accepted after publicly and so assuredly doubting its chances. And the Nieman Fellows of our year—most of whom did go to work for *PM* sometime during its first spooky year or afterwards—weren't alone in their yearning. I was told later, authoritatively, that Ingersoll went through nearly six thousand applications before settling on the two hundred odd original members of the news staff.

I was one of them. About a month after Ingersoll came to Harvard he wrote that he was counting on me to be one of the staff. I was inordinately flattered. Betty and I conferred. Back in Greenville, the *Delta Democrat-Times* was doing moderately well, well enough, anyway, not to need me at its editorial or business helm for a while. Like almost every other newspaperman who has never worked in New York, I wanted that experience. It had been a long time since those occasional assignments which the New York *Times* gave Columbia journalism students; assignments which later made me at least reasonably honest when I admitted to fellow cub reporters in New Orleans that I had formerly worked for the *Times.* We readily concluded that I would actually be benefiting the *Democrat-Times, PM,* the free world and ourselves by going to work on *PM* for a short, but undetermined period, say four or five months.

So in mid-May, I left Harvard a little prematurely and reported for duty in a converted second-story loft of a Brooklyn printing plant. Betty and the boys went to Lake Wauramog in the Connecticut Berkshires, where we had taken a cottage jointly with her sister and brother-in-law, who lived a commuter's hour from New York; and throughout the summer Don and I flew there on weekends and sometimes in midweek in his two-seater amphibian.

PM's publication date was still a month away, but a skeleton staff, to which more and more flesh was being added, had been experimenting for a month. The new newspaper was almost ready to put out trial editions.

I felt lost that first day, and never quite got over it. Except for Ingersoll, I knew no one then on *PM,* and he was a harassed man, wandering around in outward bewilderment, his shirt opened all the way, and scratching his chest. A tall Negro, who sat at the receptionist's desk—he was a Phi Beta

Kappa, but apparently not even *PM* was ready for a Negro reporter—checked me in. Ralph saw me for maybe ten minutes. I would be press editor he said and explained that *PM* would use the writer-researcher team combination perfected on *Time* and *Life*. Except for Betty, I've never had a researcher before or since. My researcher turned out to be a pretty, sarcastic blonde girl, who was about 180 degrees to my left, completely convinced that there was no honesty in any publisher, with the possible exception of Ingersoll, and raring to expose the ad-controlled capitalist press for what it was.

I didn't know anything about the capitalistic press of New York, Chicago, San Francisco or anywhere else except Greenville, and I said so, but Ingersoll believed this was all for the best, inasmuch as I was coming to *PM* without preconceived opinions. He said he wanted me to keep a close eye on the nation's newspapers and show up any rotten spots on them. Then he took me out to meet George Lyon, a stout, fatherly man, a veteran Scripps-Howard editor who had come in from Buffalo and who explained that he was Ingersoll's link with the past. George, who was one of the first to leave *PM*, took me around the city room and introduced me to the staff. I wanted to like all of them and did like a great many; but even a small town capitalistic publisher from Mississippi could detect early that *PM* was already divided and was further dividing on professional and personal and idealogical grounds into hopelessly inimical groups.

This division was brought home when I applied for membership in the Newspaper Guild. As it happened, I believed in the usefulness of the Guild and do now; my eight years as a publisher who didn't always earn minimum wages himself hadn't shut out the memory of reporters who, like myself, had worked ten hours and more a day, six days a week, for from ten to twenty dollars, with no security and short shrift if they hit the wrong key. But the New York Guild was dominated then by left-wingers and Communists. Without even knowing why at first, I became a minor issue. Since *PM* was to be a closed shop, an employee had to join the Guild to hold his job. I was an employee. But I was also a publisher in my own right, and it was argued by the doctrinaires that a publisher, a Southern publisher at that, had no business in the Guild. I did squeak through and carried a Guild card for three months.

The people on *PM* used to jab me a lot about the South. A majority of them were ordinary working newspaperfolk, decent, inquiring, idealistic men and women who had a genuine concern for the baffling region where I lived. But some were not, and looking back and knowing what I know now about their affiliations, I cannot wonder why these had little use for the minor *PM* editor who loved and defended the South, who believed in intervention long before Hitler invaded Russia, and who became bored with their dull, positive oratory which ordered a man to declare himself either on the side of the fascists—which included us in the South—or of the angels whose wings often glowed an unheavenly pink.

I am sure that a dreary, humorless, consecrated insistence upon conformity to a fixed and condescending liberalism contributed more to *PM*'s failure than did the clever, busy Communist minority itself, or the incredible mismanagement that even I could see from the cellar level, or the persistent jealousies and the professionally irreconcilable ideas as to what kind of paper *PM* should be. When *PM* was on the way out, Henry Morgan, the radio humorist, summed up in one bitingly funny sentence the essence of the *PM* news approach which was also the essence of its failure. This, said Morgan, is the way a *PM* story always started:

"My name is Minnie Moscowitz and I live on Flatbush Avenue, Brooklyn, and I think it's a shame . . ."

PM wasn't always honest in driving home its morality lessons. That summer, a Negro was lynched in Mississippi, the state's first lynching in three years. One lynching in a hundred years is unforgivable, and so is one gang massacre or waterfront terror killing. But some dedicated spirit, maybe Ingersoll himself, saw fit to invite Jed Harris, a Broadway producer who is undoubtedly a good impressario but who certainly was a prejudiced commentator, to write a guest editorial about the outrage. He began his condemnation thusly:

"Down in Mississippi, where the only forms of recreation are drinking Coca-Colas and lynching Negroes, they've done it again . . ."

I protested angrily to Ingersoll about that lie, and soon thereafter about another stupidly insulting performance in which a *PM* reviewer denounced some play or movie which had presented a certain rebel, name of General Robert E. Lee, as a decent, high-minded man. This friendliness toward a notorious traitor, commented the reviewer, was practically treason itself. Ingersoll had too much else on his mind to bother with such trivia, or to pay any attention to the argument that *PM* could never succeed simply as the voice of the phony liberals, leftists and assorted gentry of greater New York, or even the city's genuine liberals, and that it should try to reach a national audience of open-minded people, of whom many could be found even as far away as Mississippi—provided *PM* did not tolerate the kind of vicious dishonesty of which these two examples were a fatal beginning.

If I am spending what may seem to be overmuch time on these mistakes, it is because no newspaperman likes to see a newspaper die; no believer in a free press wants to see that press shrink; and no one who ever birthed a newspaper of his own or helped to breathe life into any other inanimate composite of white newsprint and black ink can be indifferent to the tragedy of stillborn *PM*. Perhaps this is Monday morning quarterbacking, but I do believe that a sizable minority on *PM* recognized what was wrong.

PM's staff was recruited from three journalistic groups, and additionally from scholarly experts who were unfamiliar with what to most of them was decidedly a lesser craft. The savants and pundits did not contribute as much to the confusion as did the professional newsmen who fell into three principal divisions: the daily or press association newspapermen, who were conditioned to getting the basic story into print as fast as possible and following up with more details for the later editions; the news-magazine writers, who sought the well-rounded picture and insisted on the background which their researchers would dig up, preferring to get the full-bodied story in tomorrow's paper rather than just an outline of facts today; and the picture-magazine graduates, who would come dashing up with a picture of a policeman falling on his rump near a gorilla cage and demand that a page of type be discarded in favor of a blowup of this amazing and unposed bit of Americana. *PM*'s pictures and maps were almost always better than the rest of the product and generally better than any other paper's, possibly because the men in that department were single-minded in their conviction that *PM* should be essentially a picture newspaper and sought to fill it with the best and most significant photographs they could produce or could buy, lavishly, from any source.

I can't help coming back to the pity of it. There were, most obviously, many misfits on *PM*, including me; not a few card-carrying Communists and fellow travelers, who were waging a class war instead of honestly trying to put out a good newspaper; and some misplaced zealots, who were lost outside their ivory towers and academic halls. But among *PM*'s two hundred news staff members there were as good newspapermen as could be found anywhere in the world; certainly the majority of the rank and file were more than adequate. I know of no better newspapermen than Bob Neville and Ken Crawford and Ken Stewart, Rae Weimar and Wesley Price and Weldon James, and many others, including Ingersoll himself if he had put his mind to newspapering.

But the staffers were not good enough to break down the wall of managing editors between themselves and Ingersoll, nor to adapt themselves to the New Day in Journalism. They couldn't overcome the public's quick suspicion that *PM* was too often more interested in making an ideological point than in telling the whole truth. They were troubled by the reaction of their fellow writing newspapermen on the other New York newspapers, whose good will *PM* certainly had at the very beginning but lost soon thereafter when respect for a new idea gave way to gibes at the Brooklyn messiahs so self-consciously and inadequately and superciliously setting the world aright.

And always, suspicion and struggle among members of the palace guard. And wastefulness. In midsummer, the national Guild held its annual convention in Memphis. At issue was control of the Guild by the moderates, led by Ken Crawford, the national president, or by the left-wingers, dominated by the New York Guild, whose chairman was Carl Randau. Both Crawford and Randau worked for *PM* and both would attend the Memphis convention. Surely, most publishers would have assumed that men they had chosen to work for them could be counted on to report fairly any controversy, whether or not they were participants. But Ingersoll couldn't have been sure. He asked me to go down to Memphis to cover the convention.

But the trip was an unnecessary expense, in more ways than one. Nothing newsworthy happened at the drearily divided convention, although the leftists were hopeful that Ed Crump would carry out his threat to run the Reds and troublemakers out of town.

I filed at least a story a day leading up to and including the New Yorkers' inconclusive victory; but there was a spate of good pictures back in Brooklyn, and also a controversy about the politics of some of *PM's* staffers, which *PM* publicized so only a few of what I hope were impartial lines appeared in *PM*.

By August, I had enough of *PM*, and *PM* had enough of me. Ingersoll told me one day that I hadn't been able to master the *PM* style, and that he was considering eliminating the press section anyway, which he soon did. He recommended that I take a couple of weeks off and go through with an earlier suggestion I had made—that I be assigned to a roving job in the South, where I could write stories of the disregarded good along with the overplayed bad and talk to civic groups about the potential of *PM* as a national picture newspaper of liberal beliefs.

Betty and I were ready to go home. I had been given a contract for a first book, the story of the lower Mississippi for the Rivers of America series, thanks to Betty's ability to persuade Carl Carmer that I could and should write it. We had much researching to do. Besides there was little doubt by late summer that the National Guard divisions would be called into federal service before very long, and I was a corporal in the 114th Mississippi Field Artillery. So we left New York and I wandered around the South for another month, especially in the vicinity of the lower Mississippi, writing and talking in *PM's* behalf. When the War Department announced that the 31st Division would be called out in the fall,

I wrote Ralph a letter of resignation and had a warm reply. The only time I have seen him since that summer was three years later, in Algiers, when he was in the Army too. His draft board had called him up in 1942, and he had noisily headlined in *PM* his six-thousand-word conviction that the board had summoned him only because its members disliked *PM*. He demanded an unequivocal ruling on the status of newspapermen, and then enlisted in the Army, in which he rose from private to major and wrote a best seller, "The Battle Is the Payoff."

PM didn't do relatively as well, either in the war years or afterwards, for it descended, in effect, from a general to a dejected private who died almost unmourned eight and a half years later. In the first receptive weeks its circulation reached upwards of four hundred thousand, but from then on the path turned almost uninterruptedly downward. Out of New York's eight million, so many of them militantly aligned with minority-group interests, with organized labor, with political and economic extremism, and with all or most of the causes which *PM* championed, it would have seemed that the newspaper could have commanded a following large enough and loyal enough to have made survival possible. The charge and the taint of Communism hurt. But what hurt *PM* most, I think, was the long accommodation of the American people to newspapers, good and bad, which give them advertising, comic strips, generally factual reporting, and not too much to despair of, and which are not guided by what the *New Yorker* magazine described as a bunch of young fogies. And Ingersoll's own personality contributed to the failure. He was given to emotional decisions, we thought, and was easily swayed first by one partisan group and then another; he listened too readily to the associates to his left, and not enough to those in the middle. He was not a good quarterback for a team that didn't have enough practice before playing for keeps, and which had proclaimed itself the world champion long before the kickoff. He commanded considerable loyalty but not much confidence among the rank and file. He was a good prima donna, but he made the mistake of hiring too many other prima donnas.

He did have at his disposal for eight years the fortune and the enduring patience and the faith of Marshall Field III, a man whom I've met only a couple of times, but for whom I have an odd admiration. Eight million dollars or so may not have meant much to Field, nor the total of the estimated twenty-five million which he has sunk into varied ventures in mass communication. The rare aspect is that he was willing to take over *PM* after its bad start and put up that kind of money without ever exercising any real control over the assorted eccentrics who lost his money for him so easily. As far as it is possible to judge, his only motive was to aid *PM*'s stated purpose. He was against people who push people around. He was unfairly smeared for everything questionable in *PM*'s short life. None of the debatable policies was his. As one of the smaller loss items in the *PM* profit-and-loss sheet, I'm glad that in Chicago he finally has a newspaper which glows with the satisfying color of black ink.

As for the personal equation, what I got out of those few months in New York was the final knowledge that I wasn't made for big cities or big newspapers or for working for somebody else if I could help it. I probably knew this all along, but it was good to make sure.

10

Us Mississippi Dragons

The day that Great Britain's Neville Chamberlain spoke of the peace in our time that the Munich shame would bring, I wrote an editorial, which if it influenced no one else did succeed in hoisting me on a military petard. The editorial was no different in content from thousands of other angry, bitter comments in the nation's newspapers, most of which made the point that unpreparedness had brought the free British to thus bow to Hitler's enslavers.

When I had finished the editorial, the thought came that never had I so much as marched in a single military formation, except raggedly as a Boy Scout, and that I must certainly typify personally the unpreparedness at which I railed. So, on sudden impulse, I walked across the street to the offices of Galla Paxton, a successful cotton broker and good citizen, who was also Colonel Alexander Gallatin Paxton, commanding officer of the 114th Field Artillery of the Mississippi National Guard, known as the Mississippi Dragons, an organization whose significance for defense was no more recognized in Mississippi than anywhere else in the country. With some faint recollection of newspapermen who held reserve commissions in a mysterious service called Intelligence, I asked Galla if he knew how I could get such a commission. His eyes held the gleam of the desperate recruiting officer when he answered, truthfully enough, that no such short cut existed unless I had received some military training in college, and suggested that if I was really interested in the martial life, the best way to enter it would be to join the National Guard. I asked him if I could join as a lieutenant, after learning the manual of arms, and he explained gently that I could not, but that as a private I could study the lessons that would enable me to qualify as an inactive second lieutenant, assuring me that most certainly, if the world kept spinning as it was, I would end up before long as an active officer. So I signed up as a Guardsman that same day, taking one year off my age on the application blank inasmuch as the privilege of becoming a National Guard private was then withheld from married citizens more than thirty years of age. Almost everyone in town, including Betty, and I am sure, Galla Paxton also, thought I had entered second childhood.

And so thought I when I turned up for drill the next Monday night. The city had built a new armory not long before, as a PWA project, but there were no blueprints for filling it with artillerymen. At thirty-one, I was a good twelve years older than most of my fellow privates, the majority of them high-school and farm boys who wanted the weekly dollar a drill, and who liked going away two weeks for camp. The uniforms we wore and kept at home between drill nights were 1917 issue: the broad-brimmed campaign hat, the itchy wool shirt, always either too tight in the neck and short in the sleeves or contrarily sacklike; the pesky, laced riding pants, and the difficult leather boots. Galla's officers of Headquarters and A Battery were mostly friends of my own age or a little younger, and none, except Galla himself, had any wartime experience. That first night, a sergeant told me where and how to stand for inspection. I felt very silly and couldn't help grinning when the immaculate majors and captains and lieutenants, whom I had never known as officers, tried not to look amused or incredulous when they saw me before them as the newest recruit. Inspection over, I waited for the command to hop to the guns and begin firing at random. I began thinking of myself as successor to the immortal Pelham of the Army of Virginia, or Captain Bragg giving the Mexicans a little more grape, or the young artilleryman Napoleon who knew how to lay down a mean barrage. I couldn't wait to get to those guns. The guns were 155 m.m. howitzers, for which there would be for the next three years a chronic and sometimes an almost complete shortage of ammunition, even during the year before Pearl Harbor when we were called into federal service.

And then came the first of multiple setbacks to my career as a cannoneer. An officer came over to me and said that I was to report to headquarters upstairs. I did and found out that Galla needed a headquarters clerk, and I was it; and I couldn't tell him, as private to colonel, what he could do with his howitzers. I was not even a member of the Greenville battery, which was a gun battery, but of the headquarters unit, which was a sort of housekeeping outfit. I consoled myself with the thought that one day I too would be an officer, and there would be howitzers for all, and I forthwith learned to keep those often senselessly detailed records every Monday night. So adept was I that in no time at all—a year and a half as I remember—I had risen from private to corporal. Additionally, I had qualified for an inactive commission as a second lieutenant, simply by reading condensed courses on gunnery, sanitation, military law and kindred subjects and taking examinations, with the answers readily provided, at odd times.

In a day when the uniform is familiar and honorable it is

difficult to believe that only fourteen years ago, the soldier, and especially the National Guardsman, who was only a part-time soldier, was looked upon by most of his civilian fellow citizens as either not being altogether in his right mind or as pathetically dependent upon the drill-night pay, which ranged from a dollar for an enlisted man to ten dollars for a captain, and I don't know what for majors and colonels and generals, who were in the military bathysphere. On drill nights, I would dress at home, and drive down to the armory, but before I backed out of our driveway I would carefully remove the broad-brimmed campaign hat we then wore, and slouch low in the seat so that no moviebound friends would detect me in uniform and shout "Boy Scout" at me. Perhaps I was hypersensitive, being much older than the teen-age privates, but I am sure that even most of the officers, spick and span in soon-outmoded boots and Sam Browne belts, felt ill at ease in the decided civilian atmosphere of 1938. They, for the most part, were young business and professional men, who had been active in their university ROTC's, and for one reason or another had joined the Guard.

Galla, then in his early forties, whom the enlisted men were to forever bless with the nickname "Bull Whip Shorty," loved military life and came in for a good deal of ribbing from irreverent friends at Lusk's cotton-exchange office. But Galla held his outfit together and made it one of the three best Guard regiments in the nation, through his own single-minded, far-seeing and stubborn persistence.

He loved boots, which, a couple of weeks after we had been mustered into federal service in November, 1940, were declared by the War Department to be improper uniform for artillery officers. I discovered this at regimental headquarters, while scanning a group of official communications, just before I was about to buy reluctantly a pair of seventy-five-dollar boots which Galla recommended. When I told him of my discovery and said that now I wouldn't have to buy the boots, he answered that every officer in his regiment would wear boots, at his order; I turned stubborn too, and refused to buy them, and for nearly three months at Camp Blanding, I was a regimental untouchable, the only officer in the 114th who was obeying the War Department instead of Galla, at a savings of seventy-five dollars. But in the early spring, a regular-army inspector changed Galla's mind and the regimental officers' footwear, and I was credited with a triumph, albeit a Pyrrhic one, since a lieutenant who bucks a colonel is not exactly in an enviable position.

Betty also contributed to my role as an outcast. Just before we left Greenville for Camp Blanding, after having manned the armory for several weeks, Galla had a farewell dinner for his officers and enlisted men and their wives. As was our unvarying civilian custom, Betty and I arrived late, which wasn't too intelligent for a regimental second lieutenant, and Betty compounded the offense. As the officer corps of Mississippi's finest struggled to their gallant feet, to the interlocking of spurs and the tumbling of folding chairs, Betty looked fondly at Galla who had come forward from his place at the head of the table to greet her, not me. In the awful hush, she looked Galla up and down—never having seen him in uniform—and said in a voice that carried to the blushing howitzers at the far corner, "Galla, you're the cutest looking thing in those boots I ever saw."

But that came later. Between 1938 and the fall of 1940, the weekly drills, so handicapped by lack of equipment and general interest, were supplemented by the Guard's two-week summer encampments at Camp Shelby in southeast Mississippi. As a private in Headquarters battery I continued, to my mounting irritation, to be a sort of office boy and clerk, and the closest I ever got to the glory of a gunner was to serve as a shell carrier, which probably isn't the military term for the saddest sack who lugs the ninety-six-pound howitzer shells to the gunners. Once, while I was thus engaged, to the great delight of a group of officer friends lounging under a clump of pine trees to escape the Mississippi July sun, the regimental chaplain, Duncan Gray, who later became bishop of the Diocese of Mississippi, all but made me desert his church, by commenting to all and sundry, "There goes the most pampered private in the American Army."

But there was no War Department pampering of the Guard. Our equipment was ancient; we didn't get enough shells for anything but the most inadequate gunnery practice; the citizenry at large thought of us as a valueless travesty of armed forces; and Guard officers all over the nation sought desperately and not too successfully to keep their batteries and companies at authorized strength. Then the first bombs fell on Warsaw, and in that dark autumn and the worser spring and summer that followed, America began to look at its own shrunken sinews, and the National Guard became more than a national joke.

Our 31st Division, the Dixie Division, made up of Guard units from Mississippi, Alabama, Louisiana and Florida, was ordered into federal service early in November, 1940. Married officers of my age and older, who were over age for the rank they held, were permitted to resign. I didn't. I hadn't become an officer until we were mustered into federal service, for my commission had been an inactive one to be authorized only when the regiment was expanded to war strength. After those two years as an office-boy private and corporal I wasn't going to miss the chance to be an officer and to have what some thought would be only a year of duty. Betty and I made up our minds quickly on that score.

I didn't know how to give drill orders, except on paper, or much about firing a howitzer, and almost nothing of military discipline. For the first week of active duty, during which we hung around the Greenville armory or drilled in the streets to the great amusement of the townspeople, I didn't even have a complete officer's insignia. I bought khaki trousers and an officer's cotton shirt and borrowed from Jimmy Robertshaw, a young lawyer-reservist, one gold bar—he couldn't find the other—and wore it until a consignment of insignia arrived at a men's store in Greenville, meanwhile covering up the unadorned shoulder by pretending in public to be rubbing it.

My campaign hat had only the enlisted artilleryman's red cord, so Betty twisted some gold and black threads into something that resembled an officer's hat cord.

Almost immediately, however, I found that I was to remain a newspaperman in thin disguise. Galla wanted a regimental paper. He got it, but the *Mississippi Dragon* had a short life, lasting only from our first week of active duty until two months later, when, in Camp Blanding, Florida, the commanding general decided he wanted a division paper. I was dragged, unresistingly, from the regimental headquarters company to division headquarters to become the first editor of the second divisional newspaper to be created in the nation, a hopeful, understaffed sheet I named *The Dixie*.

I soon learned the reason for the existence of the most junior of junior officers present. When the regiment's various units assembled at Biloxi from all over Mississippi to journey in convoy to Camp Blanding, I led the way, in the company of two noncoms who, thank the Lord, had preceded convoys before. We were simply advance housekeepers. We arranged for police escorts through the gaping towns and cities along the way, confirmed the bivouac places, and carried messages from one snailing unit to another. Actually, the movement was accomplished amazingly well, which was a tribute to Galla and his staff, and we reached that scandalously unfit campsite, Camp Blanding near Starke, Florida, more on schedule than was the camp itself. I suspect that behind the selection of that sandy waste is a juicy political story. The camp was far from finished, and it should never have been begun. We arrived there two days before Christmas.

On Christmas Eve, as befitted my relative rank, I led another convoy, this one to Jacksonville, fifty miles away. The three trucks I commanded carried the regiment's laundry. I spent my first Christmas Eve away from my family wandering around a Florida laundry and the streets of Jacksonville, returning to camp at five in the morning, just in time for another chore, that of officer of the day on Christmas.

I didn't much mind having those details, for which the G.I.'s have a vivid descriptive phrase, for such is the expected fate of secondary second lieutenants everywhere. But I did resent, and remember with wonder, some of the absurdities in which a few of my once-sensible fellow townsmen indulged in the name of military necessity or discipline. When all of us were less than a month out of civilian clothes, I watched one young Mississippi lawyer, who slightly outranked another, call his junior to attention and dress him down more harshly than an old-time overseer would correct a field hand, all because the offending officer had offhandedly challenged a statement about the number of men to be fed in one field kitchen.

When we had been at Blanding a couple of months, a battalion commander persuaded the colonel to order all officers to grow mustaches. The order went out. It didn't bother me because I already had a mustache, but I made up my mind to cut it off just to see what would happen. However, it was then that I was moved to divisional headquarters, as editor of *The Dixie,* so I never found out what would have been done to an officer who wouldn't wear boots and who shaved his mustache. In a spirit of levity, several officers, including the medical officer, wrote a letter of mock protest, pointing out that mustaches harbored germs, interfered with eating stew and in many other ways were a detriment to the beauty and efficiency of the staff. They caught hell.

Some of the situations were less innocuous. When our regiment arrived at Camp Blanding, construction was only half completed, and was proceeding at a shockingly slow and indifferent rate. Our Headquarters battery had no lights along the company street or in our tents. Captain Frank Kerr, the battery's commanding officer and a good one, sent out some of what he called his spies who liberated sufficient wire. The next day, two sergeants, who had been linemen with the Mississippi Power and Light Company, strung wire so fast and efficiently that by night ours was the only lighted area. The following day, a union agent called in person and told Frank abruptly that we'd have to take the lines down as they weren't strung by union workers. Frank told him that if he wanted those lines removed he'd better bring more than one hundred and thirty men along to do the job, because we had that many who would be waiting for them. The upshot, after the agent complained to headquarters, was a costly compromise. Our lines stayed up, but the union linesmen strung parallel wires, and after they were in place, which took a week as against the one day job of our men, our lines came down.

The lackadaisical, cynically slow completion of Camp Blanding was a continuous irritation to the troops. The emergency, with the resultant hasty gathering of workers in many cases unfit to hold down even hammer-and-nail jobs, was greatly responsible, but the average soldier doesn't reason things out. There was a running feud between the construction workers—at one time about twenty thousand men were more or less on the job, living in their own barracks—and the soldiers; there were frequent fights, particularly on Saturday nights when the two groups sought common recreation.

Some of the workers were tough customers. One Saturday night I was officer of the day, and was making the rounds of the camp with a sergeant from Greenville. Officers on O.D. duty carried sidearms, but we had no ammunition and the automatics were not loaded. The artillery shell dump was located in a wooded area of the camp. There were pitifully few large-caliber shells in it, but it did represent one of the danger spots in the camp. Adjoining it was a sawmill, erected by the camp contractors to turn out lumber for camp construction. The sergeant and I turned up at the sawmill grounds, through which we had to pass to get to the dump, soon after midnight. As we approached, we heard cursing and a cry of pain and fright, and out of the gloom of the poorly lighted grounds, ran a thin, middle-aged man, with blood streaming down his face. Behind him we could just make out a group of civilians, obviously drunk, who were laughing and jeering. The bleeding man, who turned out to be the sawmill's night watchman, told us that the men were construction workers, who were drunkenly threatening to go into the dump area and blow up the ammunition just for fun.

When these men saw the sergeant and me, they quieted for a few seconds, and then came toward us. I told them, in as friendly a way as I could, being frightened myself, that the area was off limits for them and they'd better leave. That made them angry, and they began threatening us with a beating. A couple of them started toward us, and I pulled out my empty automatic. So did the sergeant. If there's anything more dangerous than to pull a loaded gun on a group of quarrelsome drunks, it is drawing an empty one. But they didn't know our guns were empty, so they halted, still cursing. About that time the night watchman left precipitately, and I figured he had had enough. I didn't know he had gone to a shed where there was a telephone, and the sergeant and I stopped there shaking and uncertain, while the workers began assuring each other that we didn't dare shoot.

I doubt if the whole incident took more than ten minutes, but it seemed like all eternity before a truck drove up, and the biggest man I have ever seen got out. He wore a Texas hat, and carried a six-shooter on his hip. He was a member of the civilian police staff employed by the contractors to keep order among the workers. The big fellow asked me, "These the fellows been giving trouble, son?" and I said yes. He walked toward them—there were seven or eight, clustered together close to us—and without another word, caught the nearest by the seat of the pants and the collar and heaved him into the tonneau of the truck. He repeated the trick until the whole crowd was sprawling in the truck, slapping one or two of them in the process. Then he drove off with them, leaving the sergeant and me feeling very inadequate and wishing we had been trained as Texas Rangers, which, as we later learned, was what our rescuer had been.

If these assorted incidents were for me a source of consternation or sardonic delight or, often, an inner laughter at the foibles of the military, they were no less so for Jimmy Alsop, a corporal from Cruger, Mississippi, in the Delta, who was to become my close friend and associate and for a while my only staff member on *The Dixie*. Jimmy, a happy-go-lucky, undisciplined son of a wealthy planter family, was a giant of a youngster, who looked like a mildewed grizzly in the much-too-small 1917 wool shirt and laced trousers which had been issued to him, and which on rebellious principle, he refused to replace with comfortable khakis at his own expense as most enlisted men were doing.

Jimmy had a newspaperman's mind and a fighter's heart. He was so little affected by the Army's efforts to turn him into an automaton that General John Persons, the commander of the 31st Division and a fine soldier, later characterized the two of us, almost proudly, as the most unmilitary pair in his or any other command. That came after Jimmy and I—late in the evening, around headquarters, when we would be working on the next issue of *The Dixie* after a day in the field —had taken to wearing white tennis shoes with our uniforms because our feet hurt. The general surprised us one night with our sneakered feet propped up on the single desk we shared, officer and corporal, talking about working together after our military service was ended.

But the general liked Jimmy too, and I know he was almost as saddened as I was when, in 1948—after working with us awhile in Greenville and then, with our initial help, starting his own daily in near-by Greenwood—the boy dropped dead. Two years in the Pacific jungles, where he suffered combat wounds, jungle fever and a lung infection had worn his great body and weakened his heart, and Jimmy fell lifeless while playing softball with his newspaper's team. But neither of us foresaw that ending in those first zany months at Camp Blanding, where we laughed together, and put out, with the considerable aid of Second Lieutenant O. C. McDavid, another Mississippi newspaperman and a good one, the best division newspaper—we said—that any National Guard outfit could boast. And that in addition to what the Army euphemistically calls "other duties," late at night and on Sundays and whenever we could find time, without official recognition or tables of organization or transportation or any of the prerequisites that a later generation of army publicists and editors would enjoy.

Jimmy and I, enlisted man and officer, were not supposed to fraternize; but Jimmy had his automobile, driven down by a civilian, and I had good friends, John and Katherine Marshall, in Jacksonville. Jimmy also had brought along some civilian clothes. So, whenever we could get off, or whenever we had to go to Jacksonville for supplies, Jimmy would get behind the wheel, and I would sit on the back seat as befitted an officer, and we would drive to a filling station outside of Starke. There Jimmy would change clothes and I would change seats, and into Jacksonville we would drive in search of fun. If any of my fellow officers knew—and of course some did, because we would run into them—they didn't report us. Actually, our Army relationship was that of a couple of newspapermen and, friendship aside, I could not find it sensible, either in Blanding or overseas, to try to direct an Army newspaper or magazine as a military unit. Newspapermen don't perform effectively as newspapermen under chain-of-command military discipline.

I left Jimmy and Camp Blanding and the 114th Field Artillery and *The Dixie* early in the summer of 1941. Before I quit them for Washington—no greatly advantageous change—I knew a little more about soldiering than when I first cursed those sandy flats. I had also suffered an injury which was to haunt me from then on. I had run a palm or palmetto frond point into my right eye during night maneuvers, and, because of my own and the Army's neglect and a temporarily run-down physical condition, the infection that set in led ultimately to the loss of sight in that eye.

But I learned a lot about more than just soldiering in those months in a never-never land that lay between peace and war.

Even while Jimmy and I laughed at the antics of the Guardsmen, I began to respect the job that we were doing, however badly, officers and men, the military minded and the unmilitary. Looking back now I know that the nation should have thanked God for the inept Guard divisions, for men like Bull Whip Shorty Paxton and his civilian-soldier subordinates, who fashioned the youngsters of a country with no strong military tradition into an indispensable nucleus of the most powerful fighting force the battered world has ever known.

This compliment will surprise Galla. Five years after the war, when the Guard divisions were again being called to duty because of Korea and the Soviet menace, I approved editorially the breakup of National Guard units, principally because of the tragedy that could and sometimes did result when National Guard companies from a single town went into combat as a unit and were cut to pieces. Galla, who was again on active duty with the 31st, this time as Major-General Paxton, its commanding officer, wrote in rebuttal that I was a traitor to the Dixie Division, and declined to give us background information on the Greenville battery, readily obtainable elsewhere, which we wanted for a special edition. I could understand why. Galla had put his heart and soul into the creation and development of first a battery, then a regiment, then a division, and he didn't want to see its men scattered, its identity diffused, and its combat effectiveness impaired.

I almost agreed with him last year, when he brought the Dixie Division's band to Greenville at the time the 31st was being transferred from Texas to Indiana. It's a crack band, and Galla went all the way to the Secretary of War before the War Department would let him dress his bandsmen in Confederate uniforms. In their dress grays, with crossed bandoliers and tilted forage caps, the Stars and Bars of the Confederacy and of Mississippi grouped behind the Flag of the

United States, the Dixie bandsmen swung up Washington Avenue and down Main Street to the tune of the "Bonnie Blue Flag" and "Dixie" and "The Caissons Go Rolling Along."

That day the band had a new recruit. Behind the staff automobile in which the general led the parade, rode a solitary horseman. He was Phil, my twelve-year-old, garbed as an old-time Southern colonel, astride his walking horse, who, incidentally, is named Stars and Stripes. Phil held the state flag in his right hand; and though the spirited horse slipped several times and nearly fell on the mile-long line of march, the flag never dipped. Our hearts in our throats, out of nervousness for our rider and pride in the spectacle, Betty and Hod and Tommy and I kept up with the marchers for the full route. At its end, I couldn't help boasting to my dazzled youngest, "That was Dad's old division, Tommy"; and I might have embroidered greatly on the theme had not Hod, who listens too closely and remembers too long, ended the reminiscence before it began.

"Don't ask him for details, Tommy," he said.

11

Blessings on Thee, Pentagon

No traducer of the Pentagon goes unchallenged in my presence for Big P is a family shrine. The nearly three years I spent in the War Department in Washington were my most fruitful. On Army time, I completed one book which I had already begun, wrote two others and began a fourth, gaining thereby a third-floor, east-wing reputation as a hard-working officer who ought to make a career of the chair-borne military. I became in turn, and in each case almost overnight, an expert on civilian defense, the situation on the Eastern front and the political intentions and capabilities of the enemy; with time out for oversees duty with *Yank* and *Stars and Stripes,* I ended up as an interpreter of monitored enemy broadcasts and the executive officer of the Propaganda branch which Military Intelligence got around to organizing two years after Pearl Harbor. These assorted War Department pursuits gained me three promotions not counting the two that got away, and a citation for gallantry in propaganda analysis. During those years I shared with grocery-toting generals the privilege of trading at the War College's post exchange, where edibles were a lot more plentiful and considerably cheaper than anywhere else; and I also shared my aging Mercury with five fellow officers, who made up a car pool, using the gas thus saved for weekend jaunts into rural Virginia. Two of these compatriots had once been junior salesmen for International Business Machines, so our marching song each morning began: "Hail to our leader, we are proud of him, Thomas B. Watson of the I.B.M."

For all this I must thank Budge Smith, whom I first knew as Captain George Smith, Field Artillery, a regular army officer and a good friend, who was stationed in Greenville as an artillery instructor for the National Guard during the last four peacetime years. Budge never recovered from my decision to sign up as a Guard private, and every time he saw me in the vintage-of-'17 uniform he would laugh his shoulder-heaving, silent laugh; and on drill nights, we would foregather at his or our house, after I had earned my dollar for the hour-long military session, and speculate on just when and where the inevitable war would break out.

Just before the Guard was called into federal service, the inscrutable War Department summoned Budge to Washington for duty in the last branch Budge himself would ever have selected, the Bureau of Public Relations, newly organized and growing like Topsy and less normally.

Budge went to Washington, and Mississippi's finest somehow made it to Florida by overland stages.

I was in the hospital at Camp Blanding six months later when I read Budge's letter, and most welcome it was, for I was doing a thirty-day stretch on my stomach with an infected abscess, and was full of tubes and self-pity. Budge wrote that the cherry blossoms certainly were beautiful in Washington and how would I like to be transferred to the Bureau of Public Relations with a jump to a captaincy without putting in any time at all as a first lieutenant? I would have left the next day, tubes and all, but the hospital couldn't spare the tubes and made me wait until I didn't need them. By the end of June I was more or less on duty with the Bureau of Public Relations, and our reunited family was ensconced in a two-story apartment in the green, pleasant outskirts of Silver Spring, Maryland.

The less said about the Bureau of Public Relations the better, for even after all these years, my remaining good eye is still badly jaundiced. Budge, whose luck was holding out, had already been transferred from Public Relations to Intelligence; and he had also discovered to our common sorrow that there was nothing in the rule books that said I could skip a grade, so I was still a second lieutenant. The Bureau sheltered a motley assortment of regular army officers who, almost to a man, wanted to be somewhere else; bad reserve officers who had never had it so good, what with the rank few of them deserved and the pay they didn't earn; and good reserve officers who hadn't done their homework and consequently never had it so bad, since they were outranked by their professional inferiors; some good and a few able men who had been directly commissioned from civilian life, and a passel of veteran civilian newspapermen who found themselves in the delightfully anomalous position of giving orders to officers, especially in the press branch, where I first vegetated.

The duty of a press branch officer was to write releases which almost always began "The War Department announced today," and which for the sake of color and variety were sometimes changed to "The War Department today announced." Once, at the hands of a reckless young, creative genius, a story got by that began with "Today" and, as I remember, he was transferred to a weather station in Newfoundland. Two releases a day were considered a splendid output, and if a fellow wrote as many as four, he was known to be toadying for a promotion.

While in Public Relations I wrote a startlingly dull book entitled "Civilian Defense of the United States" in collaboration with a lovable older officer, Colonel R. Ernest Dupuy. He had several excellent military books to his credit, and being a colonel with a growing branch underneath him, can certainly be pardoned for sitting on the branch while I, resting in its shade, wrote the first drafts of all but three chapters of the book. C.D.O.U.S. was a quickie, designed to provide a grateful public with the newest wrinkles in wartime self-preservation. It was begun and almost finished in the three months before Pearl Harbor, thanks to Betty who somehow found her way through the mazes of the Office of Civilian Defense, directed at first by Fiorello La Guardia and soon thereafter by former Dean James N. Landis of the Harvard Law School, a notable scholar and bureaucrat who easily made headlines with a directive regarding the "obfuscation of the illumination" during air-raid alerts. That book might have been a best seller, if we had only been able—or if someone had been able—to determine whether incendiary bombs are best put out with a direct-jet or a spray-nozzle hose, a moot point because there weren't enough of either to go around if the Atlantic Seaboard had been attacked. By the time we settled on spraying, the war was well under way, and a dozen other civilian-defense quickies were on the market.

About this time, I went into Walter Reed Hospital to have my injured eye treated and was there when the Japs attacked at Pearl Harbor. I got out of the hospital the next week, after persuading the commanding officer that a fellow didn't need any eyes at all to work in the Bureau of Public Relations; but when I returned to duty, a colonel in the personnel section hinted strongly to my face that I had been faking my eye trouble; I hinted back that he wasn't exactly what I thought an officer should be, so he gave me a solemn promise that as long as I was in Public Relations and he was, I would never become a first lieutenant. He kept that promise. When the first promotions in the Bureau of Public Relations were handed out the next month, I had the distinction of being the only officer not to be promoted.

So I went to Budge Smith and said, look Budge, I am by instinct and second nature a military intelligentsia, and you got me up here in the first place, so please do something. Budge immediately recognized that Military Intelligence needed me and that the job for which I was ideally suited required me to wear a first lieutenant's silver bars, which in short order I got, and so ended my first six months in the War Department.

The intelligence assignment was a good one, save that I had almost nothing to do. I was assigned to the map room, a secret inner chamber in which an overlarge assortment of junior officers posted in grease crayon all available information as to the enemy situations on every front, as well as pertinent information concerning our own forces and supplies. It was here that I first found out something of what America was up against; for the map-room officers of necessity read the decoded secret cables that gave the true situations wherever our Military could gather it. The shock of discovering what really happened at Pearl Harbor while the newspapers were headlining the lightness of our losses, was matched a few months later when the cables told of the truly desperate condition of MacArthur's men on Bataan while the stories the public were fed made their hopeless campaign seem a stalemate or even a victory. The Japs knew better in both cases, and it is difficult to understand the mentality which presumed that the American people couldn't take the truth.

All this time the War Department was inevitably and necessarily expanding, and in due course had moved into the remarkable new building across the river, which despite its accommodations for thirty thousand military and civilian personnel, turned out in the end to be too small. The map room grew in size and ornateness and was renamed The Secretary of War's Map Room although he rarely entered it. The map room officers grew in numbers along with every other branch, but posting the situations and taking turns giving brief, parrotlike summations once a day for any interested top brass didn't keep us busy. The subject matter was fascinating, for we knew almost as much as anybody else except the highest echelons; but we were generally bored and when I had an offer from another branch of Intelligence to join a group whose duty it was to write intelligence manuals, I went along, assuring my map-room comrades that an accompanying promotion to captain had nothing to do with the decision.

Soon afterwards, in a reshuffle, I became an expert for the first time in my army career. Someone had come up with an idea for a new intelligence publication which would be restricted to less than fifty copies, beginning with one for the president and working down. It would sum up, every two weeks, the enemy's military, political, psychological and economic situations and probable developments. The idea was a great deal better than the men delegated to implement it. For some reason I was made the political expert. The military expert was a reserve major, a thorough, persevering man, who had been a schoolteacher in Michigan and who enjoyed being in the Army. The psychological expert, a second lieutenant, was a young lawyer from St. Louis whose summations read like legal briefs, and who was an able and serious practitioner of psychological interpretations, which he was here undertaking for the first time. The economic analyst had been a Princeton instructor in economics and generally knew more about our subjects, as well as his, than we did. Our boss was a loud and positive lieutenant colonel, a former State Department commercial attaché in some Balkan country, and before that a West Pointer who had resigned his commission in the dull 'twenties, as did so many good men. He did much generally meaningless roaring, mostly over punctuation and had especial trouble with periods. He was actually a nicer and more capable fellow than his behavior would lead anyone to suppose, and we found out in time that he liked to be yelled back at almost as much as he liked to yell. But none of us could truly be considered experts.

For the first few weeks on this assignment there was almost a full day's work each week, and this interfered seriously with the completion of the Rivers of America book. But in no time at all we experts began expanding, and I acquired two researchers all my own. One was a fine and brilliant girl, Jean Benton, who delighted in doing everyone's work; the other was an old friend, Private and later Sergeant and finally Captain William Ransom Hogan, lately of the Department of Archives of Louisiana State University, and now a professor of history at Tulane. Bill, whose sedentary pursuits and age hardly qualified him as a combat engineer, was in a combat-engineer regiment in training near Washington when I rescued him, knowing well that his gratitude and professional ability would combine to give me all the spare time I needed. So Bill came to the War Department as a specialist in research, which he was, and I went back to writing the book.

Our routine became simple. Jean and Bill would summarize all available data on the political outlook around the world, and turn in their summary to me the day before we four experts and our dictator were to foregather round a table to put the pieces together. For the sake of accuracy and last-minute information, I would check with the New York *Times* dispatches, and then write about six pages of succinct inside information on world politics, which was duly stamped "Secret." The end product served up by us four experts was as good a digest as any, I suppose, and I enjoyed reading it and hope the President did, but I still don't know whose hat our names were pulled out of.

Then I finished the river book, and once again came dreary boredom. I don't know how the thousands of other officers in fringe benefit jobs in and out of the Pentagon stood inaction. Maybe some of them liked it. Maybe most of them weren't the fat as far from the bone as I was; but it didn't make a man proud to be as useless as so many of us were. I know that elsewhere in the Pentagon, and in the training camps, and certainly overseas, there were many thousands of able, overworked and conscientious officers with more than enough to do, and doing it well. After all, we did win the war, even if it was in triplicate. I also know that it is unfair to single out the Regular Army for the senselessness of so much of the expansion; for too few found themselves facing too many imperatives at the same time; and some of them, as human as the rest of us, were also ambitious, and wanted their new kingdoms to grow. Even so, duty in the Pentagon in wartime was a sobering experience, and largely a desolating one; for it did seem that the overriding concern of the Pentagon's company and field-grade officers, if not the generals, was for promotion and departmental expansion; too many had the accompanying objective of sitting out the war in the Pentagon. I wanted promotions as much as anyone else, and I was happy to be with my family; but it was the tedium more than anything else, together with, I hope, some more patriotic concern, which prompted me, when the book was finished, to seek an overseas assignment as officer-in-charge of *Yank*, the Army's weekly magazine. Let's pass over that short period of usefulness just now and come back to the Pentagon again, as I did when a flare-up of hemorrhages in my bad eye brought me home to the states. From that time, late in 1943, until the end of the war, I could have checked into Walter Reed for disability retirement, as I eventually did, but duty overseas made me want to stick out the war. For a while I dawdled as a *Yank* supernumerary in the New York headquarters and in Washington with even less to do than before. Early in 1944 I accidentally became a military specialist in propaganda.

That happened one afternoon over coffee with Lieutenant Colonel John B. Stanley, who had been selected to head the still nonexistent propaganda branch which General Joseph McNarney, the assistant chief of staff, had just created. Jack Stanley, a graduate of the military academy, was a singularly literate army officer, who had been in Special Services, a branch which had over-all direction of *Yank* and other recreational and educational Army enterprises. I had served under him for a while in the Middle East. Jack wrote boys' adventure stories and boys' books. He asked me if I knew anything about psychology or propaganda. I said, why, naturally, and cited in proof a course in propaganda analysis I had taken at Harvard, not to mention two years of abnormal psychology in college, none of which either fooled or impressed him. However, he was looking for an officer who wanted to be transferred from present assignment, and I told him to look no further. From then until I entered Walter Reed Hospital, thirteen months later, I analyzed propaganda, got my lone citation and last promotion, wrote my first novel and began another which I wish I had never finished.

The trouble with the Psychological Warfare branch was that many of the old line officers thought there was nothing to such a silly business as dropping surrender leaflets and using the radio to bewilder or weaken the enemy's resistance and trying to guess what the enemy himself would do on the basis of what he was telling the people at home and broadcasting to the other people beyond his borders. That branch should have been put into operation much earlier; not that it would have shortened the war, but there was a provable need for co-ordination of psychological warfare in the field—we never achieved it—and for a close and continuing study of enemy broadcasts, enemy publications and the voluminous records of prisoner interrogation, to say nothing of the necessity to persuade some commanders in the field and some generals in Washington that lives could be saved and enemy morale weakened by propaganda itself.

Jack was the right officer for the assignment. He was imaginative, and had an understanding of mass moods and underlying meanings and he could make me work and believe that the work had meaning. By the time the war ended I felt useful even in the Pentagon.

12

Of *Yank* and *Stars and Stripes*

I would like to think that the American High Command, having decided in due course that the maintenance of soldier morale in the Middle East required the establishment of an edition of *Yank* in that theater, riffled through its file of aptitude records, picked out mine from the top-ranking handful, and agreed unanimously that I was the right man for the job.

Nothing like that happened. I got the assignment as officer in charge of a yet unestablished *Yank*—and the unexpected editorship of an equally nonexistent Middle Eastern edition of *Stars and Stripes*—because of Bruce Manning. Bruce wasn't even in the Army, though he tried hard. I suspect he sold one Colonel Edward Munson on my qualifications only because he wanted some tried company in Egypt and Africa whither he was bound as one of those special assistants to the Secretary of War for the never-realized purpose of making a documentary film about the American supply system.

Bruce has had a way of turning up when I am down in spirits, out of cash or looking for greener pastures. Once he and I and Gwen Bristow, his wife, who writes best-selling Book-of-the-Month novels, were newspaper folk together in New Orleans, and lived in adjoining apartments in a cheap and adventurous old dwelling in the French Quarter. Bruce talked me out of quitting my first newspaper job and into quitting my second, and the day he and Gwen got word that their first mystery novel had been accepted, he borrowed ten dollars of my thirty-dollar United Press paycheck, and we went out on the town. Since then he has become one of the better names in Hollywood, as writer, director and producer, and Gwen has gone her own unerring way as a novelist, and our paths don't cross as often as formerly; but they crossed in Washington in the fall of 1942, the night Bruce had wangled his War Department appointment after the doctors had turned him down for a commission.

Standing in the middle of the living room, and making like Kitchener at Khartoum, Chinese Gordon and a whole desert full of Fuzzy-Wuzzies, that slightly delirious Irishman told me I ought to come along too. I wanted to do nothing more, and said so, disgustedly adding that I was buried for life in my Pentagon rewrite job. Bruce said if I really wanted to go he'd see about it, that he had met the fellow in charge, name of Munson, and to drop by Munson's office the next day and we'd get everything lined up.

And so we did, the very next day, which is one of those Manning miracles, and don't ask me how it happened because I know only that leprechauns and the Blarney stone and the Little Old Woman of County Clare had something to do with it—or so Bruce says. Ed Munson, who later became a brigadier, and could himself have made a fortune in Hollywood playing the part of a dynamic general, was sold on me before I turned up, for Bruce had arrived ten minutes before. So was Jack Stanley, a major then, who was also going to the

Middle East as a sort of over-all supervisor of military publications.

It wasn't until after I had more or less irrevocably committed myself that I wondered what kind of fool I was being. I was irretrievably blind in one eye, though the Army didn't know that since there'd been a mix-up in the report from Walter Reed Hospital. At thirty-five I wasn't old, but I wasn't exactly combat-fit after a year and a half behind the desk breastworks. And there was Betty, holding down a full time job and with the responsibility of one seven-year-old and one three-year-old son to boot. But this was the first important task that the Army had given me a chance to do; it was an assignment overseas.

Anyway, a few weeks after Bruce and Jack Stanley had taken off, I joined them in Cairo. Bruce's careful planning had almost gone agley, for Munson had decided to send me to Australia and the Pacific; but Eric Knight, the gallant gentleman and novelist who had been selected for the Middle East, was killed with all other passengers when a military plane exploded over British Guiana under very suspicious circumstances, and so at the last minute I was shunted to the Middle East after all.

Almost nothing that happened to me in the Middle East and Africa, and almost none of my slightly mad Army and other associates there seemed either probable or even real then, and they seem less so in retrospect. Bruce and Jack were practically original settlers by the time I arrived in Cairo. Somehow the word had got out among the houseboys and assorted fellaheen that Bruce was a top-flight pasha back in the old homeland, and he was playing the part for all it was worth, dispensing largesse, graciously accepting full genuflections and recalling with gestures and an occasional Arabic phrase how he had brought law and order to the Wild West. Jack acted as his court chamberlain, and in the role of military aides to Manning were two highly unsoldierly majors, Charlie Vanda, who was as successful in radio and Hollywood as he said he was, and Ross Shattuck, another character out of Hollywood, a publicist of stars, who had been wounded in the behind during the First World War, and who let it be known to all that old Shattuck was going to enjoy this one. They lived in a villa that was much too good for them, ate Egyptian food that was much too rich for them, and undoubtedly linger on in Egypt today as a happy myth.

Especially Bruce, whose principal pleasure it was then, and always, to bring unexpected happiness to people. One night he and I went to an ENSA—the British USO—performance in the desert, given by a caste of talented, tragic Poles, once ranking stage and vaudeville stars in Poland, and now, men and women, in the Polish army in exile. Their performance was brilliant and saddening, individually and as a group, and Bruce wept throughout the show. At its end, he rushed backstage and managed to let the Poles know that he wanted to give a party for the entire troupe the next Sunday. And so he did, and it was possibly the most exotic party ever given in Cairo—American exotic—with a Caribbean string band from our Special Services, mountains of hamburgers and cases of beer, gin and whisky, and, at the end, a regular Donnybrook Fair, with the American hamburger king, a regular army sergeant cook, getting into his cups and blessing out a British colonel, fighting with a British army sergeant and ending up with thirty days' confinement.

But this is getting too far ahead of what, at best, cannot be a chronological account. Cairo, the Middle East and North Africa remain for me, as wartime experience must remain for most of us, a kaleidoscope of generally unrelated experiences, some joyous and amusing, some rankling, some satisfactory, some frightening, some sad, and all or almost all of them memorable and personally important.

My troubles as an army editor began within minutes after I arrived in Cairo. Jack Stanley told me casually that, while my assignment was to organize and begin publishing a Middle East edition of *Yank,* General Lewis Brereton, who was theater commander as well as commander of the Ninth Air Force, wanted a *Stars and Stripes* for his forces. Staff? Well, that would be my problem. A weekly of sorts had been published for some months, and undoubtedly its personnel should be available. Also, scattered throughout Africa and the Middle East were the *Yank* correspondents, roving sergeants all of them, whom I was to direct and with whose aid I would be publishing *Yank.* It sounded suspiciously easy.

Within the next day or so, I made three discoveries: We didn't have any newsprint. We didn't have any place to print a newspaper or a weekly magazine even if we had newsprint. The staff of the nearly defunct theater weekly was, except for its editor—a good newspaperman who was joyfully returning to the provost marshal's forces—completely without experience. One was a second lieutenant who knew how to type but didn't like to. Another was a young Egyptian, born in Cairo of Russian-Jewish parents, a cartoonist who had attended the American University and whose ideas of American humor and American journalism were out of the Thousand and One Nights. The third was a young English woman, pretty and bright and provocative, who was the wife of an Oxford poet turned wartime captain in the British Intelligence. These two were to become my best friends in Cairo, but that didn't make a newspaperwoman out of Joyce, who was an artist and temperamental and who was listed as a civilian secretary, which she wasn't.

But I did have more or less at my service the *Yank* correspondents, as gifted and individualistic and undisciplined and courageously enterprising a group of American newspapermen as ever lived.

I hope that someday a full and personal history of *Yank*'s overseas operations will be written. I would like to contribute the chapter on the sergeant-correspondents in the Middle East. Except for the officer-in-charge in each theater, no *Yank* staff member could be an officer and remain with *Yank*. Every one of the men under me was as qualified to be commissioned as was anyone in our Army; but they preferred to stick with *Yank*, and I would have too. They operated as lone wolves mostly, and since the Army never quite figured out their status, at least in the Middle East, they had freedom beyond the wildest dream of any G.I. Quite rightly they resented the military stratification of the British, which made most places out of bounds to enlisted men and noncoms; and they evaded the ban long before combat correspondents were authorized, by removing their sergeant's stripes from the British battle dress, which was permitted in our theater and which most of us affected, and replacing the regulation insignia with one they dreamed up, a cloth shoulder tab bearing the legend "U.S. Army Correspondent."

When I first arrived they were scattered all over two continents, but they began drifting in from the field, Pete Paris from the fighting in the desert, Ed Cunningham from a submarine trip to Crete, Walter Bernstein from Palestine, Burgess Scott and Slim Aarons, fresh from the British Eighth Army, in their jeep which was named Paducah in honor of Scotty's home town—all of them ready to help get *Yank* and even *Stars and Stripes* started, but impatient also to get back to their personally contrived adventures. Only Al Hine remained in limbo, virtually a prisoner in the Persian Gulf Command of an irascible colonel who disliked him and wouldn't let him out of that theater.

I wish I had a peacetime staff with the guts and the talent of those *Yank* wanderers. Pete Paris was killed on D-Day in the channel. Walter Bernstein parachuted into Yugoslavia where he wangled the first interview with Tito, and returned to civilian life at the war's end as a successful free-lance writer. Al Hine finally got out of the Gulf and is an editor of *Saturday Evening Post.* Ed Cunningham, who specialized in turning up in places that were impossible to reach, is in industrial publishing now. He survived an air journey to Crete which he was not supposed to have taken, the beleaguered island being at the time distinctly out of bounds for American army correspondents. Ed got there by air, through a completely worthless written order from me for him to proceed where he wished "in the interests of *Yank*, the Army Magazine." Within two days he was arrested, and I received from the British an angry cable notifying me of his apprehension and asking what should be done about him. I cabled, "Give him ten yards head start and shoot him like a dog," which was sufficiently baffling for them to send Ed back to North Africa. Scotty and Slim were the hardest to believe. If there was an army regulation they didn't violate, it was because they hadn't heard of it. Slim was a cameraman and Scotty was a reporter, and they formed *Yank*'s best team, on and off duty. I could say more about them, but I won't, for which they should be thankful. At last report, Slim was in Hollywood and Scotty an editor of the Ford *Times.*

I persuaded the British to share with us, two days a week, a printing plant which they had taken over in Cairo from its Italian enemy owners. Through the combined persuasiveness of Jack Stanley, Ross Shattuck and myself, we obtained newsprint on the cuff, payable in kind when ours arrived—a ship bearing all we needed had been recently sunk—and meanwhile billed to us at twelve hundred dollars a ton! I had my *Yank* boys, off and on, and the three aides I had inherited.

Within two weeks, a once-a-week edition of *Stars and Stripes* appeared to be no problem at all, except for news content. Front-line stories were easily had, as were a host of features about the G.I.'s in general. But we needed news from home, and there wasn't any, for Army cable communications were too crowded to schedule even a bulletin news service for the embryo *Stars and Stripes.* Our only sources were the two English-language dailies in Cairo, and the Office of War Information's news service, which wasn't at all what we or the troops wanted, being mostly propaganda about the American way; worthy stuff, but still propaganda of little spot-news value. We wanted to start off with a good yarn from back home, but up until the day before the first issue was to appear we didn't have one. And then, the Egyptian *Daily Mail* answered our prayers, with a four-line front-page story from San Francisco, reporting with utmost brevity that Floyd Hamilton, America's public enemy Number One, had been shot to death in San Francisco Bay while trying to escape from Alcatraz, and that two or three companions had been recaptured.

With only those unadorned facts to build on, I proceeded to fake a news story for my first and only time. Scotty and Ed and I agreed that here was just what the boys wanted. I wrote a lengthy story in the most graphic tabloid style, describing Hamilton's death throes in the chill bloodstained waters, the chatter of the guards' sub-machine guns, the terror of his companions. I quoted a letter which had been discovered in his cell, asking his mother's blessing and forgiveness, calling upon all wrongdoers to learn a lesson from his evil ways, and revealing that he had wanted to escape only because he was determined to enlist in the Army. Never, not even in the seven fat years, did corn grow greener in Egypt. We photographed Scotty's face and cropped the picture so that only his ominously catlike eyes remained. I curled my upper lip in a snarl which was likewise photographed. We ran these frightening facial excerpts under cutlines which read "the Eyes and the Snarl of a Killer."

The next morning, with the Middle East's first *Stars and Stripes* just off the press, I left, sleepless, for Algiers, on the other side of North Africa and with a desert war in between. My unwarlike mission was to wheedle some newsprint, press blankets and maybe even a reporter out of Colonel Egbert White and Lieutenant Bob Neville, of the *Herald-Tribune, PM* and *Time,* who were publishing a mammoth daily *Stars and Stripes* in three editions, with equipment and a staff that almost any American newspaper would have envied. When I arrived at the *Stars and Stripes* offices in Algiers two days later, I strolled over to the teletype on which news from the states was coming in. Almost the first item I spied was one from San Francisco relating that Floyd Hamilton, who had been believed to be slain in an attempted escape from Alcatraz, had been discovered cowering in a cave on the island. Here endeth the lesson in good newspaper practice.

But our little *Stars and Stripes* flourished. Within a few weeks I was being aided by one of the best and most personable newspapermen I have ever known. He was Bob Strother, who had been in the Middle East with the OWI and was newly commissioned a captain. Bob had one brother who was an Air Force general and another who was an infantry colonel, both in the Pacific, and he had recently lost his youngest brother, a pilot who had been shot down by the Japanese, which gave Bob a personal motivation for getting into uniform. Bob knew a lot about the Army and not a little about the Middle East. We occupied billets together, divided publishing responsibilities so that in time he was primarily responsible for *Stars and Stripes* and I for *Yank*, and settled down to what never became exactly routine.

We finally rounded up a good staff, which included Dick Coe, who is now the *Washington Post's* dramatic critic; Karl Sprinkle, another good Washington newspaperman, and Irwin Shaw, who tried to teach the rest of us to drink a concoction of gin, tomato juice and red pepper, and who usually worked only when he was so minded, since he aspired only to writing good novels and better short stories and remaining a chronic buck private. We also acquired, through his forthright bribery of us, one pressman whose name I have forgotten.

He was in civilian life an all-round printer on a weekly newspaper, and he was exceedingly unhappy out at Kilo Thirteen, our big supply base outside of Cairo, where he was a warehouse guard. He turned up at our billets in Ismailia House one night, his pockets bulging with an assortment of canned goods. As he pled his qualifications, he would take out one canned delicacy after another—smoked oysters, caviar, tongue and the like—and place it before us, saying, "Found this in the warehouse, captain, and there's a lot more like it." We got the idea fast enough, and as soon as we told him that he was hired if we could arrange his transfer, he left us, returning in a few moments with several cartons of assorted edibles. He told us they had been left over from the pre-Pearl Harbor days when our diplomats and civilian technicians were trying to win friends and influence people through their stomachs.

Yank was not as easy to set up, for it required a two-color press, and there was none available in Cairo where every piece of printing equipment, no matter how primitive, was being utilized for military or propaganda purposes. We were living a hand-to-mouth existence on *Stars and Stripes,* going from one printing house to another for our relatively modest press run. We discovered soon that *Yank* would have to be printed elsewhere, if it was to be printed at all. Since we received by airmail each week mats of all twenty-four pages of that remarkable magazine, type setting was no problem; all we needed to do was cast the mats of as many of the master pages as we wished, substituting up to eight pages of our own if we were equipped to do so. But those pages had to be printed, with at least the cover in two colors.

Somebody said that maybe we could find a press in Tel Aviv, in Palestine, some three hundred desert miles to the North. So I went to Tel Aviv, the first time by jeep which is no joyride. Ross Shattuck was already there as some kind of minister plenipotentiary, as far as he or I could learn, to the Arabs, the Jews and anyone else who wanted to relax in his beaming baldheaded presence. Ross was enjoying the post and Tel Aviv was enjoying Ross, and since he had forgotten more about printing and publishing than I ever knew, we set out together to find a press.

There was none suitable in Tel Aviv, that miraculously wrought city by the Mediterranean. But, after a week of searching high and low, we found a press at a printing establishment in adjoining Jaffa. Jaffa is ancient and Arabic and even then the hostility to the citizenry of Tel Aviv—the two cities run together—was marked.

The press stood in a building whose two-foot-thick walls had been erected for the knights of an early crusade, and it was owned by three brothers named Malik, who before the war had made a good living from printing multi-colored tissue wrappers for export citrus fruit. The war had put them out of business, and the press stood idle. It was a magnificent, German-built press, less than five years old, and the answer to our dreams. The brothers were delighted to lease it to us at a price which, I am sure, was considerably higher than the former net profits of their business. All that was required were a few relatively minor adjustments, the addition of a couple of gears and an extra angle bar or two over which our newsprint could be threaded, and we would be in business. The brothers were more than willing for these changes to be made, since they would not be permanent and could not harm their beautiful press. Of course, neither Ross nor I were printing-press engineers, nor were the brothers nor any of their Jaffa friends. In another day or two we found in Tel Aviv a man capable of blueprinting the necessary remodeling. He was a young, blond Jewish refugee from Germany, and he was very happy to oblige. When we told the three brothers that we had found such a man in Tel Aviv, they asked us whether he was Jewish, and when we answered affirmatively, they said angrily that he could not enter their shop because he might steal their "secrets," whatever those were. And there matters stood, with the brothers adamant in a matter that could mean the loss to them of several hundred dollars a week, until we figured a way out. We dressed the young refugee in a G.I. uniform, told the brothers that we had found a qualified American soldier, and that was that.

Yank's Middle East edition was born in the remains of a Christian crusaders' fortress in a land holy to three faiths, wherein three Syrian brothers owned a German-made press that was converted to our use by a Jewish refugee. The type we required was set by Muslim linotype operators who couldn't read English and uncomprehendingly and rapidly matched the characters. The printing operation was supervised by a British master printer, a young sergeant from London with two years of desert fighting behind him, whom our allies loaned to us. The Americans who from every battle theater sent in *Yank's* stories came from a score of national backgrounds and from every region of our own sweet and free land, with names like McKenna, Schoenfeld, Borgstadt, Ruge, Foisie, Corbellini. And out of that old, suspicious and hapless city by the sea, immemorial prey to a host of conquerors, there went each week to young American boys waging desert war a gay, wisecracking magazine whose hero was Sad Sack and whose voice was the soft slurring of an Alabama private and the clipped skepticism of the New Yorker, the twang of a Vermont mountaineer and the brash roaring of the West.

Nothing brings me more pride than the memory of my association with *Yank* and *Stars and Stripes* in the Middle East and in North Africa. When I returned home, I told Betty and young Hod of the rare moments of danger, as returning husbands and fathers do; of the times the bombs fell nastily close in Tripoli and on the crowded mountainside of Algiers; of the whine of a desert bandit's nonpartisan bullet in the safe zone above Suez and the forced landing of a lost transport plane that we as passengers had believed was only looking for a downed plane; of the undertow at Alexandria and a badly timed visit to a place named Kasserine Pass, where too many Americans died in needless ambush and the others, I among them, fled; of the angry, uncomprehending black sentry from the Cameroons, whose bayonet thrust in the nighttime at an airfield's gate came near to making useless the interpreter's shout that here were friends; of sand-fly fever, and dysentery;

the rubbled road in Sicily where beaten, disciplined men from Saxony held up the American probing, and the chatter of machine guns stirred the casual front-line visitor to a harmless turn at answering them. But what was important for me was that a magazine and a little newspaper made men smile or debate among themselves, made them mindful of home, made them sometimes, perhaps, aware that they sweated and fought for a good reason.

It is not often now that I come across the men who filled the pages of *Yank* and of *Stars and Stripes*. When we do meet, our wives reconcile themselves to an evening of listening to tall stories and stories not so tall. And always they begin with "Remember?"

Remember the typhus epidemic?

They fell in the streets, faces contorted, eyes staring, the people of Egypt to so many of whom life at its best meant no more than twenty years of hunger and nakedness. We passed them by, because we were so ordered, and we could not have helped them anyway. I awoke one morning with a typhus louse biting me, and I gave way to panic, for I had seen others die. But the Army doctors laughed and said I ought to thank God I was an American, because the American troops had typhus shots, and there wasn't a chance in ten thousand that anything would happen. . . .

Remember Bob and Rose?

Bob was a Scandinavian-American sergeant from Minnesota, blond and square-faced and blue-eyed, and Rose was a beautiful, olive-skinned girl who could count four Eastern strains in her blood, and who could take dictation in five languages. She worked for us on *Stars and Stripes* and she and Bob fell in love, and though it took some doing we finally got permission from headquarters for the Middle East's first marriage between an American soldier and an Egyptian girl. The Red Cross decked out the roof of the hotel which was the enlisted men's club, and eight brasses played a wedding march. Rose's people came, some in Western dress and some in their own costume, and I was best man; and when the chaplain's double-ring ceremony was over, Bob flung his arms around me, saying, "Thanks, Captain, thanks, Captain," and pushed Rose toward me. "You kiss her first," he ordered. "You put it over."

Remember the officer with the swagger stick?

I was walking along a crowded Cairo sidewalk when ahead of me a ragged little urchin darted from the curb into the street, his eyes on a discarded cigarette butt. Down on him bore a British command car, in too much of a hurry for the place and time. The driver slammed on his brakes to avoid hitting the child, and the car swerved and jolted to a stop. A British officer jumped out of the car and began beating the child over the head with his crop. Two New Zealanders and I reached him at the same time; we were angry and cursing, and I wanted to fight, nor was the Englishman unwilling. But a crowd gathered and the hate was there for all to see and hear and almost smell. The Britishers drove away, and I walked on, sick at my stomach, and frightened because I could see into the future.

Remember the Gezira Club?

The island in the Nile, surrounded by the city which it repelled, was an oasis, which the British had sown not long after they had made Egypt effectively theirs, which was a long time ago. There was a cool, green swimming pool at the Gezira Club, and chill drinks and cricket fields and tennis courts and all manner of ways to relax; and for allied officers the dues were fantastically low, so the Americans went there often, to the disgust of the old-timers and the undisguised pleasure of the women who were young. The Americans laughed at the men of the British Eighth Army, who were on leave, which was a cruel thing to do, even if the desert rats, in swimming, did have a zebra look. Their legs were white to just below the knee, and darkly brown from there to a few inches above the knee, so that another light stripe showed as far as the bottoms of their bathing trunks. Their necks were brown as far as a turned-down shirt collar admits the sun, and their arms were brown too, to an inch or so above the elbow, where they turned white again, and the top half of their foreheads were white where the headgear had shut out the sun. "Zebras," said the Americans, who were mostly base-wallahs and fliers, and all as nicely tanned as Hollywood would want, and with much money to spend and a forward way that the girls in the flimsy swim suits seemed to like. The British liked none of this, and I cannot blame them, but I don't know what could have been done about it except to take away the surplus money of the Americans, and nobody yet had figured out a way to do that.

Remember the Tel Aviv bartender?

Everybody called him Gus, a sad-faced, bespectacled man who had wanted to be a doctor, but Hitler wouldn't permit it. He mixed drinks and sometimes smiled at the names we gave the concoctions; names like Rachel's Tomb and the

Cossack's Kiss, to hide the sameness of vodka and lime juice and grenadine and gin. Maybe Gus is a doctor by now, for to us nothing seemed impossible in Tel Aviv, which was mostly clean in spite of its swollen numbers; a place where the milk was safe to drink and American food and American concoctions were offered in two languages, and people spoke of tomorrow with the pride and the confidence that made us think of home, and spoke bitterly of yesterday in a world that made us ashamed of man. On the beach at Tel Aviv, with the G.I.'s and the pretty girls swimming and lounging and making love, while the life guards sat on their high perches, it was not hard to think we were home again; not hard, that is, until a caravan of camels crossed between us and the sea, silhouetted against the western sky, and American voices called to each other to look at the circus. It is a good memory, the memory of Tel Aviv and the little fortresslike settlements where Jews were farmers and frontiersmen and united in their labor and their dreams.

Remember those damned censors?

The *Yank* pages from home for that week had a double-page story of a new anti-tank gun, tank-mounted, and already proudly announced in the United States and approved by the War Department for publication. But the colonel who somehow headed Military Intelligence in the Middle East, and his acquiescent censor, decided that the *Yank* story violated military security, so they ordered us at the last moment to jerk those two pages and replace them with something else. We had nothing else to substitute, and I was crazy angry anyhow and forgot that I was only a captain instead of a newspaperman; so I filled those two pages with a legend which read, in the biggest, boldest type we could find: "STORY FOR THIS SPACE PASSED BY WAR DEPARTMENT AND UNPASSED BY THE MIDDLE EAST COMMAND." But I didn't win the argument, and if anyone wants details on how it feels to be verbally chewed to pieces with no chance to chew back, ask me.

It was this experience that prompted me to flee to Teheran, on a flimsy pretext, right after I wrote and published an editorial in *Stars and Stripes* about the miners' strike, an editorial which ended wrathfully: "And as for you, John Lewis, damn your coal black soul." I thought I would catch it again, but when I returned to Cairo I found out that the editorial had been broadcast, that the generals approved heartily and that I was, very temporarily, a minor hero. All of which may be filed under the classification "Addenda on the Army Mind," though that probably isn't altogether fair.

Remember Bea Lillie out in the desert?

Her son had died in action not many months before, but she made her faces and sang of the fairies in the bottom of her garden, and we might have been back in New York or in London, instead of not so far back of the lines. The British laughed loudly and often at this gorgeously, heroically funny woman from their island, and sometimes I laughed too; but being American and sentimental, I also cried a bit, seeing them and her there and thinking of that aloof, hard-bitten people who minimize their own courage and emphasize the qualities which the rest of us dislike. I thought that night, and I have thought often since, of the calamity that would befall the world's free men, and even the world's slaves, if those people and ours ever again go our separate ways. It must not happen, and not the least of the reasons why it must not is the common heritage which Bea Lillie represented that night on a desert stage.

Remember Mahdi?

Joyce and Tommy Thomson lived in Mahdi, and so did their Egyptian friend whose name was Aziza, a wise and generous and talented woman whose brother was court chamberlain, a noted archeologist and an Oxford honor man, and in whose garden sometimes played the small daughters of Egypt's degenerate ruler. Mahdi, suburb of Cairo, was a flowery, tropic paradise where a world war scarcely ever intruded, and where Englishmen and Free French, Poles and New Zealanders and Americans, newly returned from the desert, could gather at Joyce and Tommy's and talk poetry and politics and art and journalism. At Mahdi I met the Egyptians, who could see what lay ahead, but who were unwilling or unprepared to do anything about it; brilliant, cynical, not as Westernized as they thought, with money and time both heavy on their hands and knowing that time at least was running out. They said that their way wouldn't last—and who could disbelieve seeing the beggar children with clusters of flies hiding their eyes?—and then they would laugh and murmur "maleesh" and complain because the war kept them from Paris and Lucerne. And in the streets of Mahdi, though not as many as those of Cairo, roamed the beggars and the gaunt men with doomed sight and bodies weakened with parasites, and in their eyes the vision of Death whose face was very young. . . .

Remember. . . . remember. . . . remember?

And, remembering, it is no longer possible to forget that the lands to which journeyed the sergeants of *Yank* and the reporters of *Stars and Stripes* are so very close to Mississippi and California and Ohio and Massachusetts, and that the bell of John Donne still tolls.

13

Telephone, Pyramids 5664

One day in Cairo, Gil Valle asked Bob Strother and me if we would like to go to a party that a sheik was giving for him out in the desert.

Gil, who was a second lieutenant, and I had flown to Africa together in a two-engine cargo plane which got lost over the South Atlantic while looking for a small pile of volcanic ash called Ascension Island, an incident that gave us a great deal of fright in common. He was of Cuban parentage, a personable twenty-five, and had been an assistant movie director with Universal Studios. He had been sent to the Middle East to help Bruce Manning make a documentary film about the Eighth Army and Ninth Air Force desert supply system. The documentary never was produced because the Army changed its mind, and Gil was killed later on before his first lieutenancy came through.

Bob and I thought that Gil was joking but he insisted that the invitation and the sheik were both authentic. Gil said that he had fallen into conversation with the sheik, a young fellow who had attended the American University in Cairo, during the filming of a slightly staged desert sequence which portrayed the use of camels and Arabs in the supply lines. The sheik owned the camels, hundreds of them, Gil said, and he owned the Arabs too; it turned out that he was an old hand at renting his camels and tribesmen for movie making. He had told Gil that he had become very good friends with an American director who had come over before the war to make a picture which needed camels. I can't remember the director's name, but the coincidence was that he was a man under whom Gil once worked in Hollywood. Gil had in his billfold a snapshot of the man and himself, with their wives, and when he displayed the photo, the sheik embraced him, pronounced him a friend because he was his friend's friend, and proposed a big party a few miles out in the desert beyond the Pyramids. Gil could bring ten to fifteen friends.

So a few nights later we drove to a rendezvous near the Pyramids, maybe twelve of us, including Bruce, and a New Zealander whom Gil liked, and a couple of Polish captains who had survived Russia and the long roundabout journey to the Middle East and were part of the little indomitable army which General Anders had put together from the survivors.

The sheik, and four or five of his men met us with a string of horses, all of them, as the Waverley novels say, richly caparisoned. The sheik, who was in his early thirties and darkly good-looking, was also richly caparisoned in a gold and silver galabeah. He spoke passable English and seemed very glad to see us. We shook hands all round and he gave each of us a calling card and in a few moments suggested that we ride off. I don't think there was a cavalryman in the group, but the horses were as friendly as the sheik and away we went under the stars, with the sands flowing out from under the horses' hoofs, and I couldn't make up my mind whether Hollywood got its ideas from the sheik or he had got his from Hollywood.

I kept his calling card for seven or eight years; then I lost it along with a billfold. Printed across its center, in English and Arabic, was his name:

SHEIK ALY SAWABY EL GABRY

Across the top, in smaller type, was a legend which I cannot now quote exactly but which proclaimed in English and Arabic that the sheik had camels for sale, for rent for long or short hauls and for motion-picture production. In the lower left-hand corner of the card was printed:

Telephone Pyramids 5664

We traveled maybe five miles under a nearly full moon without losing a rider. Gil proclaimed that the scene resembled one he had helped create out in the California desert, and said he was feeling right at home. The sheik talked mostly to the Poles during the ride because they and he could speak French better than English, and I tried to remember all that I had read that afternoon in the Army handbook on how to behave among Arabs. The book was one of those generally helpful pamphlets on conduct in foreign parts, which the soldiers called the "Don't Goose the Natives" series. What I recalled especially was that Arabs consider the laying of alien hands on their persons, whether in friendly spirit or otherwise, as a deadly insult, eating with the right hand as the coarse behavior of an oaf, and the drinking of hard liquor an affront to the Moslem faith.

By the light of a bonfire and the moon, we saw the sheik's

headquarters a good half mile before we reached it: four or five long, low scattered tents a few yards apart, black against the sand and very ominous-looking. Against the fire moved a few figures. When we reached the tents and dismounted and our horses had been led away, the sheik called out an order in Arabic, and a line of musicians and other paraders, maybe twenty in all, including a couple of tribal clowns, came marching toward us, cymbals clanking and reed instruments shrilling a disharmony of welcome.

After the parade the sheik led us to one of the large tents. It was lit with pressurized lanterns and carpeted with several layers of the thickest, biggest rugs I have ever seen. Along the tent walls hung Arabic tapestries in reds and greens and golds. Enough small, highly carved chairs for all of us were grouped near a table laden with glasses and bottles of Scotch whisky. Two grinning manservants began sloshing the Scotch into glasses as soon as we entered, not just a jigger or two jiggers or even three jiggers, but half-tumblersful at a time, and the tumblers were tall. I thought how considerate the sheik was to provide for the unbelievers the whisky that his faith forbade him to drink, but the sheik took one of the tumblers, too, and lifted it and said pretty intelligibly, "Down the hatch." We obeyed.

By the time we had begun our second tumblers, which wasn't much later, the sheik had taken off his outer robe, because the Scotch was making the tent seem hotter than it was. The galabeah under the outer robe was nearly as ornate, and Gil, who must not have read the handbook on how to get along with Arabs, asked the sheik how many more nightgowns he had on. The sheik said three, and grinned, and told us he liked Americans, and ordered, "Down the hatch again." By that time we were beginning to feel like blood brothers of every sheik this side of Jordan. Every few minutes our host would repeat that he liked Americans, that we had been good to his people and it was fine to be friends and brothers.

Then, after a while, he clapped his hands, and in came the tribe's magician, or maybe he had been hired in Cairo, where in every block roamed sleight-of-hand artists from five to a hundred years old. For a few piasters they would baffle the troops and beg for an opportunity to show what they could really do, which was considerable. The sheik's magician performed just a few feet from us, and at our own level, but we couldn't see through any of his bag of tricks.

When he had done, the sheik waved him out, the servants poured more Scotch, and in strutted the campus clown, his face daubed with white paint. I think he was trying to mimic the behavior of Western white people, but either he wasn't too good, or we weren't too discerning. He took stagefright, so the chief barked at him in Arabic and flicked him on the back with a riding crop and he scampered out yowling, though he wasn't hurt.

Next—the main attraction of the evening—two dancing girls entered. I am sure they had not learned their art out in the desert. They were improperly and Orientally diaphanous, pretty and highly painted, Salome's own daughters. Gil whooped and clapped the sheik on the shoulder, and the sheik didn't slice him with a scimitar. He grinned instead. He began flicking the girls with his riding crop, lightly, but the tip must have stung them, for they frowned and glanced angrily at each other and ran out of the tent before their dance was over and also before we wanted them to. We decided afterwards that they must have been imports from Cairo because if they had belonged to the sheik, they wouldn't have run out.

We probably had another round of Scotch, and the sheik took off another galabeah, but he still had his headdress on when we quitted that tent for the next one, which turned out to be the dining tent. A table, almost as long as the tent, ran down the middle, and off to one side were another Scotch dispensary and a serving table. The dining table was laid with heavy silver and loaded with a fantastic variety of foods. In the center crouched a whole roasted lamb, flanked by chickens and fish and beef filets, mounds of fruit and dishes of rice and rolled-up grape leaves filled with seasoned rice and meats. There were dates and nuts and slabs of unleavened bread and bowls of aromatic stews; altogether, I remember more than thirty kinds of edibles. The amateur bartenders went around the table again and again, half filling our glasses each time. No water or soda, just Scotch, with the sheik drinking along with the rest of us, and everyone becoming very friendly and loud.

The sheik opened the dinner by tearing off a large chunk of lamb—with his right hand, I noticed, marking up his second disregard for what the handbook said—and sharing it with somebody beside him. He preferred eating with his fingers, all through the meal, though on occasion he handled his table silver gracefully. The food and the spices and the Scotch and the warmth of the tent forced him midway of the meal to remove his headgear and the last galabeah but one. His hair was thick and cut very short. The galabeah was white and unornamented, and with his turban off, he looked like a sunburned halfback about to go to bed in a nightgown.

We ate and ate, and it was a good thing, because with all that Scotch we would otherwise have had a hard time making it out of the desert. Near the close of the dinner, which took a long time, somebody started to sing "Carry Me Back to Ol' Virginny," and the two Poles gave a few mournfully spirited numbers, and pretty soon individual singing groups were coming together and breaking up and reassembling in different units all over the tent, the singers wandering back every now and then to the tables to snare just one last tidbit or to have a glass filled again. I remember watching Gil put his arm around the sheik saying, "Sheikie, you old son of a bitch, you just got to come to Hollywood," and hearing the sheik say, "By damn, I will."

When we floated out of the tent, it was after three in the morning, but the show wasn't over. The bonfire was burning high, and in its light three tribesmen rode up, one of them leading a beautiful white Arabian horse. The sheik walked, not too steadily, to the horse and mounted him, and he and three fellow riders showed us how to handle spirited performing horses. The Arabians pirouetted, reared, danced, knelt, galloped—whatever the riders, by touch, told them to do—horses and men knit together in the desert firelight, while we clapped and cheered and told the sheik he was the best damn horseman we'd ever seen outside Ringling Brothers Circus.

Just after the exhibition had ended and while we were telling sheikie—all the Americans were calling him sheikie by then—what a great horseman and great guy he was, and warning him never to come to Greenville or New York or Plainview without looking us up, four or five uniformed horsemen appeared. Their leader was a British sergeant. The group did not appear to be an army detachment but some kind of desert police patrol, though I am sure they were operating as a British patrol and not as part of any Egyptian police force in that land which nominally was sovereign but in reality was not.

I didn't like that sergeant, and neither did any of the rest. Probably he was sleepy and irritated to find a bunch of Scotch-happy allied officers where we may not have had any business being. But there was no excuse for the way he talked to the sheik, who after all had been there—he and his forbears—

long before British police sergeants, as long as those rugs in the dining tent had been there. The sergeant was insolent and every inch the spokesman of the superior race. He asked the sheik for some identification papers which he was supposed to carry, pretty much as a detective asks a suspect where he was on the night of June thirtieth, and he was curt with us, though he saluted before asking for our identification cards. The New Zealander liked it least of all, and said something I didn't hear but which, from his surly look, the sergeant resented.

When the patrol rode off, no one felt like having another drink, and besides it was time to go anyway. A public relations major whispered to me that his commanding officer was planning to give a cocktail reception soon for General Louis Brereton, who commanded the Ninth Air Force and the American Middle Eastern theater, and why not ask old sheikie? So we invited the sheik to the party, explaining that the date had not yet been set, but that we would telephone Pyramids 5664 as soon as we knew when the party would be. The sheik was very pleased and almost formal in his acceptance. We shook hands again, and left him there, and rode off behind a couple of his guides, alternately talking about what a great party it had been and cursing the sergeant who had put such a bad taste in our mouths.

But we never saw old sheikie again, which also put a bad taste in my mouth. Somewhere further up the line the matter of inviting to the general's party the sheik who rented out camels must have been discussed and decided upon adversely, because Bob Parham, Brereton's public relations officer, who had been a good newspaperman before he became one of those blessed mortals, an Air Force semi-instantaneous colonel, told me a few days later that we'd better not invite the sheik, and that was that. I don't know why it was. Politics maybe, or policy, or the possibility of friction between a desert Arab and some of the Egyptian officials who would be at the party. I wrote the sheik a combination thank you and explanatory letter, which he had no reason to answer and did not. I've wondered since whether the sheik put into the same category the manner in which the sergeant spoke to him and what was actually a withdrawal of the invitation we had given him early one morning in the desert near the Pyramids, where we had been his guests.

I thought of the sheik and related matters eight years later when the Cairo mob gutted those institutions and sections of Cairo which we had most frequented and which, until their destruction, Westerners must have thought sacrosanct: Shepheard's Hotel, the Auberge de Turf, Barclay's Bank and Groppi's, that noble ice-cream parlor, and all the other preserves of the foreigner who came to profit and to patrol but not to rescue that grim land. Reading of that destructive insanity, I remembered the typhus-stricken beggars in the gutters of Cairo, and a sergeant on horseback, and the sterile sands where no wheat grows, and the thirty different foods in a rug-strewn tent, and an invitation withdrawn, and I didn't need a political analyst to explain that madness.

14

Concerning Betty

Betty is probably the only woman in all the roster of working wives to have her career ended by fleas. This happened in Washington, and in a roundabout fashion the responsibility rests with Mary Lou Simon, whose husband had survived the holocaust on the carrier *Franklin.* Bill Simon had been reassigned to a shore station on the West Coast and to join him Mary Lou had to give up her job as confidential researcher for Bernard Baruch, who had no mind to go to the West Coast and no inclination to give up Mary Lou's services either unless he could find an acceptable substitute. That was in the spring of 1944 .

At that time Betty had risen to a CAF-double something or other, a Civil Service rating which I especially remember because it meant that again she was making more in the Office of War Information than I was as a newly promoted major. From the time she got her first war job, a few days after Pearl Harbor, when I was that military leper, a Washington second lieutenant, until the week of the fleas, she managed to outearn me, matching promotion with promotion; and while this was a minor blow to a husband's pride, it was a means of survival in Washington.

In 1941, Mary Lou had left *Time* for OWI, which was then called the Office of Facts and Figures. That was a few weeks before Betty turned up at OFF with no provable qualifications but only the unprovable statement that she had done half the research for her husband's book on the Mississippi River. Louise Wells Baker Stroup, who had taken leave as the director of all of *Time*'s researchers for a similar post with OFF, says that Betty added, "And it's not out yet, but it's going to be the best historical book *you* ever read," which got her the job.

Two and a half years later, in 1944, our world was nearing a respite from its monstrous torment. I was back from Africa and Bill was coming home from the blazing South Pacific when Mary Lou told Betty that Betty simply had to go with Bernard Baruch because Mary Lou couldn't leave what she thought was her duty unless Betty quit OWI and took her place. She promised that the job would be more interesting and give Betty more freedom, because Mr. Baruch didn't require fixed hours or even daily appearance at his headquarters in the Carlton Hotel, as long as the facts he sought were carefully and succinctly presented.

Betty agreed to the change, and Mary Lou said she must come right away, which meant in two weeks. But Betty couldn't leave for a month; so instead of having things easier, her first two weeks with Mr. Baruch coincided with her last two weeks at OWI, which meant a good deal of overtime work, some of which she palmed off on me.

For about four months Betty ferreted out facts for Mr. Baruch and prepared them in summaries that resembled digests of the *Reader's Digest* digests, and had more fun, I think, than she ever had working anywhere else, partly because Bernard Baruch was courtly and considerate, and greatly because she delighted in having a small share in his magic. It was magic that was bi-partisan in its wonders, for she could and often did go to the Hill and there extract from Republican and Democratic senators and congressmen confidential dossiers pertaining to certain postwar matters in which Mr. Baruch's advice was sought.

It is no secret now that one such problem related to a postwar commercial aviation policy for the United States. Mr. Baruch's contemplation of the matter became all-absorbing in September, a month in which Washington and Maryland were so frightened by a polio epidemic that we sent Hod and Phil down to Florida where Betty's sister Evelyn was then living. That left us alone with Molasses, young Hod's dog, for the latest of our nurses had gone the way of most wartime household employees; and when Mr. Baruch told Betty that she would have to go to New York for two days for an aviation policy conference, we decided to put Molasses in a kennel. What we didn't know was that Molasses was host to a host of friendly fleas and that most of them remained in the house the morning I drove Molasses to the kennel and Betty to the station and myself to the Pentagon.

When I returned to a supposedly empty house that night, I was greeted, silently and painfully, by hundreds of fleas who wanted company, and found it in me. Nothing creates a greater sense of personal outrage or conviction of wifely inadequacy than to be attacked in one's home by fleas. I found a can of flea powder, sprinkled myself and the bed, and passed a self-pitying night, taking some consolation from the knowledge that Betty would be back the next night to take care of the fleas.

But she wasn't back the next night. She telephoned in the morning and said that Mr. Baruch wanted her to stay for another meeting. "Damn the postwar aviation," I said, and told her about the fleas. She promised to return the following morning.

That night the fleas were hungrier, and I moved over to the Wests', across the way, and slept on their sofa. When Betty telephoned me at the Pentagon the following morning and said that Mr. Baruch insisted that she stay still another day, I told her, not calmly, that she would have to choose between me and postwar aviation, and to make up her mind. She did, and came home that same night, and promptly bought at a service station a can of spray which got rid of the fleas. The next day she gave Mr. Baruch two weeks' notice, and soon afterwards the children came home and so did Molasses, and Betty settled down to being a housekeeper unadulterated for the first time since we started the *Daily Courier* in Hammond.

Five years afterwards, Quentin Reynolds gave a party for us in New York, and I think I can be forgiven for doing a little name dropping, for there never was a weirder assortment of characters at any small gathering. Mr. Baruch was there, and so was Toots Shor and one of the DiMaggios, Mayor O'Dwyer —that was shortly before he became ambassador-in-haste to Mexico—and that fine man, the late Judge Robert Patterson, and a couple of the Cowles, who brought along an advance copy of the first issue of *Quick,* and a high and wide assortment of writers. I told Mr. Baruch the story of how Betty came to quit him, and he laughed and looked at her across the room and said that if she had put her hair up then the way she does now, he never would have let her leave.

It's fortunate that fleas hadn't attacked me earlier in our marriage. If I had made a housewife out of Betty at any time before the fleas did, we never would have kept our newspapers going. We would also have had a bad time in Washington where, in 1940, a married second lieutenant made about one hundred and eighty-three dollars a month, and we didn't think we could take much from the *Democrat-Times* which was beginning to have a frightening turnover, thanks to the draft and enlistments, while everyone mistakingly predicted that small daily newspapers would be hard put to survive the war.

Until Pearl Harbor we hadn't thought much about our financial dilemma. When I was in Camp Blanding, Betty stayed in Greenville with the boys, but after I was transferred to Washington, they joined me for what we tried to believe would be only a few months more of the National Guard's year of active duty. When the Army doctors put me in Walter Reed because of my injury we were surer yet that we'd be out in December. We even wrote to the building contractors in Greenville, telling them that we would be building a house in the spring. What we meant was in the spring ten years later. But when I talked the hospital commandant, the week after Pearl Harbor, into returning me to duty, having decided there wasn't anything anyone could do about the eye anyway except pray, Betty said she was going to get a war job; and so she did, with the Office of Facts and Figures.

What I remember best about those OFF and OWI days of Betty's was the zeal with which she was forever undertaking new tasks, all having something to do with national and allied morale. Once she had to get Juliana of the Netherlands and a battleship together, and there was much dashing to and from Philadelphia before Juliana finally made the newsreels and the radio on an unnamed man-of-war in an unnamed port. The purpose was to encourage the allies by showing them that the United States recognized the wartime contributions of all members of the allied front, including the small, conquered countries.

After a couple of promotions or so, Betty directed a radio campaign for the collection, by innumerable patriotic little Boy Scouts, of thousands and maybe millions of pounds of milkweed floss—and it takes a lot to the pound—because floss was needed for buoyant lifejackets. But the Navy found something else while the collections were being made, Betty thinks, because for months afterward, her office was deluged with letters from scoutmasters asking what, please, should they do with the floss that was in the high school basement and the Oddfellows' hall.

She compiled a tragic and meaningful record of the unconquered little people of conquered Europe and had charge of a campaign to make the public take seriously the need for security of information. It was when I was overseas that she sided with OWI's creative writers against the "advertising crowd" in a policy debate that could be held only in America on the big question of whether information should be presented as information or whether desired results should be sold the American people like a new brand of soap. Symptomatic was the disgust of the creative writers when they discovered American women were to be told they should walk to be slim and beautiful rather than given the facts that the nation—and their husbands in the services—needed the gasoline. The lady beautiful approach won out and some of the writers resigned, but Betty stayed on because, as she wrote me, she thought there was room for both techniques.

Betty loved her OWI folks, and so did I. Most of those who became our especial friends had given up more lucrative or freer pursuits because they wanted to have a part in the war and weren't qualified for the armed services; it seemed to us then and we believe now that the critics who ridiculed the work and the motives and the over-all objectives and activities of OWI were captious or vengeful or ignorant. Surely there were no better or more intelligent Americans than Elmer Davis and Ep Hoyt, Henry Pringle and Milton MacKaye and Phil Hamburger and Philip Wylie and Archibald MacLeish. They were doing well enough before they came to OWI, and they've done well enough since.

We made lasting friends among them, thanks to Betty, whom they adopted from the beginning and looked after when I was overseas. They like to tell stories, at our too infrequent reunions, about Betty's perseverance. She was always being plagued in Washington by sudden departures of a succession of nurses—one by way of a jail sentence for drunkenness; another, a German woman, who quit because Betty objected to her telling young Hod that Hitler and the Nazis were right; a third, who left in the middle of the night because Molasses was slow at becoming housebroken. These crises demanded Spartan solutions, not for the sake of Hod who was in school most of the day and was plentifully supplied with neighborhood playmates whose mothers kept general watch, but for Phil, who was too young even for kindergarten. Betty even took him on one such nurseless day to the OWI itself, and he played around her desk unconcernedly, or sometimes tried to escape down the hall with assorted OWI's in pursuit.

And after work, there was the queuing up for groceries, the juggling of ration points for food and gasoline, the problem of getting to and from work in a shifting car pool, the task of consoling a worried husband, and trying to make ends meet and save a little—somehow all the while, even enjoying the tensions and madness of wartime Washington.

That was Betty, and what is finest about it all, in retrospect, is that Betty wasn't unique, but only one of hundreds of thousands of Bettys, who in the war years adjusted themselves to being uprooted, and to following husbands to Army camps, making homes in slums and trailers, working in factories and in war-crowded cities, the younger ones afterwards going with their student husbands to academic tenements, where the men could study while the women puzzled with them over the textbooks and bore their children, remembering the heartaches with a laugh, if they remember the aching at all. They were and are the contrasting other side of the statistics which are bad enough but are dwarfed by women such as these, upon whom humanity's destiny depends and who have no time to be afraid of the dark forest. I married one who was already like that a long time before the war.

15

"—from Jesus Christ on down"

In the summer of 1946 the late Theodore G. Bilbo yowled his way through Mississippi as a candidate for re-election to the United States Senate. Because he convinced a majority of Mississippi voters—who are a minority of adult Mississippians—that he was being martyred by interlopers from the outside world, led by the Communist party, he was re-elected. It is impossible to believe that any other senatorial election in our history ever dealt democracy a lower blow or ever sent a less worthy man to Washington to represent a supposedly intelligent and free people.

But once during that campaign, he almost came a cropper. He was speaking in Leland, eight miles from Greenville, in the little city hall auditorium, to a crowd which overflowed into the soft, river night. For an hour he had spat a frightful effluvium, evil, vindictive, hate-filled, mocking. Negroes he had put in their place by recalling that the fathers of today's black men and women, who had the temerity to seek to vote, had only yesterday eaten nigger steak for breakfast back in Africa. He told his listeners that the best way to take care of the nigger who dared to try to vote was to see him the night before election. He paid his passing respects to me, promising a skinning party when he came to Greenville, which he never did, and explaining that "no red-blooded Southerner worthy of the name would accept a Poolitzer-blitzer prize given by a bunch of nigger-loving Yankeefied communists for editorials advocating the mongrelization of the race." He repeated this throughout the state every night in that shameful summer of a state's voluntary degradation.

All this was Grade-A vote-getting technique in Mississippi. But in Leland he blundered. He complained satirically that folks had been saying lately that The Man Bilbo—on the stump he chose to refer to himself in the third person as The Man Bilbo—was anti-Semitic, which meant, he explained, that he didn't like Jews. In fact, a little Yankee girl reporter had come to him just the other day in Washington and asked him whether such reports were true.

"I said, 'Little lady, why of course that ain't true,'" Bilbo told his rapt audience. "'Why,' I said, 'I'm for every damned Jew from Jesus Christ on down.'"

The applause that time was unenthusiastic, so Bilbo raced

on to another victim. Out in the dark, I started moving through the crowd, going from person to person and asking them if they had just heard what I had heard, and if so, would they give affidavits. Six persons, who were widely known in the Delta and unimpeachable as to character, agreed.

I gathered those affidavits the next day, had photostats made of them and sent them to all the daily newspapers in the state. We wrote stories for the Associated Press and the United Press about how Bilbo was for "every damned Jew from Jesus Christ on down." I really thought we had him over a barrel, for while a majority of Bilbo's supporters didn't much mind what a man said about Jews or niggers or Catholics or Dagoes, and he said plenty about all of them, they were God-fearing Christian folk who didn't like a man getting sassy with the Lord.

Bilbo won, anyhow. He denied part of the phrase. What he had actually said, he explained, was, "I am for every *good* Jew from Jesus Christ on down." That made it sound a lot better, his followers agreed, for certainly there were good Jews. He wrote a sickening form letter to offended Protestant clergymen, recalling how he had always loved Jesus, and would never say anything so sacrilegious, and as for the Greenville editor who spread those lies, everyone knew that he was a well-known Communist who would stoop at nothing to defeat The Man Bilbo.

Accepting the distinction between a damned Jew and a good Jew, his pious supporters marched as Christian soldiers to the polls and voted for The Man Bilbo who had reverently included among his good Jews the Son of Man.

Not many summers afterwards, I was lounging on the gallery of a golf club which overlooks the loveliest of bays along the North Atlantic coast, and thinking that here and now, at least, God's in his heaven and all's right with the world. And then I heard the precise voice of the club hostess, talking by telephone to an unidentified offender, and not to just one, but one after another to every operator in that region of a hotel, inn or any other kind of hostel where the clientele was not, as they say, restricted. The manager of one of them had made the mistake of telling three of its guests that they could play golf at the club. These three had been allowed to go around, because nobody wanted to make a scene, she explained. But never let it happen again. Never send out to this club any Jew, at all, not even anybody who looks like a Jew. They aren't allowed under club rules.

It came over me, listening, that after all, Bilbo might not have been as bigoted as I thought him, or at least not as bigoted as it was possible for a human being to be. After all, in his remarks at Leland, as amended, he had been for every good Jew, while the directors of the little Maine golf club just didn't want within putting distance any Jew at all, whether rich or poor, hungry or persecuted, arrogant or humble, smart or dumb, old or young, duffer or champion. Neither presumably did any of the club's members, though later that same summer most of them attended a duo piano recital given in our barn studio, for the benefit of the local hospital by a notable husband and wife who happen to be Jews, and who performed without charge.

Man is a contradictory animal. Bilbo could be elected to high office in Mississippi by opening the flood gates of racial hatred, and in Maine I am sure he would have been booed off the platform. Yet no Jew can play golf at the Megunticook club, whereas in Greenville, our country club president for the last five years or more happens to have been a Jew, which proves perhaps only that it takes perseverance to hate Jews and Negroes and Catholics all at the same time.

I admit to a prejudice in the matter. It so happens that at almost every decisive period in my life, some Jew, living or dead, has stood beside me and helped me forward; not Jews, good or damned, whom I was for, but only Jews who were for me, when I might otherwise have been damned myself, nine of them, in all. One I knew only slightly, two not at all, and another mostly from the written word. Maybe they will gain inclusion among the good ones whom Bilbo endorsed, and, just possibly, a guest card at the golf club, though I can imagine the look on the hostess's face, if one of these nine, whose name is Jesus Christ, were to present his credentials and she were to recognize him from his pictures or from something he said—neither being likely.

I'll start with Otto Beit, whom I saw only twice, because he lived in England where he had been knighted before I was born. He was a man of immense wealth and greater charity, and he had married an older sister of my father whom he met when the Louisiana girl was visiting relatives in England. His brothers- and sisters-in-law on this side of the Atlantic presented him in time with some twenty-five nephews and nieces. He would not have been able to identify any of us, but each of us went to college without financially burdening our families; for he had a great deal of what most of my father's people had relatively only a little of, and he and his wife, my aunt, wanted the American young ones to get the best possible educations.

I was sixteen when I went to Bowdoin College in Maine, and I didn't know then anything about Jews or about what happened to people because they were Jews. There had been only one in Hammond, a tailor, who accompanied his Christian wife to her church.

At Bowdoin I met Jim Abrahamson, a year older and a year

ahead of me, and there and later in graduate school at Columbia, I learned as much from Jim as I did from the professors. He was an economist and a sociologist, and probably the most intelligent man ever to go to Bowdoin College (where he now teaches), while I was only the campus poet, who wrote love verses that I pretended were born of wide experience. I didn't ponder much over causes and effects, or look at the other side of the tracks. Jim changed all that.

In New York, we solved the world's problems two or three nights a week at an old, friendly, bare-tabled brauhaus on Third Avenue. Jim would take me to listen to his economics lecturers at Columbia, who sounded like prophets of doom and were true diviners of what was to come. I began thinking of other things than poetry and Jim Abrahamson was responsible.

One night he told me a story so memorable that ever since I have had a hard time persuading myself that I did not witness the making of it first hand. It happened at the first Armistice Day celebration, he said. He was a kid of twelve in Portland, watching wide-eyed as the parade went by, patting his feet in time to the band and clapping for the marching units. Then, of a sudden, something hit him in the back of his head, and his cap flew off and he fell from the sidewalk to the street; when he got up, dazedly, a man behind him, fists still clenched, snarled, "Uncover for the flag, you dirty little Christ killer." Jim blurrily watched the American flag go by, and his head was throbbing with pain, and his heart with a worse soreness, and when the flag had passed, he picked up his dirtied cap and ran home, crying.

From Columbia I came to New Orleans and at the end of a year of teaching at Tulane because I could find no newspaper job, the New Orleans *Item* after a few weeks' free trial conceded that I might be worth twelve and a half dollars a week. The *Item's* top reporter was gangly Herman Deutsch, who came right out of *The Front Page* because that was the way he was. He would tell me when he liked a story and when he didn't, and what was right or wrong with it, though he wasn't an editor and need not have bothered.

Three years later, when I was a publisher, and the banks had closed and reopened, and the *Courier* was still shaky and might yet have gone down, I dropped in on Herman because we were thinking of writing a play together about Huey Long. (We did write it eventually, an utterly libelous farce that we still think deserves the light of day.) Herman asked me how the *Courier* was doing. I told him not so hot, and he asked, "Would a thousand-dollar loan help you?" Just like that. Whatever I said had the sound of angels rejoicing as accompaniment. He loaned us the thousand dollars, without note or collateral or interest. That was the most money we had seen at one time since our marriage. I doubt that we could have kept going without the second linotype for which part of Herman's thousand dollars went in down payment. Or maybe it wasn't the linotype so much as the fact that somebody believed in us, which made us believe all the more in ourselves, and if that sounds trite, I'm sure I don't mind.

Betty had known David Cohn before I did, even before she entered college, for Dave, a bachelor forever, whose French Quarter apartment in New Orleans housed three Epstein heads, was often a dinner guest at her mother's. I met him there the year I taught at Tulane. After we went to Hammond to start the *Courier*, Dave would come up to see us now and then. He called on us the day after he made his decision to leave the world of business, in which he had been fabulously successful, for the world of letters. There is no need to introduce Dave and his eight books, and countless magazine essays, but I want to tell once more how he paved the way for our going to Greenville.

In the spring of 1935, Louisiana State University was celebrating its seventy-fifth year, and Huey Long was making the most of the event. One much-heralded part of the program was a Southern Writer's Conference at Baton Rouge, to which I was invited, though my only writing other than for newspapers had been a couple of poems, a flamboyant magazine short story, and a handful of denunciatory articles, mostly for the *New Republic,* concerning Long's tyranny. I hadn't intended to go, because our son was scheduled to be born most any time, and arrive he did, the day before the conference was to open. Betty urged me to attend. She was all right, so was little Hodding, she said, and so, after weak paternal protestations, I went.

The conference was quite a show, for an imposing roster of the South's writers had turned out: Allen Tate and John Crowe Ransom, and Robert Penn Warren, who was mostly poet and teacher then; Roark Bradford, and Lyle Saxon, whom I knew from the Quarter days, and many others. And Dave, who asked about Betty and the new boy. That night, at a reception, when the hotel's top-floor ballroom grew uncomfortable and hot from too many people and too much cigarette smoke, Dave suggested that we get some air on the fire escape.

We sat on the fire-escape steps, high above the Mississippi, with the barge lights glowing, and now and then the long hooting of a river tug, and the river must have made Dave think about Greenville, his home, three hundred miles north of us, where I had never had occasion to go. He told me of a brave and challenging little river city, and of Will Percy, who lived there. Dave said, "He's a saint, Will is," which I would later come to know myself. He asked me how we were doing in Hammond and when I answered optimistically, he said, "You're butting your head against a brick wall." I admitted that I knew it. "You ought to come to Greenville," Dave said. "We need another paper there. I'll talk to Will about it."

That was the beginning of our coming to Greenville, a year and a half later, with Huey Long dead of an assassin's bullet, and our paper sold, and all because of a smoky ballroom, and Dave Cohn.

Skip ten years with a newspaper fight and a world war in between. Near the war's end, we almost lost our newspaper, and didn't because of another of the nine.

After I went into the Army in the fall of 1940, to be followed in the next two years by first one and then another of our staff, the directors and I began to worry about the *Democrat-Times*. We had no way of knowing that newspapers would thrive during wartime. Will was dead, and the other Greenville stockholders were honestly concerned as to whether the paper could keep going, with Betty and me away and the staff falling apart. Billy Wynn suggested that I find someone to buy the Greenville stockholders' interest, which consisted of about forty-seven per cent of the stock, someone who was in newspaper business, and who could give the paper the management it so badly needed.

I found someone, all right, just before I went overseas—a fellow officer with sizable newspaper holdings. He bought out the Greenville men and some of my stock to boot, for he insisted on fifty-per-cent ownership, and managerial control for two years, at the end of which time a buy-or-sell clause would become effective. He was an extraordinarily successful, and extraordinarily purposeful person, and I believed him when he told me that the buy-or-sell clause would never be invoked, that instead we would go on acquiring papers after the war with me directing the editorial policies and him handling the business end. What he didn't tell me was that he didn't mean it. I ought to have read our contract more closely, especially in respect to the buy-or-sell clause, which set down that if either partner wanted to buy out the other at the end of two years, he could make an offer. The person to whom the offer was made had the choice either of selling at the offered price or buying instead at the same price. That was standard practice in such clauses. But there was a little phrase to which I paid no attention, thinking ahead to other newspapers after the war, for I liked him and respected his business acumen, not realizing that it was being tested on me. The phrase said that in the event the buy-or-sell clause was invoked, the purchaser must buy the "entire creditor position" of the seller for cash. A time limit of ninety days was fixed during which the partner first approached could make up his mind.

I went then to the Middle East, and he went to the South Pacific and his general manager got busy. He did a fine job of putting the *Democrat-Times* into good shape. During the next two years, the manager acquired for my partner and put in his name the outstanding obligations of the newspaper. That included the balance of the annual payments owed to the original owners of the *Democrat-Times,* the outstanding preferred stock held by the Greenville men (which he surrendered to the paper and for which he took a mortgage instead), and the notes on a larger newspaper press which was bought soon after his organization took over the management. Each of these items—the annual payments on the paper, the preferred stock and mortgage, and the notes on the press—were, of course, being liquidated in monthly or annual payments and were neither past due nor due in full, and they totaled about eighty-four thousand dollars.

In 1945, in the very week the buy-or-sell clause went into effect, I received a formal letter from my partner informing me that he was invoking the buy-or-sell clause, and that if I chose to exercise my right to buy him out, I must also buy for cash his "entire creditor position," which he listed, all eighty-four thousand dollars' worth. He must have been sure I couldn't raise anything like that, for he offered me for my fifty per cent of the paper only twenty thousand dollars.

I had guessed the blow was coming. There had been no secret about his acquiring the preferred stock, and I had discovered after returning from overseas that he had personally financed the purchase of the press and bought the newspaper notes from the original holder, the Smith family. But there was nothing I could do except act dumb and wait for the two-year period to end. I didn't think I could do much about it anyway if things went as we had begun to suspect they would.

No one likes to be played for a zany, and we had ninety days, but we had in sight only about thirty thousand dollars at best, which was a long way from enough.

We hadn't, however, counted on Joe Weinberg, who was the president of the Greenville Bank and Trust Company, and we hadn't counted on Milton Starr, a Tennessean whom we had come to know in Washington, where he was serving without pay as a major consultant in War Production.

Joe Weinberg is in his seventies now. He was born in Greenville when it was not much more than a steamboat landing. He had prospered there through his men's clothing store and his faith in the town's future, buying real estate when others were selling; even in the great flood year of 1927, while the water sloshed five feet deep in the streets, he ran a full-page ad in the old *Democrat-Times,* telling his fellow citizens not to lose heart but to stick to Greenville.

So, in late March, when I was still in uniform, we decided that I should get a few days' emergency leave and fly down to Greenville to see Joe Weinberg. He might, he just might. . . .

I flew down the next week, and it took me nearly an hour to tell my story to Joe Weinberg and to answer his questions. At the end he told me that he would lend us forty thousand dollars, which was all his bank could lend to one person under its charter, and did I think I could raise the balance? I assured him that I could, though I didn't see how, and he said something so unusually pleasant that I'm not going to put it down here; and after that all we had to get was about thirty-five thousand dollars.

That next week, with not much more than a month to go, Milton and Zaro Starr asked us to go with them to a party for some of their fellow Tennesseans at the home of Allen Tate, who was then the resident poet at the Library of Congress.

Betty had brought Milton home for dinner one night in Washington, early in 1942, though I had been rather provoked when she suggested that we have him out. She had met him at the Office of War Information, where she was a veteran of a month or two, and she said that he had seemed sort of shy and lonely when she talked to him but that he shared our interest in the South. So Milton came to dinner, and he did seem both shy and informed, and we liked him. When Zaro, his wife, came up later, we liked her too, and we became good friends.

We found out, in time, that Milton owned a chain of motion-picture houses in the South; and at the Starr home we were forever meeting a variety of people, poets and playwrights, congressmen and movie makers, generals and privates, politicians and teachers, mostly with some tie or another to Tennessee and all with a tie to Milton, who was good at unraveling knots, and listening, and setting people straight.

Anyway, we went together that night to the Tennessee party, and sometime during the evening Milton and I fell to talking about the happy inevitability of victory in a few months over Germany and Japan. Milton asked me how it would feel to be running our paper again after nearly five years in uniform. I said that we might not go back, and told him something of our predicament. I remember that he became very angry and said that he wanted to help in whatever way he could and to be sure to phone him the next day so that we could talk the matter over at a more propitious time. I promised I would.

But the next morning, when I told Betty about the conversation, we agreed reluctantly that we should not bother Milton with our woes. So I didn't telephone him. A couple of nights later, he telephoned instead, and asked me why I hadn't got in touch with him because my story was worrying him, and to come on over.

Before the evening was over, Milton had our financial house in order. He would put up the necessary thirty-five thousand dollars, and for it would receive my partner's fifty per cent. If I wanted to buy him out at any time, he would sell to us for just what he had put in. If not, he would be happy to remain as a silent partner. The next month, we went down to Greenville together, and I tried to be nonchalant in the bank which had acted as escrow agents when I handed over a check for one hundred and four thousand and some odd dollars and cents, and got back our newspaper. And now, seven years later, we've repaid Joe Weinberg, and we've repaid Milton Starr—as far as money is concerned. The

Delta Democrat-Times is ours, but every now and then I have a recurrent nightmare, in which I discover too late that I have just signed a legal document including the phrase "the entire creditor position of the seller."

Now in all of these episodes, the men who walked with us past one milestone after another were our friends, except for the English uncle whose relationship was both nearer and more distant. This is not true of two others, both dead before I knew who they were, who represent that genius for creative philanthropy which so singularly has characterized Jewish leadership. One of them was named Guggenheim and the other Pulitzer. In 1945, on quitting the Army, I was granted a writing fellowship which bears the name of the one, and in 1946, I received one of the newspaper awards which makes the name of the other synonymous with America's creative best. In each instance, the effect upon me, as it must be upon any recipient of these prizes, was galvanic. I had been writing books before I received a Guggenheim fellowship; and I had been protesting editorially against racial and religious injustices for a long time before our editorials won a Pulitzer prize. But the Guggenheim fellowship made me think for the first time that maybe I might become a pretty fair writer, and the Pulitzer prize induced more people at home to concede that there might be some merit in what we were saying. I wonder if Joseph Pulitzer, warrior and perfectionist and lover of justice, and the heirs of John Simon Guggenheim, could possibly have known what their visionary gifts would mean to the hundreds of men and women who receive them; and whether another notable Jewish philanthropist, Julius Rosenwald, could have foreseen the smashing impact of his benefactions in the South upon men indifferent to justice, and upon men and women and children for whom the Rosenwald Fund opened the doorway to hope. We do have recognition, we, the recipients, say; we do have some merit, we are not writing or speaking or painting or teaching in the darkness.

Six whom I knew as friends and two who were friends of hopeful, ambitious Americans. And another. . . .

Last spring, a fellow Greenvillian came to me, somewhat hesitantly, and asked me if I would accompany him on a Roman Catholic retreat at Pass Christian on the Mississippi Gulf Coast. His reason was sound enough, if a little roundabout. He was a Catholic himself, and a former alcoholic, who through the Church and Alcoholics Anonymous had defeated his enemy. Because he had enough money to do as he wished, he was spending most of his time and much of his money in working for alcoholics and his faith. Inasmuch as most Mississippians are Protestants, the law of averages makes it inevitable that Mississippi's alcoholics are also overwhelmingly Protestant. But my friend believed that the young Jesuit priest who directed the retreat could help Protestant victims, at a special retreat for alcoholics, as much as he had helped him, if only they could be assured that there was nothing up the sleeves of the Jesuit gown. He thought that if I, an Episcopalian, a sort of middleman so to speak, and no prohibitionist, would go to a retreat, I could talk to the AA's afterward and allay whatever fears they might have about entering a stronghold of papists.

I said yes on three counts. I liked the man who came to me, and had marveled at his comeback. I wanted to do anything I could to help any poor devil who was a victim of dipsomania—and we have lots of them in dry Mississippi. I was intrigued at the prospect of three days of monastic silence and of self-searching and reading and observation of Catholic teaching.

So I went to the retreat, and it was a rare spiritual experience. Young Father Sheridan was a dedicated Jesuit shock trooper, slangily contemporary when it was appropriate, hypnotic, mystical and sure. I went the whole way—except for making a confession—fumbling through the rituals, at first self-consciously, from early morning to well after nightfall. Instead of my confessing when my turn came, the Father and I had a good talk, during which, as a reporter should, I finally had him telling me about himself instead of my telling him about myself.

I talked in Greenville the next week to the county AA chapter and told the members that Father Sheridan didn't ask a man what his brand of religion or brand of whisky was, and to try him. Several did, which helped them and made my friend happy.

But I didn't tell them of one morning's instruction, because it might have frightened some of them off. At each of the four-a-day lectures in the chapel, called Instruction, Father Sheridan spoke of the kind of conduct that in sum total would add up to Christian living. As an aside, I must say that whatever criticism members of other faiths may make of the Catholic Church—that it is matriarchal, authoritative, masochistic, intolerant—no fair American could be mistrustful of the goals of morality for the individual, for the family, for the Christian, for the state, for the human soul, which that young Georgia priest set for his listeners. On this morning Father Sheridan devoted himself to a subject that does not ordinarily command the respectful attention or the approval of all Americans. He talked, not in generalities but in angry, reproachful specifics, of the great gap between human behavior and the ideal of the brotherhood of man and the fatherhood of God; of the deprivation of the civil rights of Negroes in Mississippi, and our calculated effort to deny even self-respect to those Americans of another color. He struck hard, and as he spoke of man's inhumanity to man, of Jew-baiting and all our shallow contempt for our fellowman, the chapel was filled with the sound of God's rage.

Father Sheridan was authoritarian, all right. I doubt that anywhere in the South a Protestant minister could get by with tongue-lashing a congregation on our regional and national indecencies to our fellowmen. Listening to that intense, black-robed young man, I was aware that he was trying to change his listeners' prejudices and folkways by the force of his belief and by the authority with which his church had vested him, and I felt a passing, Protestant qualm at the power that backed him up. Then I asked myself, why not? If we wait for each man's heart to change, without some kind of spiritually generated compulsion, we may wait too long, and another compulsion, dreadful and earthly may intervene. The young priest in his chapel was invoking the compulsion of the spirit, while all around our western islands of freedom, the Soviet compels by terror the equality of the living tomb of state servitude, wherein men are not black nor brown, nor Catholic nor Jew but are indistinguishably enslaved and equally driven.

Father Sheridan was not demanding obedience to democratic law, nor was he inspiring a fear of knout and torture chamber and execution squads. His was instead a restatement of the law of a young and ageless teacher, a rabbi of Palestine, a Jew, who was hailed and feared and mocked and tortured to death as the Christ; a Jew divine for two thousand years, a Jew whose fellow Jews have been slain, not by David's tens of thousands but by the millions in our Christian time; a Jew who animated this priest in his chapel, and the Roundhead, and once, presumably, Theodore Bilbo, who said he was for good Jews beginning with the Jew Jesus; a Jew who most surely helped my friend to quit his drinking and told him to help others who were weak as he had been; a Jew of compassion whose story of the good Samaritan is there for all of us to read.

16

Faulkner, Fish, Fowl and Financiers

We who enter the lists as protectors of the fair name of Dixie, astride the good steed Southern Change, sometimes ride that stalwart charger into the ground. From his back we hurl defiances: the South is no longer the heartland of ignorance, for we most certainly have as many writers as once we had readers and, ergo, are cultured. The South is ceasing to be America's farm problem child, for we are restoring our land's fertility and diversifying our crops and replanting our forests. The South is learning to live the good, dietary life, having abjured its late dyspeptic allegiance to meal, hogmeat and molasses. The South is just what the Northern industrialist's doctor ordered, for we have sunshine, plenty of willing workers, a variety of raw products, a growing consumer's market, and the nicest sites for new plants that you ever saw. Sure, we're on our way.

All this I believe. All this I preach, believing. In all this, I rejoice. But sometimes, and especially on one January day in 1950, I have wished that these evolutionary revolutions wouldn't happen so fast and in one place and all together. That day should go down in Southern history, Greenville appendix, as the time that the Four F's descended on us together. Those F's are not related to draft status but stand instead for Faulkner, fish, fowl and financiers, and in their joining lies a moral.

First, take Faulkner.

For reasons least known to ourselves, Ben Wasson, Kenneth Haxton and I organized one low-water night some time back still another addition to the multiplicity of publishing houses whose directors dream of an America that will some day read instead of write. Ben—who once wrote a novel and thereafter left Greenville for New York and Hollywood, and eventually came home from the Navy with a bad stomach and a yearning to take things easy—conducts for us the only full-fledged book page in Mississippi. He is also one of that very select group whose members are personal friends of William Faulkner. Kenneth inherited a large share of a Greenville department store which he may not have wanted because his business duties take away some of the time that he prefers using to buy records, play records and write yet unpublished novels. His record collection, let it be said as an additional aspect of the Greenville legend, happens to be one of the largest private collections in the country. The records fill a large music room, overflow into nurseries, porches and bedrooms, and spill over into an outbuilding.

None of this explains, nor can we, why the Levee Press was organized. But it was, capital three hundred dollars, with free office space and printing at cost, courtesy of the *Delta Democrat-Times.* As may someday be stated in the charter and by-laws we haven't yet drawn up, its purpose was to publish limited, signed editions of new, relatively short books—"novella" sounds better—by established Southern writers. The *Democrat-Times* bought some good-looking book type, and we were in business. In a few months, we brought out our first volume "Music from Spain" which Eudora Welty in Jackson gave us. The edition sold out because Charles Poore of the New York *Times,* and everyone of the handful of reviewers to whom we sent copies, gave us favorable reviews. Charlie's was not only favorable but funny.

BOOKS OF THE TIMES

BY CHARLES POORE

Eudora Welty's fine story, "Music From Spain," is the first book from the new Levee Press at Greenville, Miss.—a state that is enjoying a lively literary renaissance these days. The story Miss Welty has to tell is as impalpable—and as real—as smoke. It is one day's fantastic adventures in the life of a remarkably prosaic man, a Milquetoast, a Walter Mitty, if you will, who for a brief interval lives far beyond his mental and emotional income. As overture to each chapter there is a musical thingumajig that still eludes me completely, though I have had this house's "Dr. Faustus" expert making an impressively infernal noise with it at her piano.

That's the main criticism to be made of the book. There should be more, if only to bait the lit'ry lions of the Delta. They take umbrage as briskly as a man listening to New Year's resolutions reaches for a grain of salt. They're able, nimble and eloquent. One false word about Mississippi authors and you'll have a posse of them after you quicker than you can say: Hodding (Dewey-for-

President) Carter, William Faulkner, Herschel Brickell, Ben Ames Williams, David L. Cohn, Stark Young, Elizabeth Spencer, Tennessee Williams (all right then, look him up), David Donald, Mildred Topp, Nash K. Burger, Frances Gaither, Ben Wasson, Lucille Finlay, Maxwell Bodenheim, Charles Henri Ford, Hubert Creekmore, Shelby Foote and Eudora Welty.

SLAP IN THE FACE DOES IT

The scene of Miss Welty's balladlike tale is San Francisco. There, amid the cable cars and the hilly clatter of that Asia-facing town, her hero, an imperfectly transplanted Mississippian, is living out his life of quiet desperation. One morning, before proceeding to his watch-mender's work, obscurely stirred, perhaps, by the Spanish music he heard the night before, he hauls off and slaps his wife in the face. Just like that.

The act of violence is pure catnip to his soul. A swaggering bruiser now—in his mind, at any rate—he leaves her among the ruins of domestic felicity and breakfast dishes. Out in the bright incalculable street he is guided by destiny and Miss Welty to a strange encounter with the mysterious foreigner who plays music from Spain.

All sorts of private discords and frustrations bubble up through the gray quagmire of his mind. The tragic loss of a child, the unhappiness of his own prolonged infancy, the trapped bleakness of his marriage, the overweening patronage of contemptuous employers, do their devil dances through his head. But it's clear enough when the day's bizarrely realistic adventures are irrevocably over.

The Levee Press was founded by Hodding Carter, the Pulitzer Prize-winning editor and publisher of the *Delta Democrat-Times*, and Ben Wasson, editor of the DDT's book page. Their next venture will be William Faulkner's "Dangling Clause." "Music From Spain" is a handsome example of bookmaking. It will be of particular interest to all who have admired the wonderfully skillful and perceptive writing that have made Miss Welty one of the truest creative writers in America.

When Ben had said, "Let's publish a Faulkner," Kenneth and I laughed at him, even though we knew they were good friends. Ben fell back on his dignity and telephoned Faulkner that night, and in a few days Ben and I drove over to Oxford, about a hundred and twenty miles away, for an evening with the Faulkners. It was a memorable evening with an at-first-reticent genius. When it was over, Ben and I returned home with an original manuscript which William Faulkner at first had suggested be called "A Dangling Clause from Work in Progress," and which we had finally shortened to "Notes on a Horsethief." It was good, even though a few readers have since complained that they never before had read thirty thousand words divided into only three sentences. Between the time he gave us the manuscript and its publication, Faulkner won the Nobel Prize, which made the little book even more of a collector's item, but that comes later.

So let's leave the first of the four F's for a while, and move on to the second.

Which is fish.

When we began building our house out in the country a little way from Greenville, we thought that it would be pleasant to make a small lake out of a three-acre cypress brake which stretched for about six hundred feet across the very front of our acreage. From the brake—which was dry in the summer, moist in autumn, marshy in winter, and wet and green in spring—rise the more than thirty lovely, wide breeched cypress, feathery-leafed and long-lived, and old when the Delta still waited the cotton planter's coming. The lake would surround the cypress and reflect them and the home that we would build.

The bulldozers and draglines came to deepen the slough into a lake, and behind them followed two small, almost naked Negro children, who killed water moccasins with willow switches at ten cents a snake and collected more than five dollars from thankful me. Finally the lake was finished, and because I had been writing and reading editorials about farm fish ponds, we said this lake must be a home for fish, which are food and also fun to catch. I wrote to the state and federal agricultural agencies and explained that I was a visionary Mississippian who had dug a lake, ready for fish to balance our diet and stop erosion and give joy in this dreary world, so please send us fish to make our dream come true, one tenth of them bass and nine tenths of them bream and damned be the wandering cow to whose legs cling the egg of the catfish.

So we settled back to wait for the second of our four F's, which was fish.

And then came fowl.

Our twelve acres cried out, we told ourselves, for an Oriental intensity of use. Whereupon we put in a half-acre vegetable garden. We planted scores of fruit trees. We installed in the stable at Christmastime two saddle horses and a burro. We designated a distant hollow as the future home for a few choice pigs, and we turned loose in the pasture four sheep and, for a very short while, three goats. Looking over our work, we pronounced it good. But we agreed that something else was needed. Not a cow, for cows are very confining, but chickens.

The extension department recommended a hundred layers and sent us free of charge seven books and a set of chicken house blueprints. Up went the latest in hen houses, close to the stable complete with fenced-in yard as recommended. My good friend Trickey Hicks, who manages the Quaker Oats Company's Greenville branch, told me that what I wanted was day-old baby chicks, and he offered to order some extra special white Leghorns from somewhere in Florida. Into the brooder room, which had been added at one side of the hen house, went an electric brooder, against the coming of the little one-day-olds. Eggs, we told ourselves, were the answer to our rising agricultural overhead. They would pay for the horses' feed, and when each faithful hundred stopped laying, we would reward them with a cool place in the deepfreeze.

All in all, those twelve acres would present an emphatic answer to the dastards who said the South preferred to raise nothing but cotton and buy all its vittles at the commissary or the supermarket. So about mid-January my friend Trickey ordered one hundred and fifty day-old chicks. They would be in, he said, in a week or ten days. But that hatchery must have caught up on its orders just before ours was received.

And now for the financiers.

Unless one has helped to seduce an industry from the North, or even from somewhere else in the South, he cannot really appreciate the headiness of such a triumph; and the more our fellow citizens above the Mason-Dixon line holler "kidnapers" and "socialists" and "thieves'" and "unethical enticers" at us, the more enjoyable is the seduction. After all, we Southerners have been shoeless unfortunates for a long time, the pitied, bottom one third of the nation, serving as the fertile seedbed for America's industrial manpower, a supplier of raw materials to be processed elsewhere, and all in all the best of horrible examples of what happens when a region is almost wholly dependent upon an agricultural economy, and one-crop agriculture at that, with everybody beyond our borders pitying and criticizing and making urgent recommendations that we mend our ways. It was inevitable that the South should go hunting for industry; and it wasn't strange that Mississippi, the poorest and least industrialized of the states, should be the first Southern state to authorize by act of its legislature an industrialization program in which state and local governments become so allied with industry as to bring loud and angry shouts of state socialism from areas where manufacturers who are expanding, or who are unhappy where they are, have heeded the Southern sirens.

Mississippi's plan—it is called the Balance Agriculture with Industry program, or BAWI for short—was authorized by the state legislature way back in 1938, but it creaked along almost unnoticed until three or four years ago. The BAWI was the creation of a business-minded conservative, the wealthy governor named Hugh White, who was re-elected to a second nonconsecutive term in 1951. Under the plan, municipalities or counties are permitted to float bond issues, the proceeds from which are used to build plants for an industry with which the municipality has successfully negotiated. The bonds are backed by the full faith and credit of the town, city or county. The industry, which must have been approved by the state Agricultural and Industrial Board as solvent and otherwise acceptable, retires the bond issue with rental payments over what is usually a twenty-year period. At the end of that time, the plant is to be sold to the industry for a dollar. In the interim the plant thus erected remains the property of the municipality. The industry does not pay any property taxes on the plant for these twenty years, since the building is owned by the city, nor does the industry have to put up any of its own money to build it. Nice.

Most of us in Mississippi like that program. By mid-1952 some sixty plants had been built or were in prospect, which meant industrial jobs for more than thirty thousand Mississippians—not a great number for an industrial state, but portentous in ours, where agriculture has accounted for more than eighty-five per cent of our income.

But as late as 1950 Greenville hadn't lured a single industry, though by that time we were trying hard. We were handicapped by the disinterest of some of the citizens who were out of sympathy with any plan that might raise wages in general, make farm labor scarce, or change the size and complexion of Greenville. Northern industrial visitors, whom we entertained hopefully, group after group, seemed to prefer counties where the population was not as lopsidedly Negro as was ours; several of our sister cities thoughtfully warned prospects that Greenville had been flooded out in 1927, so why not move farther inland from the river? The Chamber of Commerce finally took up a collection and employed an industry-locating service which, from its headquarters in New York City, eventually informed us that an old, highly successful but otherwise undesignated industry was looking with interest upon the South in general and Mississippi in particular as a site for a new plant which would employ more than six hundred workers, and that a delegation of officials and technicians from the plant would soon visit us.

By the time this delegation arrived, just about every loose hatchet in town had been buried. Politicians, bankers and businessmen, hitherto divided into the factions with which smaller communities are especially plagued, displayed to our guests such unaccustomed solidarity and brotherliness that it was difficult sometimes not to grin in each other's faces. One afternoon we took out the advance guard of visitors and about twenty townsmen on the *Mistuh Charley*, the *Democrat-Times'* cabin cruiser which is unofficially also the city's welcome wagon. We were armed with refreshments and a portfolio of statistical data which proved that Greenville's climate was most salubrious, that the Mississippi was the world's most tamed river, that our people were most eager to work, that our health and happiness and patriotism were most unblemished, and that if any envious critics in Jackson or Vicksburg or Meridian denied these truths, they were just a bunch of damnable liars. Before the afternoon cruise was over, lifelong carpers were backslapping the city's guests and each other, and I was linked arm-in-arm with two badly off-key songmates who had been recommending for years that I should go off somewhere and die. What made it really enjoyable was that the strangers from New York State were the pleasantest of companions.

I am not laughing at our behavior. I am actually proud of it, because we proved that we could close ranks for the common good. In all truth, we had just what this industry—which turned out to be one of the nation's leading carpet manufacturers—wanted. It was good to discover that we were as attractive as we told the industrial world we were. Almost everyone joined in a campaign to put over the requisite $3,750,000 bond issue—the state's largest BAWI bond issue up to that time—not just by the required majority, but as one-sidedly as possible. For a month all news of the world, the nation and the state of Mississippi and Greenville was subordinated in the *Democrat-Times* to the greater glory of rug making, the desirability of rugmakers as industrial neighbors, the importance of a multi-hundred-man payroll to a little cotton-supported city of thirty thousand, and the civic duty of every citizen to vote yes. Since the industry was just as enthusiastic about having Greenville build its plant as we were about building it, the company's public relations men kept us supplied with photographs, news stories, diagrams and all possible material about the life and the works of one Alexander Smith and the truly splendid one-hundred-year human and industrial record of the company he founded.

What they didn't supply and we couldn't dream up, the Agricultural and Industrial Board provided, notably full-page suggested advertisements and a portfolio of slogans, statistics and sample ballots.

In the special election Greenville authorized the bond issue by a vote of 3106 to 32, and that's as unanimous as any city could be.

So pleased were the officials of Alexander Smith that they voted to hold their annual directors meeting in Greenville some two weeks after the election, coincidental with the annual banquet of America's most satisfied Chamber of Commerce. They offered as the banquet speaker, William Ewing, a friendly gracious man who was the company's president. All manner of parties were planned, the more enthusiastically because we were welcoming new neighbors and not just fishing for a maybe-so-maybe-not delegation of strangers. One event, of course, would be a cruise on the gentle father of waters with our *Mistuh Charley* as part of the joyful armada.

The date was set for January twenty-third.

At about eight o'clock in the morning of January twenty-third Estelle Faulkner telephoned from Oxford that her husband had just decided that there was no sense in unpacking the crate of nine hundred and fifty books we had expressed to him a month before for his signature, and recrating them to ship them back to us; instead he had put the unopened crate in his station wagon earlier that morning and was on his way to Greenville where he would shortly arrive and begin autographing books.

A half hour later I found in the morning mail a letter from the State Game and Fish Commission, notifying me that our order for five hundred bass and five thousand bream fingerlings—the proper balance, said the accompanying pamphlet —would be delivered to us on January twenty-third at eleven A.M., not in Greenville but in Indianola, twenty-eight miles to the east, which was a distribution point more nearly central for all the fish pond builders whose orders were on that particular fish tank truck. "Don't forget to bring some receptacle, such as a clean oil drum," the communication added, "and to keep the water aerated on the return trip by stirring or else the little fingerlings will die for want of oxygen."

Only minutes afterward, Trickey Hicks, my Quaker Oats friend, telephoned. Yes, the one hundred and fifty day-old chicks had arrived and they were as healthy a bunch of little things as he'd seen, but we'd better get them in the brooder house just as soon as possible, seeing as how it was pretty cold and he was afraid to keep them cooped up in the boxes in his warehouse. Say about an hour; make it ten o'clock?

And then Everett Rogers at the Chamber of Commerce telephoned. The directors of Alexander Smith were arriving at the airport very soon. They should be met by the welcoming committee. . . .

Betty said that when I telephoned her I was screaming, and that I said Fish Faulkner and Chicken Smith were almost here, and for the love that she bore me and the children, do something quick. I remember only that I told her firmly that the chicken problem was hers and to have the gardener put two empty, clean oil drums—luckily we had several around the stable—in the station wagon and meet me at the office at ten-fifteen sharp. Betty protested that she had to get things ready for the boat ride, and was Faulkner really coming and what did he drink because surely we had to have him out that afternoon, and she had never wanted chickens anyway, and besides she. . . .

And just then William Faulkner ambled into the *Demo-*

crat-Times midway in time, as it turned out, between the chicken and the fish.

Ben Wasson, whom I had alerted, saw him first and smuggled him into my office. We sent out for the crate of books and in a few minutes the two doors to my office began popping open and shut and open and shut as the word got around that Mississippi's greatest was signing books. Everyone on the paper found some excuse to come in and ask me a question and, just coincidentally, to be introduced to William Faulkner, who seemed only mildly disturbed by it all. We set up an assembly line at my desk with Ben opening the books to the proper page for autographing and shoving them at Faulkner, who signed standing up, or rather in a half-crouch, which made my back ache. As he signed each book, a girl from the bindery pulled it away from him, blotted the signature and stacked the book in the box from whence it had come.

I had to go for the fish—or was it the chickens first?—but hospitality dictated that I do something for a man who had driven one hundred and twenty miles just to stand up in my office and sign his name to copies of a book for which he could have received far more than our limited edition's twenty-five per cent royalty could bring him at only six dollars a copy. So I asked "Beer?" and Faulkner nodded vigorously, without missing a stroke of the pen. I sent to Al's Café, a half-block away, for a bottle of beer, and it should be recorded for the factual-minded that William Faulkner's ratio of signed books to beers turned out that day and the next morning to be sixty volumes of Faulkner to one bottle of Budweiser.

Then I sped home to my wife and little chickens. Trickey had arrived before me, with his cheeping burden, and he and Betty were in the brooder house, but something was wrong.

The electrical outlet into which the brooder should have been plugged just wouldn't work, and the chicks weren't happy. We gathered all the extension cords we could find in the house—for irons, radios and lights—joined them, bored a hole through the wall between the hen house and the brooder room, and plugged one end into the hen house light socket. The heater contraption began glowing just in time; the chicks got warm; Trickey began spreading mash and water and cracked corn and, I guess, pablum, around; and behind his back Betty gave me an if-I-ever-get-you-alone look. But I couldn't wait, because in forty-five minutes the fish would be arriving in Indianola.

So Wolfe, the gardener, and I filled the two oil drums with water, I took a big egg beater from the kitchen for aeration purposes, and off we went. We were on time in Indianola but the fish truck was already there. The attendants ladled out bass and bream until they figured we had the required number. Wolfe draped himself most uncomfortably over the oil cans in the back of the station wagon and whipped up wind waves with the egg beater while I drove. We didn't lose a fingerling.

We made it, Betty and I, to the hotel in time to help roll out the carpet for the rug makers. I wondered whether we smelled like fish or a baby chick or a Nobel prize winner or all three, but no one seemed to notice anything.

The board of directors of Alexander Smith added up to quite a delegation, mostly New Yorkers, who had come for a good time, and that afternoon we tried to give it to them. The boat ride was successful. We asked Faulkner to come along, but he said he'd rather finish signing and go on a boat ride the next morning; he'd have a drink with us between the boat ride and the Chamber of Commerce banquet, which he also resolutely declined to attend. After the boat ride,

Faulkner and Ben came out. We had a drink; we checked on the chickens; we sensed the surging of happy little fish among the roots of ancient cypress. Betty and I left them and went to the banquet where everyone basked in the light of victory and said nice things about each other. Bill Ewing made a civilized talk, the retiring president of the Chamber of Commerce told of the achievements of the past year, and his successor, taking over the gavel, said he hoped he could do only half as well, because an industry like Alexander Smith didn't come along every year.

I hope not, I said to myself, not on the same day with Faulkner and fish and fowl—and we all went home.

The next morning Faulkner completed his chore and he and Ben and John Gibson and I went aboard the *Mistuh Charley*, and cruised around and talked about duck hunting. We tied up just after noon and walked over the levee to the *Delta Democrat-Times*. It was then about twelve fifteen and my secretary asked, "Did you forget that you were to talk to the Kiwanis Club at noon today?" So I told Faulkner good-bye and got to the hotel just as the Kiwanians were finishing dessert and settling back to slumber through the program.

So I talked about the new Mississippi, which was diversifying its agriculture and restoring its soil and bringing in industries and producing more writers to the acre than any state in the union. I knew all about it.

17

Northern Penobscots and Southern Politics

For at least a hundred years all manner of canny folk have had their go at Southern politics. It is improbable that anything new can be said. But since the South's tribal politicians have been responsible for almost all of the anxiety and occasional despair which I have experienced in the past twenty years, I feel an urge to take a look at their innards, too.

However, I want to begin with a different tribe, of whom Mr. Shea of the Maine Penobscots reminded me.

Mr. Shea spoke one Maine summer night to the members of the Camden Historical Society, a group distinguished by the unrelated variety of its stored-away acquisitions and its low dues of twenty-five cents a year. He is, himself, a Penobscot Indian from near Old Town, and he has sold Indian baskets and geegaws in an old Army tent at Lincolnville Beach for twenty summers. But Mr. Shea is also a personage in his tribe, for whom he has sat in the Maine legislature as a non-voting tribal representative; he is, moreover, an authority on the language, the history and the mistreatment of the Penobscots. He spoke to the Historical Society on Indian treaties and his tale of the white man's injustice and double dealing and word-breaking was such as to impel Betty and me to drive the next day to Lincolnville and there buy a lovely basket, as if to wash from our consciences the spot that does not out. But no one seemed overly concerned that night about the treatment of Mr. Shea and his fellow red-men, reduced now to a dwindling six hundred, herded on a reservation under the casual guidance of an agent, who like so many agents is, as Mr. Shea says, a political man.

A day or so later I chatted with an earnest and informed summer visitor from Massachusetts who, despite his concern over Democratic pilfering, had declared himself for Governor Adlai Stevenson. During our political conversation he suggested, with some irritation, that the behavior of many of the South's delegates to the recently concluded Democratic convention was motivated by racial bigotry, and not by more patriotic considerations. The South, said he, had the mistreated Negro too much on its mind, and why couldn't Southerners at least compromise on civil rights?

While ordinarily the last task I would ever undertake is a defense of Southern politicians—who are indefensible as often as not, as is the case with politicians everywhere—the memory of Mr. Shea was still green, or red, and I could not help summoning the Penobscots as allies.

I said, yes, the South did have the Negro too much on its mind, as did the national conscience, and we had in Mississippi one million of the nation's fifteen million mistreated Negroes; but wasn't it too bad that there were not one million mistreated Penobscot Indians in Maine instead of six hundred, and fifteen million mistreated Indians in the United States, so that a contrite nation could ever remember and seek to redress past and present abuse, as abominable, victim for victim, as any suffered by the Negro, free or slave?

I recalled a monument I had seen in Senator Hubert Humphrey's state of Minnesota where United States troops had executed not a few captured ringleaders of an Indian uprising occasioned by the inferior savages' desire to recover stolen lands and to preserve what was left of them. The punishment was meted out, the monument revealed, in the same year that United States soldiers from Minnesota were liberating Mississippi slaves and preserving the Union by killing other Mississippians and burning their homes and destroying their crops.

Neither as colonials nor as free and independent and sometimes hypocritical Americans, I said, have we kept account of the massacres, the thievery, the gross dishonesty and cruelty that has characterized our treatment of the dark-skinned Americans who were here first and were free until the colonials came along, and who fought back as long as they could afterward, and were not honored for their hopeless heroism as, say, the colonial Negro Crispus Attucks, has been honored.

I had no statistics available, but I surmised that had the Negro in the South been as systematically exterminated or herded voteless and voiceless into reservations as Indians have been for three hundred years, permitted by the white father whose wards they were to go hungry and naked and to be robbed, there would be no Negro problem for Southern and Northern politicians to batten upon, for the very simple reason that there would be not enough Negroes to matter, just as there are not enough Indians to matter, either in terms of conscience or politics. I said further that except for Oliver LaFarge in the Southwest and the tiny organization which he leads, there was no national group as militantly and effectively interested in the Indian as, for example, the Southern Regional Council is concerned with the Southern Negro.

In a peroration worthy, I hope, of the late John C. Calhoun, I said, assume now that one hundred years ago the economy of Massachusetts and Maine and all of the Eastern states had rested upon the reluctant backs of those Penobscot and assorted Indians, and that instead of just killing those who wouldn't knuckle under, you had paid your good money with a bad conscience for them; assume too that the South's economy at that time had been in no wise dependent upon the field labor of the Penobscots, and that the South's political objective was to maintain a strong central government, dedicated to the expansion of Southern industry, the maintenance of the South as the nation's financial center, and the perpetuation of Southern political mastery by westward expansion, which didn't allow any enslaved Penobscots around, only some free Sioux survivors. Assume that an itchy-fingered Mississippian who liked Penobscot Indians had galloped north at the head of a posse or mob, recruiting a few red warriors on the way, and had holed up in the Springfield armory until the Green Mountain Light Infantry had dislodged and hanged them. Assume that along about this time, William Faulkner's great grandmother, who wasn't named Harriet Beecher Faulkner, had written a book about how the New Englanders had killed and pillaged and polluted the Penobscots, so feelingly and so truthfully that all the South was ready to come to the aid of the Indians. Assume that New England didn't like this bellicose attitude and had signified its renewed intention to resign as it had once offered to do back in 1812. Assume that because of a legally untested belief that the states were indissolubly united rather than federated, the South had dispatched the First Virginia Cavaliers to Boston Harbor and that a loyal Home Guarder on shore had decided to try out a new breech-loading Indian killer on the haughty Virginians. Assume that during the war which followed, the president of the Southern nation had decreed that all Penobscots and other Indians in the territory not even conquered by the victorious Dixiecrats were hereinafter free and entitled to the land taken from them for the past three hundred years, including all real estate in Boston, most of New York state and whatever they wanted in New Jersey, if any, with interest compounded at eight per cent; and, following the glorious Southern victory and the occupation of all principal cities and county seats, assume that the president had enfranchised the Penobscots, disenfranchised the New Englanders, enrolled the naturally grudge-bearing braves in the occupation army, and invited his compatriots to come up North and help themselves to the loot.

Assuming all this, I asked, and knowing that in Boston today even an Indian could make a good race for the Assembly if his name was Shea and he campaigned against Great Britain, would you be surprised if for the next two generations following this hypothetical war for Indian freedom, a lot of New England politicians would know just what side their platform was buttered on?

My friend said all that was absurd because he didn't hold anything personally against the Penobscots, and his own ancestors had never owned any Indian lands that he knew of, and besides, he was talking about the way the South had the Negro too much in its mind.

I said then that I was ready to admit that the curse of the South is the shadow of the Negro over all its decisions, and especially its political behavior. And I told him another story, which has nothing to do with Indians, and something to do with me and much to do with the point we both were agreed upon.

Just two years ago, I said, we had a congressional election in our district in Mississippi to choose a successor to a fine elder statesman who after some twenty unopposed years in the House of Representatives had decided to call it a day. The congressman was both a lawyer and a planter, and fair-minded and progressive in both pursuits; and whether or not a candidate has anything else to his credit, if he is a lawyer or a planter, he has a pretty good political advantage in the Delta. During the campaign to choose a successor all of the present and the living past members of the legislature, and almost the entire bar in our county, endorsed a planter who had spent some thirty years in the legislature, and who, being well past fifty, was considered safe and sane. He was a likable fellow, and the only thing I really had against him was his defense of the use of the lash in the state penal farm, but he didn't seem to measure up, lash or no lash, so I offered the *Democrat-Times*' support to another candidate named Frank Smith.

Frank was young and cautiously liberal, an artillery captain in World War Two, and a former newspaperman who had once worked with us. He had gone from newspapering to Washington as legislative assistant to Senator John Stennis, a decent small-town judge who had, amid general rejoicing, succeeded Bilbo in the Senate. After his stint in Washington, Frank had been elected to the state Senate for one term, during which he brashly decided that he was of congressional caliber. As far as I know, he isn't even related to a lawyer or a planter, but that didn't faze him because, as it turned out, he had as not the least of his qualifications the largest and most loyal bunch of aunts and uncles and cousins in all Mississippi, most of them voting in the Third Congressional District.

Frank was a natural politician. The first time we got together he accepted my offer of editorial support and printing credit, but suggested that the paper keep quiet until after the first primary. He was sure that he would be in any run-off and he reasoned that when a newspaper gets behind one candidate in a first primary field of three or more, the others double up on that candidate and the newspaper. Moreover, in our case, the danger was compounded because whoever my newspaper supported was tagged by his opponents as a nigger-lover by association. Frank thought we might as well put off that evil day for a while.

To almost everyone's surprise but his own, Frank went into the second primary only a few votes behind the candidate of the older citizens. The *Democrat-Times* then began firing, and our salvos were double-shotted with impatience and with loyalty to a fellow newspaperman and like-minded Mississippian. One whiff of inky grape in the closing days of what ended as a very bitter, personal and mud-slinging campaign, caught the Delta's generally recognized political boss with—as we later described the event—his political pants down and hit him in his gubernatorial aspirations.

He didn't like what we wrote, nor do I blame him, and he came back at us the night before election day as master of ceremonies at a monstrous rally for the man of his choice. I was, he declaimed, a man of very dangerous and un-Southern ideas and, to quote exactly, "unfit to live in a decent white, democratic society"—or maybe with a capital D.

I heard him only on the radio, for the rally was held in another town thirty miles away, and I was myself scheduled to speak in less than an hour at another meeting which had to do with a long quest for citizenship. This was a gathering of a newly formed Negro Voters' League, and I had been invited several weeks earlier—before we had announced our support of Frank Smith—with the specific request that I talk only on good citizenship and not in behalf of any candidate. I had accepted and, knowing that my presence would be interpreted in some quarters as proof of intent to mongrelize the white race, and that my words would be distorted, I took with me James Robertshaw, a young Greenville lawyer, as witness to what I would say. No other white persons attended that meeting.

I kept to my text, which concerned the Negroes' duty to vote their individual convictions and never as a Negro bloc or for money or in response to impossible promises or a vengeful appeal. But the memory of the radio voice rankled. I had been told soon after entering the hall that almost all of the Negroes had listened earlier to my denouncer. When I finished, I asked everyone who had heard that speaker to raise his hand. Almost the entire audience did. Then I repeated that I was not telling anyone how to vote, but added that when I left the Delta it was going to be because the good Lord called me and not because this man told me.

Frank carried every precinct in our county, including the rural boxes where no Negroes voted; and he won almost every other county too, narrowly; so a newspaperman succeeded a lawyer in Congress, a phenomenon which I think should happen more often. I am sure, of course, that the relatively few hundred Negro voters in the county voted for him, and why not? He hadn't gone out of his way to bring in a spurious racial issue, or to call up the old, dread ghosts, or to denounce anyone whom the Negroes knew to be their friend. How can they be blamed for voting a bloc, in and outside the South, as long as their color continues to be in itself a political or an economic issue? The Negro will stop being a bloc voter only when the demagogue's voice is stilled in Harlem as well as in Georgia, and only when his wants and his interests and his rights are generally regarded as identical with those of his fellow citizens who are white. That time is distant.

The average Southern politician has done nothing to hasten the day. Many white Southerners and others believe it is because of Reconstruction alone that the specter of race haunts the political scene, but this is true only in part. The racial ghost was being laid in the South, politically, soon after Reconstruction; but the post-occupation period was marked by political emergence of the South's little people, the poor white farmer and tenant, as the Populist movement dramatized the domination of banker and lawyer and planter and the accompanying neglect of the small farmer and his generally desperate condition. Only by appealing to the racial ill will of the Southerner could the so-called Bourbons divide and conquer the dispossessed Southern yeomanry whose color was too often the only discernible difference between themselves and the Negro. The Bourbons did just that, calculatedly linking the Populists and the Negroes together and calling for a politically unified white South as the only protection against Negro domination. The appeal was especially powerful in those states and counties in which the Negro was a majority of the population, or a near majority. The Populist leaders tried then to outdo the Bourbons in their racism, in terms more violent and more inflammable, so as to rid themselves of the politically fatal taint; and in the end the poor whites of the South were the losers even more than the Negro, who had generally a little less to lose and much less to hope for than did his despising white economic counterpart.

The cruel strategy has persisted. Vardaman was the most obscene of the race demagogues of Mississippi, but it was he who outlawed the abhorrent convict lease system, and not the planters who scorned and hated him for his indecencies even while they held in bondage the fever-ridden black convicts rented to them by the penal farm.

Bilbo and Rankin all but matched Vardaman's grossness, but Bilbo and Rankin, for their own measured reasons, supported and even sponsored state and federal legislative proposals for the material benefit of the little man. It is true that the Southern race demagogues are at the same time often markedly liberal in other respects and that by and large they formed Franklin D. Roosevelt's most solid bloc whenever the interests of the small man, who is especially the Southern man, could be advanced. Rankin really hated the dissimilar in race and religion; Bilbo probably did not, and his pretense that he did may be to his greater discredit.

Of all the Southern demagogues, only Huey Long didn't match race-baiting with race-baiting. When some of his opponents, all else failing, tried to tie the Negro around Long's neck, he simply laughed them off the hustings. The people wouldn't believe it, and besides the vision of wealth sharing shone so bright before their eyes that they couldn't even see the black man's shadow.

That was the legacy of the war of the upper- and middle-class South against Populism, which was all before my time, and I'm sorry I missed it. The Bourbon victory left the soul of the South scarred, and the body of the South more ill-clothed and ill-housed and ill-fed than it needed to have been. Now the Negro is again a specter at the ballot box, but the voices are less venomous and threatening because the white South is less fearful and more educated in democracy's meaning, and also because the Negro is less fearful in the South and has allies here and elsewhere to whom his vote or his democratic rights in the abstract are important. The loudest race baiter is no longer the surest winner, as old John Rankin finally discovered on an August day in which Mississippians can take pride.

What too many people elsewhere refuse to recognize is that the Southerner or non-Southerner is not necessarily a bigot because he declines to accept a civil-rights program in one package and defends the principle of the minority's right to unlimited debate or argues the constitutional case for decentralized government. That kind of indictment is racism in reverse, and it is as unwholesomely practiced in a New York City as is its opposite number in a Southern legislature.

A patient, moderate Southerner, Congressman Brooks Hays of our neighboring state of Arkansas, has proposed a middle course in respect to civil rights, to which I subscribe, but which has met the opposition of the irreconcilables at the two extremes. His "Arkansas Compromise" recommends abolition of the poll tax by constitutional amendment rather than by act of Congress. He is sure that thirty-six states would approve such an amendment, and he would vote for it himself, but he, like many of us, believes federal legislative action to be unconstitutional.

He would leave the issue of segregation on common carriers to the federal courts, which have already outlawed such segregation in interstate travel but have not ruled on segregation within the states. He would establish a fair employment commission, with persuasive and advisory but without coercive powers, similar to the wartime FEPC, and he has consistently said that the American economy and humanitarian considerations alike demand the full integration of the Negro in industry. He would leave initial jurisdiction in lynchings to state courts, but whenever a federal attorney believed that law officers and courts had failed to take proper action, he could go into federal court and show cause why jurisdiction should be transferred to that court.

Of all the proposals, the recommendations for fair employment legislation have been the most bitterly contested; they present the most basic of the constitutional problems. I have soldiered with Negroes, I have worked beside Negroes, and so have most Southerners. I have opposed editorially the establishment of color bars to employment and any wage differential based upon color; I have not found it offensive, in Africa or in the War Department or on my father's farm or in my garden, to have a Negro working with or near me. But that happens to be my own attitude, and I didn't achieve it under compulsion. I believe that persuasion is a more effective and democratic weapon than compulsion anyway, and that it can be as unfair to compel a man to hire a Negro or a Jew or a Baptist or a Catholic, if he is unwilling, as it is un-Christian and undemocratic for him to refuse employment on such grounds.

All of which simply adds up to a conviction that men are more readily led than driven.

In respect to granting these rights, a majority of white Southerners will not easily be led or driven, and there is more to their stubborn resistance than simply a susceptibility to demagogic oratory. Determination upon continued political mastery is near the center of this hard core of resistance to change, and with it goes a traditional suspicion of a strong, central government. Southerners of honest convictions, no less than the stump orator, will defend the thesis that the state and the community should bear the principal responsibility of government, and that the founders of the republic knew this when they devised the mechanism of self-government. But beneath and beyond these traditional and rational defensible attitudes lies the ultimate issue, which is essentially sexual in nature and cannot be ridiculed away or legislated out of existence. Southern preoccupation with racial issues and Southern determination to keep the two groups socially separate arise from an ancient folk decision of the Western white man not to intermingle with other races except on fixed, shoddily one-sided terms dictated by the white male alone.

I share this insistence upon sexual separateness, for I can see no good coming out of a blood fusion of the white and Negro people of the United States; but, knowing that almost all miscegenation has come from the illegal, surreptitious union of white man and dark-skinned woman, I find detestable the hypocrisy of those Southerners who condone or ignore this one-sided miscegenation; and I cannot believe that the racial amalgam will be effected any sooner if lynching is made a federal offense, or Negroes are permitted to use the Greenville public library, or are allowed to sit next to white people in public conveyances and in public places. Miscegenation doesn't take place in movie theaters or busses or libraries. No one can honestly deny that there was more miscegenation on a single large plantation a generation ago than there is or ever will be in a Southern university where racial bars to admittance no longer exist. Nor are the dark-skinned people likely to be as intent upon lightening their complexion if color is not made the determining element in giving or forbidding them full citizenship and acceptance as human beings worthy of respect.

And now, to come back to the Southern politician, I think that it is unfair to blame him solely for traditional Southern racial attitudes. It is also unfair to indict him for his sins of omission and commission without praising him for what he has managed to accomplish against a background of conflict. After all, the city council of Greenville is made up of part-time

Southern politicians; and these politicians have in recent years been untypical enough to authorize the employment of Negro policemen and the building of a Negro public swimming pool, neither of which is required in any civil-rights proposal.

Washington county, of which Greenville is the county seat, is also run by part-time politicians, called supervisors, and those gentlemen were also untypical enough a year ago to put the county about six hundred thousand dollars in debt so that a modern, relatively low-cost hospital could be built, principally because there were no adequate hospital facilities for Negroes. Incidentally, an equal amount was contributed by the state of Mississippi, under the terms of the nationwide federal-local-state hospital-building program which Mississippi's legislators, all politicians, were the first to take advantage of. Those same political legislators have enacted a visionary medical-education plan for students of both races, under which the state pays for the schooling of approved applicants in return for a pledge to practice medicine in the state for five years afterwards. Their political whimsies have prompted them to appropriate sufficient funds to give Mississippi one of the best, if not the best of public-health services, with traveling x-raymobiles and the most successful venereal-disease-control program in the nation; and this in a state where more than ninety per cent of the venereal-disease cases are among Negroes.

Everyone has heard of the Bilboes and Rankins of Mississippi, but not of the day-in- and day-out efforts for justice on the part of Mississippi judges and justices, educators and legislators and sheriffs, all of whom are politicians or dependent in one way or another upon political action.

And I imagine if these decent fellow citizens of mine could have heard Mr. Shea of the Penobscots, they would have been as indignant as I was at the treatment of his people.

18

Just What Is a Lynching?

A long time ago I saw the body of a Negro woman dangling from a tree the morning after a mob had lynched her. Even now I sometimes see that body in my sleep. But the chances that my sons will ever come across the corpse of a lynch victim are, statistically, at least fifty times less than my own, and that is what I prefer to think of in my waking hours.

The crime of lynching is the only one in the calendar of capital offenses which has steadily declined for a quarter of a century to the nonsymptomatic point. If the South should be ashamed of the lynchings that are still committed—and it is—it should also be permitted to take sober pride in the record. But there are too many who would not permit us to do so, who even dispute the record itself, and who insist that only through federal legislation can the scarlet blot of the mob be erased. Their voices are loudest during political campaigns, but they are never stilled. Nor are they always or even often fair, and it is this unfair and unchanging refusal to recognize what the South itself is doing that makes the Southerner's task more difficult. I would like to tell here the story of the other side, and of the calculated refusal of the professional critics of all things Southern to admit that there is another side.

In the late fall of 1949, three young white men, who had been drinking heavily while driving about Chickasaw County in Mississippi, became engaged in a profane dispute with a Negro farmer whom they accused of refusing to draw his wagon to one side quickly enough after they honked their horn. One of the men, who later successfully pleaded self-defense, struck the Negro in the head with a tire tool and killed him.

The assailant and his two companions were indicted for murder. The trial of the principal defendant was conducted in another Mississippi county, public resentment against him in his home county being considered by his attorney to be so strong as to necessitate a change of venue. He, and later his companions, were acquitted on their testimony that the Negro had first cursed and menaced them with a harrow point.

Tuskegee Institute, the fine Negro college in Alabama, had issued its annual report on lynchings some time before the trials. The report listed this slaying of a Negro by three white men in a spontaneous, drunken quarrel as one of the three lynchings for 1949.

At about the time of this slaying, four Negro youths, also presumably either drunk or under the influence of narcotics, accosted a middle-aged white man in Brooklyn. They cursed and attack him and when the brief melee was over, the white man was dead. The Negroes were not apprehended. This murder was not listed among the lynchings for 1949.

Go back to 1943. In June of that year there occurred the most sanguinary race riot of the six such major outbreaks of the war period. This was the Detroit riot which began in a crowded recreational park with spasmodic fighting between whites and Negroes, and turned into a large scale conflict after two stories circulated—one that a white man had thrown a Negro woman and her baby from the Belle Isle Bridge, and a complementary rumor that a Negro man had shot a white woman on the bridge. White sailors were apparently the first perpetrators of mob violence. The rioting continued for a week. Thirty-four persons were killed, twenty-five of them Negroes. More than two million dollars' worth of property was looted or destroyed. Army occupation, after martial law was invoked, cost one hundred thousand dollars a day. More than a million man hours in war production were lost.

In the same year, race rioting, after a white woman reported that she had been raped, took two Negro lives in Beaumont and resulted in a half-million dollars in property damage. In Mobile, Alabama, scores of Negroes were beaten in a less savage riot when the white ship workers protested the upgrading of Negroes. Out in Los Angeles the "Zoot Suit Riots" with Mexicans, Filipinos and, secondarily, Negroes as the victims, brought injury to scores of the zoot suiters. Their assailants were principally service men who were infuriated by rumors that gangs of zoot suiters had been attacking soldiers and sailors. And in Harlem, a bloody uprising of Negroes was precipitated after a white policeman shot and wounded a Negro MP who allegedly interfered with an arrest. The policeman also was wounded. Many white civilians were attacked, although policemen were the principal targets of the Negro mobs. Four Negroes were killed by the police, between five and six hundred persons were injured, most of them Negro, and five hundred persons, also predominantly Negro, were arrested for burglary, assault, incitement to riot and receiving stolen goods. Property damage and theft directed solely at white establishments in Harlem amounted to nearly five million dollars.

None of these deaths was listed as a lynching. Neither was there any organized demand in Congress or elsewhere for legislation giving the federal government full police authority to prevent or terminate race riots, to prosecute participants, or to hold to account the cities in which they occurred. Yet, there were six more deaths in the North alone during 1943 in just the publicized race riots than in the South by lynching during the entire period from 1943 until today, even if we accept as lynchings in fact all crimes so described by Tuskegee.

Quite properly the social and economic causes of the racial tensions in the North—job inequality, poor housing, smouldering racial antagonisms, lack of education—were widely cited as reasons for the Detroit and New York riots, and pleas were made for remedying these evils. No similar explanations were made in respect to the Southern riots. Neither were the two reported lynchings in the South that year interpreted in these terms. Incidentally, one of these was hardly a lynching, but a mortal third-degree beating by law officers in Florida of a Negro who allegedly resisted arrest. Its inexcusable fatal or near-fatal counterparts could have been discovered in many states North of the Mason-Dixon line.

Intermittently during the postwar years the West Coast has been plagued by violent strikes of longshoremen and other maritime workers. In one strike, a group of non-union stevedores who attempted to unload a ship which had come through from strikebound Hawaii, was set upon by a group of union longshoremen who had pledged themselves to respect Harry Bridges' Hawaiian blockade.

Acting effectively as their own police force while the regularly constituted police failed to act, the longshoremen broke the back of one strike-breaker, who died later, and severely injured others. This was only one of a number of familiar acts of violence attendant upon the stormy course of labor-management relations in the United States, in which neither side is guiltless.

There was no outcry in Congress for federal legislation to deal with labor-management bodily conflicts, nor did Tuskegee or any other investigative agency suggest that such incidents might also deserve the lynching label.

In the early spring of 1950, one Charles Binaggio of Kansas City and his bodyguard and "enforcer" were shot to death presumably by two or more gangland executioners. Binaggio, a racketeer and political power in Kansas City Democratic politics, had fancied himself as a successor of Boss Pendergast. He had apparently made promises that he couldn't keep. After that mistake, his political connections could avail him nothing. He was knocked off, so the story goes, because he failed to deliver what he had promised—namely an even more wide-open Kansas City. He had been tried by gangland and sentenced to death. Despite the smelly discoveries of corruption and close relations between politicians and racketeers in Missouri, and even despite the fact that there have been nineteen such unpunished and even unsolved murders in Kansas City within five years—more than the lynching total for the nation in that period—no spokesman for the administration demanded federal legislation to deal with lawlessness that the state authorities are obviously unable or unwilling to curb. Nor was Mr. Binaggio's untimely end listed anywhere as a lynching.

Shortly after the Tuskegee Lynching Report for 1949, in which the slaying of the Mississippi Negro by the drunken white men was set down as a lynching, Representative Thomas Abernethy of Mississippi wrote a letter of protest to Dr. F. D. Patterson, the president of Tuskegee Institute. Like many another Southerner in and out of public office, Mr. Abernethy is sensitive to criticism of the South which he considers unjust. He is also proud, as are all Southerners, of the reduction in lynching during the past twenty years. Here, in part, is his protest to Dr. Patterson, a copy of which he sent to me.

The generally accepted version of a lynching cannot, by the most liberal construction, be reconciled with reports in this particular case. All lynchings are murders. On the contrary, all murders are not lynchings. According to reports, this might have been a murder but definitely not a lynching.

If I correctly understand the Institute's latest report, it now classifies all unlawful homicides for which three or more people are responsible as a lynching. If this is to be the criteria, then the Institute has materially departed from the generally accepted version of a lynching. If this is to be the criteria, then, no doubt, the filing compartments of the Institute will hardly be of sufficient size to index card and file records of the many deaths resulting from mob violence in our large cities, particularly those in the northern areas. It is most significant that a death which results at the hands of a mob in a northern city seldom is carried as "news" outside the particular city in which the violent act occurred. But just let such take place in a southern state and immediately almost every newspaper, magazine and periodical in the entire nation headlines the act, especially if it has resulted in the death of a negro. . . .

The Institute has in the past been widely admired for honest intentions in compiling what has been accepted as an accurate and factual tabulation of lynchings. In classifying this particular case as a lynching, the Institute is losing claim to accurate reporting. In treating with silence the prompt, aggressive and diligent action of law enforcement authorities in the County, the Institute has left the impression, though probably not intentional, that this incident has gone without notice or action within the County. I, therefore, contend that your report has wronged the people of my County and my State. It has without the slightest foundation in fact reflected upon the high esteem which these people merit and enjoy. As for yourselves, it has reflected discredit upon the honest intentions of the Institute in compiling accurate tabulations of lynchings. It is not too late for you to right the wrong which you have done my people and for the Institute to recapture full confidence of the public. These can only be accomplished by either withdrawing the report entirely or the issuance of an amended report deleting the Chickasaw County incident.

Dr. Patterson's reply cited the Institute criteria for lynching, decided upon at a bi-racial conference at Tuskegee, held on December 11, 1940, with representatives of the Southern and national press, the Association of Southern Women for the Prevention of Lynching, a white group, the NAACP, and the officials of the Department of Records and Research at Tuskegee in attendance. "A lynching," he explained to Mr. Abernethy, "must include these factors: (1) There must be legal evidence that a person was killed; (2) The person must have met death illegally; (3) A group must have participated in the killing; (4) The group must have acted under pretext of service to justice, race, or tradition."

In making its annual survey of lynchings, Tuskegee Institute performs a valuable service to the country. Moreover, the four requirements for lynching as listed by Dr. Patterson seem altogether fair. The first three are clearly necessitous. The fourth criterion—"The group must have acted under pretext of service to justice, race, or tradition"—provides the basis for the Southern protest both against what is excluded from and what is included within its meaning.

Let's look again at the several crimes or alleged crimes which I have outlined. They included an inter-racial slaying in Mississippi, an inter-racial slaying in Brooklyn, race riots in the North and South, a labor slaying, and a racketeer-political murder. Each unquestionably meets the first three requirements. What about the fourth?

If it can be argued that three drunken Mississippi youths were acting under pretext of service to "justice, race or tradition," it can be just as strongly argued the offenders in all of the other incidents were likewise acting under one or the other of these pretexts. Certainly the rioters of Harlem and quite possibly the young Brooklyn muggers had racial motivations, and were driven also, as the sociologists emphasize, by a warped desire to protest injustice. Certainly the attacks upon strikebreakers by organized strike enforcers are made under pretext of service to what is by now an established tradition as well as a singular idea of justice. Certainly the gangland executions of Charles Binaggio and his henchman were in tune with the requirements of underworld justice, not to mention Kansas City tradition, and possibly in service to race also, since Binaggio, a leader of the Italian-Americans of the city, may have incurred racial animosities among the Negro or other race groups in that turbulent city.

Yet only the Mississippi case was cited as a lynching. Federal intervention is persistently demanded only for the kind of crime which is defined, at least emotionally, as the killing of a Negro in the South by two or more white men. And this despite the provable fact that among the five kinds of lawlessness here cited, only Southern lynchings have shown a steady decline during the past twenty-five years.

Street gangs—Negro and white—continue to thrive and to add to the roll of unsolved murders, rapings and robberies in every large city, while local police appear powerless to curb them. In the crowded cities of the East and Midwest, inter-racial clashes are increasing because of the pressures of the new Negro immigrants from the South and the multitudes with whom they come into contact. Yet there has been no demand for federal laws against race riot; not in 1943 when such rioting took more than fifty lives in the nation; and not today despite the recurrent racial fights in Chicago, in Detroit, in Washington, in New York; not despite the shameful Westchester riots which were at least as anti-Negro in origin as they were anti-Communist.

Within the recent past at least four senators have introduced nearly identical anti-lynching bills. In the House, ten representatives have likewise offered similar proposals. Some of these measures define a mob as being composed of two or more persons, others three or more. One of the proposals, that of Representative Celler of New York, carefully excludes gangster and labor killings from the terms of his bill. Most of them incorporate the principle of mass guilt and mass reprisal which was brought to its ultimate of perfection by the Nazis in the past war. Under this concept the political subdivision, county or town in which a lynching takes place would be subject to a fine which would be paid to the victim's family.

All of the proposed measures give the federal government complete authority to investigate, prosecute and punish the perpetrators of a lynching. The most punitive measure, perhaps understandably, is that proposed by Representative Clayton Powell, the Negro congressman from New York City. Under it, two persons comprise a lynch mob. A lynching is considered as having been committed or attempted when two or more such persons "*commit or attempt to commit violence upon the person of any citizen or citizens of the United States because of his or their race, creed, color, national origin, ancestry, language, or religion, or (b) exercise or attempt to exercise by physical violence against any person, any power of correction or punishment over any citizen or citizens of the United States or other person or persons in the custody of any peace officer, or suspected of or charged with the commission of any criminal offense . . .*"

Powell's bill would make derelict law officers subject to a fine and/or imprisonment not exceeding five thousand dollars and five years, and subject the political subdivision in which the crime was committed liable to a payment of from two thousand to ten thousand dollars compensation to the next of kin of the victim or victims.

It is interesting to speculate on what groups of two or more culprits would be considered members of a lynch mob under a strict interpretation of this measure. Two Boston Irishmen setting upon a venturesome Ulsterman who wore an orange necktie on Saint Patrick's Day? Two anti-Semitic fundamentalists from Kansas beating a Jewish boy? A group of young Zionists attacking a German athlete on a visit to this country? A pair of outraged New Jersey Catholics mauling a Jehovah's Witness? A gang of New England college students beating to death a fellow student because of his antecedents and attitude? Two West Coast one-hundred-per-cent Americans kicking in the ribs of an unoffending Filipino?

None of these incidents is imaginary. They have happened and happen over and over, and they are, in varying degrees, violations of man's dignity and right to self-respect.

But are they the activities of a lynch mob? Under Powell's definition, yes, if anyone wanted to make an issue of it. Moreover, if the violence by two or more persons because of the race, creed, national origins, ancestry, language or religion of the victim constitute the act of the lynch mob, why do not similar offenses committed because of the political ideology, the labor concepts, the racketeering activities or the social status of the victims?

What I am trying to say is that the various anti-lynch bills all have a basic political motivation. The home states of most of the authors of these bills have heavy Negro voting populations. Two of the authors are Negroes themselves. Large and growing Negro populations are politically opportunistic. A brilliant publicist for the Negro, Bucklin Moon, has boasted of them that they hold the political balance of power in the most populous key states of the nation. They want an anti-lynching bill, largely because it symbolizes, however unrealistically, a protest against and even a victory over long-time discrimination which is almost exclusively associated with the South. This potent, largely naïve mass vote is an invaluable prize. The professional spokesmen for this racial group and the politicians who must win approval from these spokesmen must satisfy it and keep its solidarity alive.

There was nothing particularly uplifting in the fraternal war between young Franklin D. Roosevelt, Jr. and Representative Powell for the honor of first presenting an anti-lynch bill before the 81st Congress. There is little encouragement to Southern citizens who have fought lynching successfully—although a good deal of encouragement to our enemies abroad—in such blunderbuss statements as that which prefaced the favorable report of the House Committee of the Judiciary on the Case anti-lynching bill on March 23, 1948:

"Millions of Americans," the report solemnly began, "are presently held in an inferior status by the threat of lynch law, kept alive by state condonation."

If 1952's one lynching in the South succeeded in keeping millions of Americans in an inferior status, what spiritual inferiority must result to millions of other Americans because of the many times that number of deaths in labor violence, condoned apparently not only by state but by the federal government in those areas in which they occur? If lynching is kept alive by state condonation, what about the decline shown in the comparative figures beginning with the first year that Tuskegee began keeping records?

In 1882 there were 113 lynchings. From that year until 1892 more whites than Negroes were lynched. In 1892 there were 231 lynchings, 92 ten years later, 63 in 1912, 57 in 1922. By 1932 the lynchings had shrunk to 8, by 1942 to 5, in 1949 to 3, counting the debatable one, and in 1952 to none. Aside from the reduction in the number of attempted lynchings during this period, if the state and its subdivisions are derelict in their duty, how can we account for the mounting disproportion between the number of victims lynched and the number of lynchings averted by police action? In 1940, Southern officers saved 28 persons from mobs, 21 in 1941, 17 in 1942, 11 in 1943, 5 in 1944, 17 in 1946, 31 in 1947, 6 in 1948 and 14 in 1949.

If the argument is advanced that lynching is still condoned by the people of the Southern states, how then interpret its virtual eradication?

For generally obvious sociological reasons, Negroes commit more major crimes of violence—murder, manslaughter, armed robbery and assault—against white persons than white persons, in and outside of the South, commit against Negroes. However, much of the nation's press considers the slaying of a Negro by a white person, particularly in the South, far more newsworthy than the slaying of a white person by a Negro. The slaying of the Negro in the "road hogging" incident was widely reported and commented upon editorially. I doubt that the story of the decapitation of a white woman in our county by a Negro, who was duly tried for murder and finally adjudged insane, got past the press service relay points.

Yet it is news, and good news, that Negro murderers and rapists can be held safely in Southern jails today without threat of mob action. These contrasting present and past attitudes of the white South provide the true basis for deciding—aside from constitutional objections—whether a federal lynch law is necessary.

This transition from condonation to condemnation reflects in a regional manner the progress of American society from its backwoods past to the present. Violent, extra-legal action against real or fancied wrongdoers has always been a uniform characteristic of thinly settled frontier regions where organized police power was weak and unable to preserve order. And this has been particularly true in time of war, internal strife or the anarchy of the ungoverned frontier.

Even the word "lynch" itself is remindful of that past. It is a verbal adaptation of the name of Charles Lynch, a patriotic if choleric Virginian who during the Revolutionary War punished the lawless by summary execution. Nor was he unique in the popular support he received. The Regulators of the Revolutionary period, the Vigilantes of the early West, the Whitecaps, the old Ku Klux Klan, all of these were approved of by many if not a majority of their neighbors. Concerning the Vigilantes, the Encyclopedia Britannica grows almost rhapsodic over the men who "cleared the western forests, valleys and mountain passes of horse and cattle thieves and other robbers and outlaws, gamblers and murderers. This was especially true of California and the states of the far west."

The states of the deep South, after the Civil War, went through a tragically anarchistic period. Most of them were almost as frontier in their governmental structures and population distribution as was the West of the Vigilantes. Additionally, they were beset by an enduring racism which distinguished between offenses committed by Negroes and by whites, and were confronted also with the problem of restraining a newly freed, largely primitive and frequently hostile Negro majority. The South became the legatee of the summary and illegal punitive action which in the American past was not peculiar to it alone.

I am sure that much of the argument for federal intervention in lynchings today is based upon this past record. Of the total of 3,905 lynchings recorded since 1882, eighty-two per cent were committed in the South. But it is to the present and the unmistakable trend toward the future that the white Southerner points, aware that in so doing, he becomes arbitrarily classified by most of the proponents of federal intervention as a defender of lynching. Yet such defenders in the South today are both infinitesimal in number and discredited in the communities in which they live.

The Southern opposition to a federal anti-lynch law is, both emotional and rational, traditional and legalistic, based upon regional devotion as well as upon a conviction of the continuing need for constitutional division of responsibilities between state and federal governments. The continued agitation provides capital for Southern demagogues as well as Northern demagogues; but Southern opposition to the proposed legislation is by no means confined to the politicians. That should be made clear. Nor does it rest upon approval of lynching or a system of relative justice any more than upon a purely emotional base.

As to the constitutionality of the anti-lynch proposals, proponents of federal legislation argue that the 14th Amendment provides them with the legal right. In related part that amendment reads:

> No State shall make or enforce any law which shall abridge the privileges or immunities of citizens of the United States; nor shall any *State* deprive any person of life, liberty, or property without

due process of law; nor deny to any person within its jurisdiction the equal protection of the laws.

It is argued by Southern constitutionalists that these prohibitions refer to abusive action by the *state* and not by the individual citizen, and protect the individual against such discriminatory or abusive actions only when performed by the state. At least half a dozen decisions of the Supreme Court have affirmed this interpretation. And many leading authorities on the American Constitution have held that the Constitution clearly describes that the police powers are reserved to the several states.

Of course, determined individuals and organized zealots, as well as some jurists, have a propensity to disregard earlier constitutional interpretations or court decisions. And it might well be argued by the sincere humanitarian that were so shocking a crime as lynching increasing yearly in the South or elsewhere, while the governments of the several states appeared either unable to cope with the crime or were covertly approving it, and were a majority or even a large minority of the citizens approving such murders, the federal government could and should intervene as it did to halt kidnaping. If a reading of the annual FBI reports on the rising incidence of all crimes—except lynching—should convince the worried citizen that state and local police and courts are powerless to prevent mounting lawlessness, then it could be argued also that the federal government should take over all police power.

The truth is that every factor, save one, which should determine the need for remedial legislation indicates that federal anti-lynching laws are not needed. The one exception is the general reluctance of Southern juries to punish members of a lynch mob. Officers do arrest mob members, grand juries do indict them, prosecutors proceed against them with vigor. But it is an unhappy fact that mob murderers have little to fear from a jury of their peers on those infrequent occasions when a lynch murder is committed.

It is highly doubtful, however, that the transfer of a lynch case from a state to a federal courtroom in the South—even with a mandatory change of venue within the state as prescribed in some of the anti-lynch proposals—would bring about this needful final metamorphosis. The jurors would be drawn from the same general population. The defense attorneys would be the same. The emotional antagonism against federal intervention would be stronger. It is not a change of courtroom but a change of heart that must bring mob murderers to justice in the South.

I know that this change of heart is taking place. Juries in the South are today convicting white offenders against Negroes—white rapists, murderers, Ku Klux terrorizers—whose victims are Negroes. Approximately one hundred towns representing each Southern state and including my own now have Negroes on their police forces. The urbanization of the South has meant more modern police systems, and this modernization is in considerable part responsible for the decline of mob violence and the prevention of lynchings.

In March, 1950, I covered the trial of three degenerate white men for murder in Kosciusko, Mississippi. While two of them had stood guard, the third had shot to death three Negro children, fatally wounded their father and wounded their mother in an orgy of drunken revenge. The killer, an ex-convict and notorious consorter with Negro women, had suspected that the parents had made complaints which had resulted in his arrest for molestation of Negro women soon after he had been released from the state penal farm.

The state sought the death penalty. The prosecuting district attorney was savage in his prosecution. The governor, the legislature and the newspapers of Mississippi were unanimous in their demands for a sentence of death for the killers. One of the killer's accomplices, who was tried first, received a life term. The other, who was the third to be tried, was sentenced to only twenty years because of a number of mitigating circumstances. Few Mississippians believed that the actual murderer would escape with less than a death sentence. But two jurors, who were later excoriated in public print by several of their fellow jurors and by state and county officers, held out for life imprisonment. And so a murderer who deserved the death penalty if ever it was deserved and for whose life the great majority of his fellow Mississippians clamored, did not pay a debt commensurate with his crime. Ironically, shortly after the murders were committed, Tuskegee announced that it was withholding judgment as to whether or not they would be classified as lynchings, and finally decided that they were not lynchings.

I realize that the basic question remains. How can the perpetrators of this almost vanished crime be punished?

A federal statute won't do it. Only reason, education, spiritual appeal and local censure can reduce the one and two and three lynchings a year to none, and make Southern juries look upon all men as equal in the sight of the law. Federal legislation, I believe, would not only fall short of its purpose but would infect far more of the body politic than it would cure. And in their restrictive definition of lynching and in their exclusion of other crimes certainly as deserving of federal scrutiny, the proponents of federal lynch laws are as guilty of discrimination as are the Southern juries which refuse to convict Southern offenders against the peace and dignity and bodily security of Negro fellow citizens.

19

Charlie Burton's Field Day

This story that Charlie Burton told me is mostly his although it also greatly concerns the two thousand Negro farm owners in the Yazoo-Mississippi River Delta region of Mississippi, who now meet each August at the Stoneville Experiment Station for the Delta Negro Field Day. And besides Charlie Burton and these Delta farmers, the story has to do with the unsung handful of Negro men and women who are county agents and home-demonstration agents, and who are so directly responsible for the progress of the two thousand and the 189,330 other Negro farm owners in the South, most of whom started out as tenants or sharecroppers on a diet of hogmeat, cornmeal and molasses, and no acquaintanceship with cash money to speak of. Their transition is the most remarkable witness to change in the agricultural South that I know.

Charlie Burton is a slim, black-haired man who looks ten years younger than his forty-two years. He looked younger still back in April, 1940, when he became the first Negro county agent in cotton-dedicated Washington County, Mississippi; a rich underdeveloped farming area, two thirds of whose sixty-five-thousand population is made up of Negroes. That was when I met him.

A Negro county agent was a rarity in the South back in 1940; and a lot of Washington County's plantation Negroes were chary of Charlie Burton, a college-educated man who had done more teaching than farming and who went around telling people to raise and put up their own vegetables and meat instead of traipsing to the commissary. He also spent considerable time, it was said, at the government station in Stoneville, a place where white people were doing funny things with cotton and other crops. All of which was true, especially Charlie Burton's interest in the station.

The Stoneville station between Greenville and Leland is a branch of the Mississippi Agricultural Station at Starkville and it is famed principally for its field-laboratory experiments in cotton varieties. But the station's agricultural scientists—some state-employed, some federal, and some under the joint direction of state and federal governments—have always been concerned with other agricultural problems and experiments too, as was Charlie Burton even when he first came to the Delta. From the very beginning he began persuading Negro farmers to visit the station and discover what they themselves could do if they asked questions and followed directions. To his surprise he learned that not a single Negro farmer in the county had ever been to the station.

"They said that we Negroes weren't permitted there," Charlie told me one day when he was giving us a story of the forthcoming eleventh field day. "I knew they were wrong, and told them so. By and by it occurred to me that the best way for them to get acquainted with the station would be to have a field day. Dr. Homer McNamara, who was head of the station then, and all his staff liked the idea mighty well. We picked a day in August, 1941, and I started spreading the word that the first annual Washington County Field Day would be held at the station for Negro farm owners. It wasn't planned to be Delta-wide then, and no more than maybe two hundred county farmers turned up. But even that took a little doing the first time."

We helped him, not sure that anything would come of the idea, with stories and editorials. But the success was Charlie's. The field day wasn't the only time Charlie Burton had tackled something that took a little doing. It had been like that all along. He had been raised in the small colored community of Carter, Mississippi, which had been named for a grandfather. School facilities were practically non-existent, so when Charlie was eleven his father moved to Yazoo City where there was a school for Negroes that extended through the tenth grade. When he finished that grade, he went as a boarding student to Alcorn High School, one hundred miles away, the secondary-school department of the state's principal college for Negroes, Alcorn A. and M. Six years later Charlie Burton was graduated with honors as an Agriculture major.

That was in 1933, and there were few Negro agents then in Mississippi, so the young graduate found a job as teacher of the fifth, sixth, seventh and eighth grades in the plantation school of the progressive Dockery plantation near Clarksdale in the heart of the Delta.

But Charlie wasn't content with being just a schoolteacher. In the afternoons and on weekends and in summer he worked with the Dockery tenant farmers, encouraging them to plant gardens, vaccinating their livestock and preaching sanitation. His employer was impressed and asked the state and county to provide a full-time vocational agriculture teacher at the Dockery school. The teacher was Charlie Burton, and he remained at Dockery until May, 1940.

"I'm especially proud of two programs we started back there," Charlie says. "We had the best sanitation program in the South at that time. With voluntary help we put down more than three hundred sanitary toilets, screened more than three hundred homes and installed sanitary fountains in the churches and schools. The county and state health departments heard of what we were doing and helped us go a lot further. They sent in a team of doctors and nurses, who made malarial and syphilis tests of all the families on Dockery plantation. A clinic was set up in the school, and everyone who showed infection was treated free at the clinic. As far as I know that was the first work of that kind to be done in Mississippi."

All the while, with the encouragement of his forward-minded employer, Charlie had been spending extra hours going from house to house and showing the tenants how to can meat and vegetables. Early in 1937, Mr. Dockery had an old house remodeled and equipped for use as a canning plant. Certain canning days were designated, and the tenants brought in their produce for canning free of charge. That was the other accomplishment in which Charlie takes especial pride.

Then, in April, 1940, came the offer of a post as Negro county agent in Washington County. He and his wife talked over the idea and decided to move, for the field of service was wider, the pay was higher and Greenville offered better opportunities for their children. Mrs. Burton, a graduate of Rust and Alcorn colleges, was to earn still another degree in 1952 when, having left her three children at home, she completed graduate studies in child welfare at the University of Indiana, returning to a post in the county welfare department.

And so, in the early summer of 1940, Charlie Burton came

to our county and found that the Negro farmers didn't think they were wanted at the experiment station. He found other more factual handicaps among the county's Negroes. There were only fifty acres in improved pasture among the Negro landowners. Their corn yield averaged about sixteen bushels an acre. Livestock was scrawny and inadequate, and there was only a handful of small, unsanitary one-man dairies. Their cotton yields were almost uniformly low. That was the background against which Charlie Burton organized the Field Day for Negro farmers.

The Negro farmers were self-conscious at the beginning of the initial tour of the station's experimental plots, but it didn't take them long to thaw out. By the time of the noonday chicken barbecue they were asking plenty of questions. At day's end, the farmers and the station's staff were alike enthusiastic, and Dr. L. I. Jones, director of extension service in Mississippi, recommended that the event be made Delta-wide the next year.

The day's program is more ambitious now than it was then. According to their interests, the farmers, more than two thousand of them in 1952, tour the various experimental fields, where the station's specialists demonstrate the work being done. At noon they gather for a huge barbecue, and with them gather also scores of white Mississippians—agronomists, state officials, planters, equipment dealers and businessmen. The feast of chicken, slaw, rolls, coffee and ice cream is paid for by such organizations as the Delta Farm Bureau chapters, the Mississippi Power and Light Company, the Greenville Production Credit Association and the Goyer Company, an unusually civic-spirited wholesale house in Greenville. The barbecue meal itself is prepared by the Delta's Negro home-demonstration agents, devoted, able women who are transforming the interiors of thousands of Negro farm homes and changing the health and housekeeping habits of their occupants.

There is nothing patronizing in this commingling of white and black Mississippians. From Washington and elsewhere have come as speakers such outstanding Negro leaders as Dr. A. H. Furr, field representative of the Farm Credit Association; T. M. Campbell, extension service field agent; Sherman Brisco, information specialist for the service; Fred Neal, director of Tuskegee's Country Life school; President J. R. Otis and former President W. H. Pipes of Alcorn, and President Lawrence Davis of Arkansas A. and M. From the platform with them have spoken such white leaders as Jesse B. Hearin, president of the Production Credit Association of New Orleans; Rex Brown, president of the Mississippi Power and Light Company; Alfred H. Stone, elder statesman, former Delta planter, and director of the State Tax Commission; Ransom E. Aldridge, president of the Mississippi Farm Bureau; Oscar Johnston, president of the fabulous, British-owned Delta and Pine Land Company, one of the world's largest plantations; and Owen Cooper, the young Mississippi economist who now heads the new Mississippi Chemical Company, producers of anhydrous ammonia fertilizers. Nobody talks down to the audience.

Nor is there anything superficial in the results that the Stoneville station and the Field Days and Charlie Burton and the Farm Security workers and the farmers together have achieved. Those pitiful fifty acres of improved pasture have grown to more than two thousand acres in special pasture demonstrations alone. The corn yield has jumped from sixteen to thirty bushels. Cotton yield has risen an average of thirty per cent because of better land use and the station's directions for insect control and use of pure seed. A general livestock sanitation program has led to the establishment of sixteen Grade-A dairies among Negro landowners. At latest report, there was only one other Negro-owned Grade-A dairy in the state outside of Washington County.

Between Field Days, Charlie spends a lot of time selling the farmers on new ideas. He persuaded some Negro farmers to plant soybeans five years ago, but the small landowners had no sure way of getting them harvested. So in 1949 he helped a farmer named Mose Mason buy a combine, putting up some of the money himself and co-signing a note, so that Mason could do custom harvesting of soybeans. With this assurance, other farmers planted soybeans, and the combine paid for itself in the first year. In 1950 two other Negro farmers bought combines for custom harvesting of the crop that vies with cattle as proof that the cotton Delta no longer puts all its eggs in one basket.

In the spring of 1952, Charlie talked fifty-nine farmers into planting okra on a total of about a hundred acres that hitherto hadn't paid taxes, and made a deal with a canning plant to take the crop. Before the season was half over, and despite the drought, eleven farmers had already made more than a hundred dollars an acre on their crops. Now they're listening to Charlie's suggestion that they try red peppers next year as a cash crop on their heaviest, stiffest land.

I have attended about half of Charlie Burton's Field Days, and have met there or on their farms scores of the farmers whom Charlie told back in 1940 that they would be welcomed at the experiment station. I wish I could write at length about some of them: men like Mose Mason, whose diversified one hundred and twelve acres produce wheat, soybeans, oats, orchard fruit, truck crops, pasture and cotton; John Jordan of Black Bayou whose six hundred and forty acres put him in the planter category, and Will Higgins who profitably farms three hundred and twenty acres; Dave Watson, whose new, growing dairy herd is already bringing him a check for two hundred dollars every two weeks; George Jennings, who was the first Negro landowner in Mississippi to win first place in a Memphis Commercial Appeal Live-at-Home contest; and Prentis Johnson, who was the first Washington County Negro farmer to give up cotton growing altogether in favor of beef production. They represent the hopeful other side.

The average size of Negro farms in our county is only sixty-one acres, but it is in some of the smallest ones that Charlie Burton takes especial pride, and particularly in the FSA farmers who came up the hardest way and have paid off. A dozen times or more a year Charlie guides to these little farms, and to some of the larger ones, a variety of visitors from Scandinavia and Germany and France and England and India and wherever else the State Department recruits those thoughtful guests who had not heard of this side of the South. Often I go with them, and my own pleasure in what I see never lessens. Charlie and his farmers show those questioning strangers the pastures and the pantries, the fruit and vegetables in the quart jars, the meat in the small smoke houses, the chickens and the hogs and the cows and the refrigerators, and Charlie tells them how things were once but will not be again.

I could add personal testimony. Fifteen years ago our *Democrat-Times* didn't have one hundred Negro rural subscribers. Now we have more than three thousand. That single statistic indicates what is happening in education, income and interest.

Now and then some of these travelers who have heard only distortions concerning the less happy side of the South are with us in August, and attend a Field Day. Charlie doesn't have as much time for them then because on those days he is one of the busiest men in the state. But they have no lack of other volunteer guides, white and Negro; and guides are not really needed at all, for they can see for themselves the well-dressed men and women, talking the talk of farmers the world over, and talking too of how it once was and how it will be for their children, whose small feet, unlike the feet of their own childhood, know the feel of earth that is their own. On such a day our guests from overseas lose quickly a great deal of the skepticism they brought with them, and if they talk long enough to Charlie Burton they lose it all. For when Charlie Burton talks he communicates the happiness that comes to a man who can measure his own life's achievement in the brighter lives of his fellows.

20

Mrs. Means Married Woman

One fall day in 1951 our receptionist-switchboard operator said a Negro woman wanted to see me. I told her to send the caller in. She was a well-dressed woman in her thirties and not too much at ease.

I am sure she expected a rebuff after I asked what I could do for her, for she told her story with not a little difficulty. She identified herself as the wife of a Negro physician who had settled in Greenville some months earlier and had established a good practice and a position of leadership among Greenville's Negroes. She had been named chairman, she said, of the Negro section of the Red Cross drive, and what she had come to see me about was our newspaper's failure to identify Negro married women with a *Mrs.*, giving instead either their unadorned names, as Lucy Jones and Mary Smith, or departing from factual reporting, listing only the initials of their husbands if their own first names could not be learned.

She ended with a request that if her name should come up in any further stories about the Red Cross or anything else, we either give her recognition as a married woman and a self-respecting citizen or not print her name at all.

I might have brushed her aside with the usual comment that this was the established policy of the paper and of most Southern newspapers from time immemorial. Or I might have evaded the issue by saying that I would like time to think about it since, if I complied, I would be violating one of the longest-lasting of deep Southern taboos.

But I took neither of these courses because I felt that something very consequential was happening in my office, something important for more than just the unusual fact that a Negro woman was asking me, with dignity and reasonableness, to recognize in our news columns that she was married. "Mrs.," she said, "just means married woman." For behind her request was the persistent, long-unanswered demand that we—not just we of Mississippi, or of the South, but the Western white people who are an amalgam of so many anciently blended bloods—recognize that what the darker peoples of the world require and must get from us is a recognition of their right to human dignity and self-respect. That demand, I thought, is part and parcel of the tangled reasons why Americans and Englishmen and Turks and Filipinos and Puerto Ricans are dying in Korea; dying in battle against an Oriental people to whom face was paramount and in whom the social condescension and racial vindication of imperialism had aroused murderous hatred of the Westerner, a hatred fanned by the Communist incitement into a will to destroy all the good which had at least partly offset the mistakes and the evils of Western exploitation of the Orient. Through this doctor's wife, I thought, speak the people of India, of Egypt and Iran, Morocco and Malaya, and Africa and Mexico and of every land where the white conqueror and the white trader and governor have drawn a demeaning line across another's country.

Face, dignity, self-respect—the words became a chant in my ears: *Face, dignity, self-respect. Mrs. means married women, China, Africa, India, Malaya.* I asked myself, am I more afraid of what some of my newspaper readers might say—I knew what some readers most certainly would say—than I am of this bursting resentment, this cascading protest of the people of color against our denial of dignity? I asked myself also: What have I got to be afraid of? Afraid that somebody will write or telephone to us to cancel their subscriptions to a damned, nigger-loving paper? Afraid of economic reprisal or social retaliation? Afraid that our usefulness in larger matters will be impaired by our violation of the taboo against permitting a Negro self-respect?

I had faced these fears in other trials, and I knew I wasn't afraid. I knew that this was my own self, wrestling with the credo that I had been taught with my first words, and now I was trying to break away from that union of pride and condescension and habit and caution that lies behind the refusal to give all married women a common dignity of recognition and offers instead a conscience-salving substitute. . . . *I love Negroes as long as they keep their place. Why my old nurse was just like my mother. I was raised with the funniest little nigger boy and we used to fish together, but Mrs. doesn't mean married woman, it means a white married woman, and the other kind are just named Nellie, and their husbands are named Jim, and when he grows old we call him Uncle unless he is a doctor or a professor or a judge or a congressman or an officer in the armed forces, anything but a Mr. married to a Mrs., because that's different, and if you give them an inch, they'll take a mile.*

All right, I thought, let's see what will happen. I said to the Negro doctor's wife, "You're right. There's no sense in it, and we'll change." I'll not soon forget the look in her face; not gratitude, which would have been out of place; not relief or triumph, but a look, instead, of surprise and accomplishment and great dignity. She said, "Thank you, Mr. Carter," and left.

I mulled over the way to tell the staff. I knew that other Southern newspapers, large and small, had taken this step, some time before, a step which had been denounced by certain Southerners as a blatant acknowledgment of "social equality" and a letting down of needful bars. The Atlanta papers used Mrs. and so did most of the newspapers in North Carolina; but our nearest big-city-newspaper neighbors didn't, despite their unchallenged control of the metropolitan field; and maybe they hesitated because their non-city subscribers lived principally in rural Mississippi and Louisiana and western Tennessee, and the management, being smarter than I was, had decided that the deep South wasn't ready.

Wasn't ready. . . . That was another shibboleth. Maybe Greenville hadn't been ready, fifteen years before, when we published a news picture of Jesse Owens, who was coming to the Delta to demonstrate, at a little all-Negro town's seventy-fifth-anniversary fete, the co-ordination that had just won him four Olympic firsts. The next day I was told, violently and often, that Mississippi newspapers didn't print pictures of Negroes. But we kept on printing such pictures when we saw fit, and now nobody even bothers to mention it. Some had cautioned us that our people weren't ready when we urged the extension of the ballot to qualified Negro citizens and the removal of the poll tax; when we bespoke the equalization of education in Mississippi and the rightfulness of the Supreme Court's order to admit Negro students to Southern graduate schools, and the wisdom of employing Negro policemen in our town, as we now do, and of spending tax money, dollar for dollar, to build Mississippi's first Negro public swimming pool, and Negro hospital facilities and schools and playgrounds. I looked back over each debatable issue and I remembered some people had said we Mississippians weren't ready; and Bilbo braying every night during that campaign summer of 1947 that I was a mongrelizer, a homoculous (it means "mud-dwelling") liar, and telling my fellow Deltans that I ought to be skinned and put in a basket and toted out of town. But nobody had skinned me, nobody had toted me out of town, nobody had ostracized me or promised economic retaliation; only a few had threatened me, and they anonymously.

So what was I afraid of? Was it so unconventional in Greenville, Mississippi, in 1952, to admit in print that a married Negro woman was a Mrs.?

On the joined principles that there is strength in unity and that misery loves company, I telephoned the Atlanta headquarters of the Southern Regional Council, a sensibly motivated inter-racial organization which, without fanfare or much capital, has been a notable instrument in bringing the races closer together and in insisting on first-class citizenship for the Negro in America.

I asked the Council for a list of Southern newspapers which used the courtesy titles with Negro names. When I read the list which arrived airmail, special delivery, the next afternoon, I was both surprised and strengthened in my abrupt resolve of the day before. About a hundred Southern newspapers were using the titles, altogether or to a limited degree. These newspapers ranged from the South's largest to many which were smaller than ours and were published in regions considerably less tolerant than the Delta. The accompanying letter said that the list was not complete. So at least a hundred newspapers in the South and Southwest, out of some three hundred dailies and two thousand weeklies, were also violating the taboo. If they could, I told myself, we could.

When I talked to the staff after making the decision, Charlie Kerg—who is loyal to the *Democrat-Times,* the United States and the Greenville Bucks of the Cotton States League, in that order—said that he'd go along. David Brown, who is from small-town Louisiana, George Stroud, who writes agricultural and general county news and is from Arkansas, and Bob Tims, the newest staff member, who went from the Mississippi Gulf Coast to the Air Force and afterwards to Harvard and Oxford, each asked me why we hadn't done it before, and commented that it was high time. Lou Crump suggested a campaign to teach everybody good manners to everybody else, chortled that it was just grand, and dared an imaginary host of enemies to start anything. Gene Roper, older than the rest, and a veteran of copy and editorial desks of a dozen larger newspapers in the South, was cautious in his comment, saying the innovation might stir up unnecessary trouble. But nobody objected, either in the news department or the advertising department—where I had half expected a protective protest—or in the composing room upstairs although there was a good deal of comment.

Of course there was considerable talk when the first *Democrat-Times* appeared under the unannounced new policy. I must say our readers got the full treatment, although unintentionally. The second lead story had to do with the Red Cross campaign. A late story had come in from the Negro division of the Red Cross. Gene used it in bold-faced type, Mrs. and all, as a bulletin preceding the original story.

That night I had several telephone calls, not from critics but from friends who wondered whether we might really have gone too far this time. I told them that we'd wait and see. It had all become for me a fantastic exaggeration of nothing, this worrying about such a change in the day of the atom and the hydrogen bomb, in the mid-century of freedom's peril, in the hour of world doubting by black man, brown man, yellow man, white man, as to where they should ally themselves, whether with the power of world communism which promises bread and revenge, or with Western democracy which struggles toward the ideal of man's dignity.

The next day another friend dropped by to tell me that while he personally approved of the new policy, he had heard a great deal of criticism, and that some of our advertisers didn't like it. I thanked him, and after he left, I telephoned several of our larger advertisers. When they sent out bills or mail advertising to Negro customers and prospective customers, did they or did they not use the courtesy titles? They did, answered all but two. Did they let Negroes try on dresses or suits or gloves in their stores? Two did. Did they or didn't they try to get and hold Negro business? They did try. Did they want to reach as many Negroes as possible through the advertising columns of the *Democrat-Times*? They did. Did they know that in the past fifteen years, while our over-all circulation had grown from thirty-one hundred to nearly thirteen thousand, our Negro subscription list had increased from less than three hundred to more than five thousand? No, they didn't. And did they really object to our using "Mrs." before the names of Negroes in those relatively infrequent stories of Negro participation in community life, Negro educational achievements or War Department stories that Private Willie Johnson, son of Mrs. George Johnson, had been seriously wounded near Panmunjon? No, they really didn't.

Of course, a good many of my fellow citizens did object. But they were wraiths as concerns any bad effect upon our circulation, our advertising lineage, our friendships and the even tenor of our lives. It took me a long time to find this out, or to decide to want to find it out, and it may seem to the non-Southerner, or even to some of my fellow Southerners, that I am devoting too much time to too-small an incident and too-minor a decision. But I do not think that the incident was really small or that the decision that came from it was inconsequential.

A few months later I met a gaunt young priest, just returned from a year's brutal captivity under the Chinese Reds. He was a missionary priest serving the Negroes of eastern Arkansas, across the river from us. He was an intense, consecrated man, and because I wanted to talk with him, I asked if I could drive him home after he had spoken to a service club of his experiences in captivity before the Reds had sentenced him, almost miraculously, to perpetual banishment instead of death.

As we drove along he asked me what I did, and when I told him that I published the Greenville paper, he smiled and said that he had just heard something about me from one of his Negro Catholic parishioners who had come to see me a few months before. She was the doctor's wife, who proudly had told the new priest of her visit and its results.

"We talk about face as if it were important only to the Chinese," Father Sullivan said. "It's as important to all of us as to any Chinese alive, whether we know it or not. What you've done is more important to our Negro brothers than if you'd built them six new high schools. I think it's more important to God."

I think so too.

21

Prof., Be Lenient

The kindest thing to be said about the year I taught freshman English at Tulane University in New Orleans, is that long before its end, all of us—faculty, students and myself—were in agreement that I had stopped looking for newspaper work too soon. But the year was unforgettably revealing as to the sad state of secondary-school education. My classes weren't altogether average, for the word got around that I was just twenty-one, a football fan and easygoing; and so coaches, alumni and fraternities conspired to pack my classes with a disproportionate number of beefy freshmen on whom they were counting for a Rose Bowl team the next year. Even so, it was difficult to understand why a good many of my students had been given a high-school diploma and admitted to one of the best universities in the South.

One of my prodigies was a mountain of muscle who, everyone said, would surely become an All-American guard. Somewhere along the way he may have learned to read and write, but he must have found these talents unnecessary after he became big enough to make the high-school team. On the cover of his mid-term-examination blue book, he wrote "for gods saikes prof, be lenant" and departed the academic life with five failures in five subjects. I did what I could. Each week I would let the flunking footballers guess what would be the score of the next Tulane game, and pass the man who came the nearest to being right.

Two students represented the other extreme. It was difficult not to lecture exclusively to them. They were brilliant, bored and as out of place in the class as I was. I didn't worry about most of the football players, but I was bothered by the predicament of the few unusual or above-average students among the mass of inadequately prepared, indifferent or incapable classmates. I still am.

Between the extremes stood the students who simply had an insufficient foundation in basic grammar. Almost all of Tulane's students came from Southern high schools. Not three out of ten of those in my classes were ready for college freshman English or even for what I remembered of high-school senior English. When I gave the class a list of one hundred words to spell, not tricky or unusual ones but just relatively ordinary two- and three-syllable words which some of them sometimes even used conversationally, less than half the class spelled fifty or more of the words correctly. The two exceptional students yawned and made perfect grades. So did a few others. But too many of my students didn't know how to spell or to read with understanding or even to pronounce the longer words in the freshman anthology of English literature.

I have since been told by educators that in respect to grammar and spelling and composition, the high-school graduates of today are in even worse case than were those whose eyes used to go blank in 1928 when I talked about unity, coherence and emphasis.

Not until 1945 did I have any further personal experience with the problems or the conduct of public-school education. Newspaper editors have no business on school boards, which are generally as controversial as any element in the body politic, but I hadn't arrived at that conclusion when we came home from the Army. A school board member had resigned. Just why the City Council thought to appoint me to his unexpired term which had about a year to go, I don't know. When I was asked if I would like to be appointed, I said yes. I thought that, if I were a member, the *Democrat-Times* would at least be able to get more detailed accounts of what went on at school board meetings.

It had been the custom of our school boards, despite loud editorial protest, to go into executive session whenever a division of opinion or the need for another policy decision existed. This behavior was stupidly ineffective, since a newspaper can always find out what goes on at closed meetings especially if there is a difference of opinion among the closeted members, because the losers can't help talking. So I became a member of the school board, which was divided that fall on two issues. One issue arose from a three-to-two decision to let Chinese children attend the white public schools. The other issue was the high-school superintendent, who had been a member of the Greenville school system for twenty years, during which time he had risen from a coaching post to director of the public schools. The two issues were related though the relationship was not vital in the school war.

In Greenville lives the second largest concentration of Chinese Americans in the South, some four hundred, most of them engaged in operating neighborhood grocery stores in the Negro sections of town. The Chinese men came originally as levee builders and railroad workers and usually without their women, because of the Exclusion Acts. These womanless pioneers created yet another racial group in our community, the Negro-Chinese, who stay apart from the Chinese-Chinese.

The state's constitutional prohibition against the mixing of races in the public schools sets forth that there shall be separate schools for non-Caucasians; but its framers were unaware that Greenville someday would have its own Chinatown. The Chinese ban has been disregarded everywhere else in the state, for outside of Greenville there weren't enough Chinese to create a situation if their saffron-skinned children enrolled in the white schools. But the Greenville Chinese had posed a problem for nearly forty years, and the efforts at solution were contradictory and weird. A Chinese man or woman could sit in the white section of the movie theaters. A Chinese man could also take a Negro girl to the movies, as some did, but then he must sit in the Negro balcony. The Baptists encouraged the Chinese to attend Sunday School in their building on Sunday afternoons and to become Christians; but when Chinese were stricken ill they were not permitted to be patients in the King's Daughters Hospital, until recently our only white hospital, although the King in question is Jesus Christ, a physician of whom it is not recorded that he determined racial origins before he laid upon the sick his healing hands. Only the inadequate Negro hospital was open to them. Nor could the Chinese children, meaning the Chinese-Chinese children, attend the public schools. So when the Chinese-Chinese families began to grow, the parents made a deal with the city fathers. They agreed to build a little one-room grammar school if the city would supply the teacher. The Council agreed.

That was years ago. By the fall of 1945 many a Chinese child had stopped going to American schools when he finished the six grades in the one-room schoolhouse, though he continued in a special Chinese school which the colony operated so that their children would remember their parent language and learn something about their racial past. Those who wanted to go to high school and whose parents could afford to accommodate them, were sent to near-by public or parochial schools, and some even went as far away as Memphis, one hundred and fifty miles distant, where the presence of a few Chinese children in a classroom apparently was not considered a yellow peril.

Then, in 1945, at the reiterated recommendation of the school superintendent, the school board voted three to two to let Chinese children attend the public schools. When a few Chinese kids enrolled that fall, the reaction of some of our citizens was akin to the explosion of a truck load of Chinese firecrackers which make a lot of noise but cause little damage. Today Chinese students play on the football team and the school band, win class offices and almost invariably are in the topmost scholastic group. The other students don't worry about their presence, proving, of course, that the young are dangerously radical. It was my privilege, incidentally, to help send through college the first Chinese graduate of the Greenville High School, the oldest of a widowed mother's several children. He is a senior now at the University of Michigan and will graduate with a degree in engineering and a reserve commission in the ROTC.

While the implacable enemies of the superintendent were relatively few, some among them had power in the community, and the admission of the Chinese children to the public schools was only one reason for their opposition, and a lesser one. The superintendent had gone far in instituting "progressive" methods of education, and the resultant effects among the student body in respect to mental and civic discipline had not been altogether fortunate. He was a stubborn and sometimes a curt man who believed in what he did, and he cared little if some people did not approve of his policies. He was also a brilliant and devoted public-school careerist who later went—rather precipitately since he lost the fight—to the deanship of the University of Mississippi's School of Education, where ironically he indirectly exercises far more influence upon the public schools than he ever could as superintendent in Greenville. Worst of all, in the eyes of some of his critics, he had attended Teachers College at Columbia University. I had put in a graduate year at Columbia myself. That winter the name of Columbia became a hissing in the streets. The storm troopers gathered strength and girded their loins. Columbia and communism and traitors and educational imbeciles became synonomous.

One morning a somewhat hysterical voice questioned me over the telephone: "Do you as a school board member know that our schools are being run by an atheist, a Catholic and a Jew?" The "atheist" was the superintendent. The high-school principal was indeed a Catholic, and the Junior High School principal was Jewish. I said, "Lady, I like all three of them, but I doubt if I could get along with you, and what's your name?" She snapped, "I thought so," and hung up, and I suspect that was when I became a sacrificial goat.

Somewhat later I wrote an editorial in which I probably should not have referred to the lady crusaders as frustrated biddies, but I did it because of that telephone call. The school board then stood three to two in favor of the superintendent. The board members are appointed by our six-man city council, with the mayor voting only in the case of a tie. My seat was due to be vacated next since I had been appointed only for an unexpired term.

When the battle was joined, the specific issues were whether the schools should be investigated at all, and if so, whether the investigating body should be selected by the Parent-Teachers Association, the parent half of which was dominated by an overwrought critic of the superintendent. She was a woman of great personal charm, unusually well educated and high in Greenville's social hierarchy. I had no objection to an inspection of the school system though we preferred the word "study" to investigation. In fact, an examination of the school system seemed under the circumstances a good idea, but not under the direction of the parent members of the P.T.A., whose leaders had already committed themselves to an all-or-nothing goal of getting rid of the superintendent and—though I didn't find out until later—to getting rid of me too, and replacing me with someone who would vote to replace the superintendent. The teachers kept quiet as teachers usually must do.

The embattled ladies arranged for a mass meeting of the Parent-Teachers Association at which the debate as to who should conduct the investigation would be resolved. It was announced that no one but the P.T.A. members and the school board could attend. For fifty cents anyone could belong to the P.T.A., and the ladies went to every sympathetic soul who had a spare half-dollar in his pocket. They enrolled many new members including several dozen who had never before and would never again show an interest in the public schools.

On the night of the beautifully stacked meeting the high-school auditorium was filled. Speaker after speaker arose to denounce Columbia and all its works, the low state of our public-school system and the shortcomings of the superintendent, and to urge that the P.T.A. be put in charge of a survey of the schools. Only in such a way could the P.T.A. leadership be vindicated, they said, and the slurs which the *Democrat-Times* had cast upon America's mothers be answered. The evening's climax came with an oration by a childless World War I hero, a dramatic, militant man who knew that Columbia was up to no good, and who that week had paid a half-dollar for his first P.T.A. membership. Despite frequent differences of opinion, he and I are friends, and we were sitting next to each other on the second row that night, when he rose to speak. The reputation of Southern womanhood itself was at stake, he said, and Greenville must vindicate its own. Would the citizenship listen to such mental characters as this school board member—here he made a roundhouse gesture which almost took off the top of my head—or would we clean house with the ladies wielding the broom? I chirped "Hooray," a sally which no one except Betty and I thought either appropriate or funny. Soon thereafter the vote was taken. A thunderous shouting signified complete confidence in the ladies. The negative vote was perfunctorily called. Nay, said the superintendent. Nay, said Betty. Nay, said I. Motion carried.

Within a few weeks the City Council considered the appointment of a school board member for a full term, as my time was about to run out. The P.T.A. leaders took turns telephoning the councilmen. At the next meeting three councilmen voted for me and three voted for the ladies' choice. The mayor chose not to vote, and the decision was postponed. The following month one of my adherents was absent, so the vote was three to two for a compromise selection, which was a wise decision. I was replaced by a good man. The superintendent, who for four months had shared with me a secret, but who was just Irish enough to stay in the fight even though his future plans were already made, announced through the *Democrat-Times* that he had accepted the deanship of the Graduate School of Education at the University of Mississippi.

I am not sure who was the ultimate victor in that fight, but I know the cause of public-school education wasn't aided. An honest, unscholarly committee did finally investigate the school system and came up with a fair if sketchy report, the contents of which were duly printed in the *Democrat-Times* and as duly forgotten. An aftermath to the unpleasantness was Betty's decision to go into P.T.A. work herself; and so she did, and became president of the P.T.A. of each of the elementary schools which our boys attended.

The progressive techniques have now been modified. The citizenry has overwhelmingly approved bond issues for four new schools. No one worries any more about Chinese children in the public schools. But some of us are still concerned about what our children are learning or not learning.

Our personal concern began in the spring of 1949 when young Hod was about to finish grammar school. The three of us had many conferences and finally agreed that it would be better for him to go to a scholastically more difficult school for the next four years. He had not had enough to do in grammar school. All his marks were A's; he held class offices and participated in group sports. His school work came too easily, for his classes were geared to the lowest common denominator, and I remembered my students at Tulane. Hod's young, eager mind was lying fallow. He took the entrance exams for Exeter and though he passed them creditably, he and we were alike shaken by the differences between the grades he received on those examinations and what he was getting in the same subjects at home. We left him in Maine at summer's end, and a couple of weeks later he entered Exeter.

After his first two years at Exeter we had another family conference. Hod liked the school. He had done well. He had studied under some exceptionally good teachers, had become proficient in tennis and basketball and had discovered that what he liked best was literature and history. But, said our sixteen-year-old son, who had shot up to six feet and a wistful maturity, there was another side to it. Exeter was seventeen hundred miles away. All his life he had been jumping from one place to another, what with moving from Louisiana, and the war and our summers, and going away to school. He felt rootless—that was the word he used—because he didn't seem to belong anywhere, and we might as well know that in spite of all the fun he had at Exeter, he had been homesick much of the time. Besides, he added, soon he'd be in college and afterwards would come the Army or work elsewhere, without his ever knowing much about Greenville or Mississippi. Exeter had taught him how to study, he said, and that was true, and he thought that between his outside reading, and the family's own interests, he would gain as much from Greenville in his last two years as he could at Exeter, and he surely wanted to try. We mulled over the problem through the summer. His mind was unchanged in September and so he entered the junior class in Greenville High School.

What I say now is not so much a prideful parent's account as it is a skeptic's awareness that our public schools just do not measure up. With no visible effort, Hod made A's in every course. He was a member of the debating team which was runner-up in the State Debating competition. He played varsity tennis and was on the varsity basketball squad. He was president of the Latin Club and business manager of the annual, was selected as one of two delegates to Boy's State in which young students take over the state government for a week, won both history medals that the school offered and at the end of the year was elected head cheerleader and president of the next year's Senior Class. These assorted chores and occupations and honors still left him plenty of time to fall in love with a succession of schoolmates, go to a dance a week (almost every night during Christmas holidays), read more books than I did and twice wreck our automobile. While he is popular, healthily extrovert, agile and intelligent, the only way that such a record can be explained is in terms of the difference in the competition, the instruction, and the courses offered in Greenville and in Exeter; and this means that there is far too great a difference in what the public-school student gets as a foundation and what the minority who can attend good private schools receive. Somehow the gap must be narrowed. The proposal to divide high-school students into groups according to their talents and interests is not a new one, and it is being followed to some extent in many high schools, including ours. The above-average student should be given especial attention and not held down by his fellows whose lack of interest or ability necessarily slow down the educational process. But the school board or the school administrators who speak openly for such a policy run the risk in my town, and I suppose everywhere else, of being accused of intellectual snobbery or undemocratic ideas; and so, not only my sons, but millions of young Americans are handicapped.

Next to national defense, public-school education is our biggest business, but it was not until the very recent past that any over-all attempt had been made to inspect that business. About two years ago I was asked to become a member of the National Citizens Commission for the Public Schools, an organization interested only in the improvement of America's public schools. None of its members are professionally identified with educational, religious or political groups; individually they reflect many different kinds of experiences. The Commission's financial support comes from the Carnegie Corporation and the General Education Board. The Commission members include Gardner Cowles, president of the Minneapolis *Star-Tribune;* George Gallup, who directs the American Institute of Public Opinion; Beatrice Gould, the editor of the *Ladies' Home Journal;* Palmer Hoyt, publisher of the Denver *Post;* Roy Larsen, president of *Time;* Walter Lippmann; Victor Reuther, director of the C.I.O.'s education department; Beardsley Ruml, the economist; Harry Scherman, president of the Book-of-the-Month Club; Louis Seltzer, the editor of the Cleveland *Press;* Bernard Young, editor of the Norfolk *Journal and Guide,* a Negro newspaper in Virginia; Charles Allen Thomas, vice-president of the Monsanto Chemical Company; Stanley Marcus, executive vice-president of Nieman-Marcus Company; Lester Granger, director of the National Urban League; James G. McClure of North Carolina, president of the Farmer's Federation, Inc.; Neil H. McElroy, president of Proctor and Gamble, and others. It is not a group which sane persons would accuse of radical leanings or of hidden special interests, although some on the lunatic fringe of our society have made just such assertions. In this organization or in similar ones which may develop from it or join with it, I see the only sensible and possible means of meeting the challenge to the public-school system. The

Commission's goals are basic: to help Americans realize how important the schools are to an expanding democracy and to arouse in each community the intelligence and will to improve our public schools instead of leaving them alone until an emotional issue brings irrational participation in school affairs. Its members want the best in education to be made available to every American child on equal terms and insist that public-school education should be constantly reappraised and kept responsive both to educational tradition and to the changing times. The Commission is advisory in its nature, but it has succeeded in forming nearly two thousand non-partisan citizens' committees pledged to work for better schools in their communities. It sponsors workshop conferences and serves as a sort of clearing house of information and encouragement to citizens' committees and other educational groups throughout the nation.

Whatever good the Commission or related groups can accomplish will probably not be done in time to help my own children. Nor can such organizations alone succeed in warding off the attacks upon various aspects of public education by the irresponsible groups of super-patriots who have brought fear to too many high-school and college campuses in the land. They cannot alone defeat the intemperate critics and the unqualified censors. But they can act in behalf of the unready child, the voiceless teacher and the minorities who stand against the mob mind.

I think of the freshman athlete in my Tulane English class and my high-school son's unchallenged mind, and of the mothers of Greenville who organized to scalp a high-school superintendent and to encourage a nonsensical concept of a great American university, and I know the three images are related.

22

It's Not Always Christmas Eve

Christmas Eve is the one night in the year which we share with others only in our own home. This has been so since Hod was a four-year-old shepherd, swathed in a shawl and a scarf-turban standing guard in the living room over an imaginary flock of sheep. With him were a Joseph from down the street, all of eight, and Joseph's younger sister, who that night was freckled-face Mary, three very junior Wise Men, and a host of neighborhood angels and fellow shepherds. The story of the Nativity which the children acted out that night was the first of thirteen such presentations which our boys and their friends have given each Christmas Eve. Now Hod is seventeen, and for two years he has been protesting that he is too old and that he has played every part but Mary and has outgrown even the striped robe which I brought from the Holy Land, together with other articles of Palestinian attire which give colorful reality to the telling of the Christmas story. Nevertheless, he remains a member of the cast, and I suspect that he will have a part for some time to come, because he really likes it and we like it and so do Phil and Tommy, who this year will move up from lowly shepherds to become Wise Men.

Christmas Eve is the family's night. My brother's younger daughter is a blonde, plump Mary now. The rest of the cast is made up of a few faithful repeaters, young Biblical troupers, and an unstable list of one- and two-timers. The audience are the parents of the cast and always Lou and Brodie Crump and sometimes a few friends who have no children. We are crowded together, for the cast has always played to a capacity house, whether in our first small house in Greenville or the Washington apartment or our home in the country, which I am sure was planned by Betty so that the playroom wing could also be a dressing room, the hall a stage, the dining room a hideaway for an offstage chorus, and the living room a ready-made auditorium.

The Nativity in Greenville.

The living room lights are dimmed and we, the audience, wait expectantly, all but Betty who on Christmas Eve is hostess, costumer, producer, vocal strengthener of the chorus and prompter. From the dining room comes some unsaintly giggling, and we suspect Tommy. Then in the Delta night, the sound of young voices:

O, come all ye faithful,
Joyful and triumphant . . .

Hod's voice, only a year ago breaking in adolescent uncertainty, rises deep and true in harmony with Phil, who is a reluctant stalwart in the boys' choir at St. James's. Tommy, we fear, may break off at any moment into "Home on the Range," which he prefers. We hear Mary's determined alto and the other voices, and the parents single out the chanters who are their own; and at the first hymn's end, an illusion of holy quiet in a distant, long ago land possesses us.

From the dining room emerges a somewhat nervous Mary, beautiful in the hand-brocaded silk that came from the real Jerusalem. Behind us she recites the words of the Magnificat:

My soul doth magnify the Lord
And my spirit hath rejoiced in God my saviour. . . .

The unseen chorus in the dining room begins "O Little Town of Bethlehem," and Mary is joined by Joseph, a son of the desert who is sure of his lines, for his mother has coached him over and over so that he won't repeat his bobble of last year. Nor does he. Together he and Mary walk among us to the double doors that separate living room from hall. Above the doors is fixed a bright star, the star of Bethlehem, and beneath it Joseph begins St. Luke's story of the first Christmas Eve:

"And it came to pass in those days that there went forth a decree. . . . And Joseph also went up . . . . unto the city of David which is called Bethlehem."

When he is finished, Joseph opens one of the hall doors, ever so slightly, and he and Mary enter into the still hidden stable. The children's chorus sings of the shepherds:

"The first Noel the angels did say
Was to certain poor shepherds in fields where they lay."

Then the chorus singers also pass through the living room until they stand beneath the star, sometimes three shepherds, sometimes five, little boys, middle-size boys, even now and then a boy big enough to be Joseph if we had need of more than one. But always, whether the shepherds be many or few, there must be left behind in the dining room three Wise Men and at least one angel. The shepherds keeping watch relate what they have seen, and an angel appears from behind the doors to bid the shepherds have no fear. Perhaps the angel will double as the multitude of the heavenly host, if we are short on multitudes:

> *"Glory to God in the highest*
> *And on earth peace, good will to men."*

The huddled shepherds follow the angels through the doors. The three Wise Men, older boys with Hod, their long practiced spokesman, approach in majestic procession singing: "We Three Kings of Orient Are." They are dressed in monarchic splendor, with beads and Mardi Gras baubles pinned onto their shawls and bathrobes and sheets, and their turbans sparkle with dime-store jewelry. Now, we share the wonders of the Epiphany. No Herod mars the peace of our night for the tyrant is with us only in the recitation which the third Wise Man concludes:

"And when they had opened their treasures, they presented unto him gifts; gold and frankincense and myrrh."

Only then do we, the audience, see beyond the veil of time. Unseen small hands open the folding doors. In the hallway, framed by a draped screen, sits Mary, gazing down upon the glow that comes from a flashlight hidden in a straw-filled basket. Beside her stands Joseph and around the Holy Family hover the angels while the Wise Men kneel and the shepherds crowd close in adoration. The children begin to sing the last hymn and we join in reverently:

> *"Silent night, holy night,*
> *All is calm, all is bright. . . ."*

When we have done, somebody says, "That was beautiful, children"; the lights go up and the members of the cast seek out their parents or go to a table where cookies and punch are their earthly reward, and the spell is ended for the time. The grownups talk together for a while, and then our friends and their children go out into the Christmas night to their own homes. Our family gathers close together, happy and excited and not too severe with Tommy, whose bedtime is now far behind him, and who is insisting without much hope that he go with us to the midnight services at St. James's.

Betty and I are content, suffused with the richness of what we share on this night, and on other and ordinary nights; for neither of us has discovered anything as precious as a family in harmony or anything as sure and certain as the family core at the universe's center or anything that can quiet our doubting as much as the spell of the holiest night, when we can believe with the mystic and the poet and the child in the miracle of God's grace.

On such a night I am very sure.

But it is not always Christmas Eve.

The preference of the Protestant South for the evangelical sects is no historic accident but the inevitable result of the revival of its spiritual life in a place which a century and a half ago was a southwest frontier at a time of democratic discontent with old forms and a popular reaction to moral excesses. This revivalism thrived among a rural people whose spiritual natures were less likely to be awakened by reason or a quiet faith than by the catharsis of the camp meeting and the fundamentalist devil. It followed inevitably that in the hands of simple, religious extremists, sectarian faith became a bludgeon. In the name of religion the South once vindicated slavery, and in Mississippi today religion is invoked by loud fanatics to defend the mockery of prohibition, and to damn the nonconformist who doubts that hell fire awaits the dancer, the tippler, the smoker, the papist, the Jew. And so it is not always Christmas Eve. . . .

Every Sunday morning the small-town radio stations of

the South are appropriated by an extraordinary assortment of evangelical preachers. Some of them are gifted, sensitive and kindly men but too many of the others are intolerant fundamentalist ranters whose voices rasp with hate for the unbeliever and who shout warning to the lost souls who disagree, all in frightening gibberish, which is calculated to fill the temples that rise in anarchic multiplication of sects. This shocking performance is the right of every preacher and every dissident; but that right, if abused, can become an actual threat to an objecting minority.

I remember one preacher who took advantage of an invitation to speak at Greenville's annual interfaith Thanksgiving gathering to make unsubtle jibes against Jews and Catholics and to preach a sickening sermon that reflected only his own bigotry. It has always seemed to me necessary to stand up to such people. Once, in the late thirties I exchanged unpleasantries with some Jehovah's Witnesses, a priest who thought Father Coughlin above reproach and an evangelical preacher who sought to discourage a movie benefit show on the grounds that all movies were immoral and so were the people who produced them—all within a few months of each other.

The Jehovah's Witnesses took exception to an editorial condemning that sect's anti-Catholicism, with specific reference to a meeting which some of their itinerant spokesmen had held in Greenville. They put a hex on me. For more than a month I received almost identically worded letters of denunciation of my "papist and AP controlled newspaper." The letters came from more and more distant regions that finally included Mexico, Canada, Alaska and England, which was no tribute to our circulation department but simply resulted from the reprinting of the editorial in a Witness publication. The letters died out in a few weeks, however, and within a year some more Witnesses came to town and asked us to print a notice of their meeting, which we did, together with another critical editorial. That time we had no letters.

I regretted the Coughlin incident because we liked the priest who was locally involved, but the dispute didn't end our friendship and it was good to discover that the Catholics of Greenville didn't go along with their shepherd in his admiration for the notorious political priest. It all came about when I read in *Time* magazine some letters from indignant Coughlinites who were canceling their subscriptions because of that magazine's treatment of their hero. I got to wondering if there were any Coughlin disciples near by so I commented in an editorial that Coughlin was a liar and unpatriotic and a disgrace to the cloth, and suggested that if any of our readers didn't agree and wanted to cancel their subscriptions as *Time*'s communicants had, they should just let us know. The Greenville priest wrote the only reply. Father Coughlin, he said, was a gentleman, which I was not; a man of truth, which I was not, and a great leader, which I was not. But the defender represented a minority of one in his parish. The day after his letter appeared, a delegation from St. Joseph's Church came in to assure me that the parishioners agreed with us and not with the priest on the matter of Father Coughlin. When I next saw their priest, at a wedding reception, we shook hands, lifted our glasses of champagne to each other's health and kept quiet about Father Coughlin.

I was less successful in making friends again with the minister with whom I disagreed about movies, Sunday or otherwise. And I haven't been able to convince our Baptists that Mississippi's prohibition law should be repealed. They are made of unyielding stuff. They dominate Mississippi numerically and politically, and there is unconscious irony in the complaints of some of their clergymen that the Catholics indulge too much in political activity. No more political-minded citizens can be found anywhere than Baptist preachers when the prohibition issue is raised. It is reasonably certain that if a reincarnated General Sherman were to run for governor of Mississippi as a prohibitionist and Marse Robert E. Lee opposed him as an advocate of repeal, General Sherman would be elected, because more than seventy-five per cent of our population are Baptists who are committed ideologically to an eleventh commandment: "Thou shalt not drink"—an admonition which has not prevented dry Mississippi from consuming illegally more whisky per capita than do the adjoining wet states of Arkansas, Louisiana and Alabama.

I don't begrudge the churches their political activity for it is as inevitable among large, powerful denominations as is politics within the churches themselves. It is asking too much of organized human beings to expect them not to react politically and with group force when their tenets are involved. But when they do resort to political action, the only antidote is to treat them as politicians and not as sacredly untouchable Baptists or Catholics or Episcopalians or Zionists or whatever.

During one of the recent foredoomed efforts to substitute a local option law for statewide prohibition in Mississippi, the chairman of the legislature's so-called Temperance Committee, herself a Greenville lawyer and advocate of state-controlled liquor stores, found herself deserted one day by her fellow committee members and encircled by a couple of hundred Baptist ministers who had descended upon the state capitol to make sure that a temperance committee minded its manners. Two of these preachers were pastors of Greenville churches. They did not conduct themselves well. One of them suggested that any woman who opposed prohibition was of doubtful virtue; the other said that if the hell's lightning of repeal were to strike our beloved state, the continued good conduct of Mississippi's womenfolk, including his own, would be highly improbable.

The performance of these ministers was horrifying. I wrote that they had disgraced both their ministry and their manhood by their sorry action and suggested that their clerical usefulness in Greenville was over. But they and their congregations disagreed with us, and they are still here.

We followed this up with a survey of the opinions of other citizens on the repeal of prohibition. Among those we questioned were the Presbyterian minister and the pastor of the largest and oldest Baptist church, a man who had not attended the meeting in Jackson and who was regarded by many of us as being more level-headed and tolerant than some of his fellow ministers. I liked him. We had first known each other in Louisiana. He had been a chaplain in World War II and was a gifted burry-tongued Scot, popular and active in the community. Once he had courageously written an open letter in my defense when a Bilbo henchman had lied about me. As with the priest, I was sorry that the minister and I disagreed violently, and I am telling this story only because all laymen ought to know the spiritual danger they create when they punish or try to bring into line the minister of independent spirit or unpopular beliefs. The danger exists especially in those churches in which a minister's tenure is completely dependent upon the whim of his own congregation, for his sense of insecurity is stronger than it would be otherwise. Our reporter quoted the Presbyterian minister as being forthrightly for legalization and state control, although he was a teetotaler. The reporter quoted the Baptist minister as saying that he was personally and strongly a dry but in agreement that prohibition was not the solution. I wrote a complimentary editorial.

The next day the Baptist minister said he had been misquoted. We printed his denial. The Presbyterian minister, to the contrary, said that he had been correctly quoted, which left some of us wondering how it was that the same reporter could so correctly report one minister and so incorrectly report another on so direct and simple a question. Later on in the week a group of Baptist laymen inserted a large advertisement in a Memphis paper and our own, declaring their faith in their preacher's integrity, Christianity, loyalty and support of prohibition.

We didn't know until some days later that the quotation and his denial had become a celebrated incident in Mississippi Baptist circles. I found this out over coffee one morning when a friend gibed that our newspaper didn't mind printing news about other people's law suits but treated our own troubles differently. I asked him what he was talking about and he grinned and suggested that I read the papers. I checked with the wire services and the Jackson and Memphis newspapers, but I could not find a story about a lawsuit in which we were involved. Eventually, a Baptist friend told me that the state Baptist church newspaper had printed a story to the effect that the Greenville minister was suing us. We procured a copy of the little church paper and found in it a story which related that we were being sued on charges of slander and libel. The story even named the lawyer who had been employed. I telephoned the lawyer and asked him what it was all about. He said that there had been no suit filed and that there wouldn't be. The minister had come to him to discuss the feasibility of suing us, and he had advised him that it would be senseless. The weekly church newspaper printed as fact a story that had never happened. I don't know where it came from, but I suppose it got the monkeys off our minister's back.

In August of 1952 the embattled drys of Mississippi easily defeated a modest proposal which would have enabled the State Legislature to permit counties to decide whether to have liquor on a local option basis. But the Delta voted for local option two to one. It is still not clear to me and never will be what is the evil contradiction between the eggnog which I serve my own rector and any visiting friends at Christmastime and the practice of a faith which has endured for two thousand years.

Organized religion is easily derided because of the hypocrites that it may house, the fanatics it may produce and the distortions which hating men can make of obscure texts. The non-churchgoer says that he doesn't attend services because he can't stand to attend church with Bill Jones, who is the meanest man in town, or Ed Smith, who is a downright thief, or the Brown woman, who has her nerve to be acting like a saint. But if such people are prompted to come to church, through some inner compulsion, whether it is fear or remorse or acknowledgment of weakness, I want to see them in a pew every Sunday. I am more afraid of the people who go to church because they consider themselves upright than of those who go because they know they aren't; and I would be a whole lot more afraid of a world in which there were no preachers than I am of ours in which some of them are preoccupied with keeping Mississippi dry. They and I believe in the man of Galilee. I do not think that Philip, my son, would have come home one afternoon with a beautiful story if Christ had not once walked among men.

Phil told us that a new sixth-grade boy, who had just transferred to his school at Eastertime from another town, had come out for spring baseball practice. The boy was a spastic who walked jerkily and had almost no control of his movements, but he wanted to play, Phil said, and the boys let him. They did more than just let him play. They conspired to make him think he was really a baseball player. Phil was pitching when the spastic child came to bat, and he and the catcher and the infield showed what teamwork can accomplish.

"I pitched him four balls," Philip said, "and that got him to first base. Then the catcher threw over the second baseman's head on purpose, and the kid got to second base. We got him to third base sort of the same way, and then I pitched an easy one to the next batter, and we let the hit go for a home run." Phil's eyes were shining. "Dad, we worked that kid all the way around the bases."

23

In Heaven or Maine

For the twenty years before her death my mother would, at the least provocation or even without one, take from an album of family photos an enlarged snapshot which my brother describes as Shakespeare among the lilies. I was Shakespeare and nine years old.

But it isn't really accurate to call that portrait a snapshot. It was taken in Maine one summer soon after I had presented to my mother a poem which, I said, had been written among the lilies in the garden of a relative who had a near-by home on Penobscot Bay. The picture was posed. I had lied poetically, because the poem had been written in the room I shared with a cousin who dreamed then of a fishing career. I had carried the finished manuscript to the lily bed, and therein implanted myself until a relative with a camera approached.

But the poem was portentous, and it is as an augury of the future that I offer it in merciful condensation.

QUESTION AND ANSWER

Beautiful angel of the skies
You are very, very wise;
Could you tell me where to go
Where the waves dance to and fro;
Where the grass is O so green
Where dark clouds are seldom seen,
Where the air is cool and sweet,
Where the birds sing tweet-tweet-tweet,
Where the sky is nice and blue
Tell me all these things, won't you?

The angel answered in accents mild
In Heaven and Maine, O innocent child.

Poetic license aside, Maine is still the closest to Heaven that I've yet come, and the place I'd be willing to settle on for a celestial abode.

Our family had spent a summer in Maine before I wrote that doggerel, and we returned several times afterward, but not every summer as did my grandmother Carter and some of our aunts and uncles and cousins. That was better in the long run, for in the long intervals of absence, Maine remained as a goal and a dream. The summer after I was graduated from high school, certain that I would go to college in the South, the family journeyed once more to Maine for a family reunion. There were some thirty first cousins among those present and one of them, who was also my best friend, easily persuaded me and less easily my parents that Bowdoin College was the place for me at least for one year. Not the shades of Hawthorne and Longfellow, but the knowledge that I'd have Maine all year round was what made up my mind. So, in the fall of 1923, I entered as the class baby and the only deep Southerner in that class, defensive and quickly provoked about the nether regions from whence I came.

A frank and skeptical dean explained to me that I was really an experiment since my high-school credits were inadequate for admission by the college's standards. Instead of one year, I stayed all four.

In the beginning I was often angry at the challenges of student and teacher to attitudes and customs and versions of history that I had thought unchallengeable. But at the end of those four years, and ever since, I have been grateful to the teachers and fellow students of that small unostentatious school, where the teacher and the taught could draw very close together, and where a youngster who liked to scribble was no queer fish at all but could almost rank with the athlete. A devotion to learning, a respect for the teaching profession, a certainty that the middle ground was the best, a Yankee independence of thought and action, the academic tolerance for the nonconformist student—those are for me the hall marks of the Bowdoin academic culture, deep-rooted, earthily provincial, resistant to sudden change.

Even the Maine winters I liked, with wet-combed hair freezing on uncovered head as we hurried to chapel in zero weather. I liked the ceremonial afternoons for tea at a professor's home, and the more ceremonial nights in the dark meeting hall of the fraternity which was founded as a literary society and persisted with difficulty in that tradition.

The one historic landmark I never adjusted to was the old Congregational church, immediately adjoining the campus, in which, so goes the Bowdoin legend, Harriet Beecher Stowe wrote *Uncle Tom's Cabin.* It seemed a direct affront, especially because the college used it for commencement exercises.

But by my junior year I could accept almost with equanimity the roster of Union generals among our college great. As editor of the annual I got even with one of them, fine old Joshua Chamberlain who became a Bowdoin president, for in a dedicatory survey of Bowdoin's sons, I chronicled briefly that he commanded at Little Round Top and then gave my literary best to tell how the vastly outnumbered but finest army the world had ever known was turned back by superior force and entrenchments. I ferreted out comforting counterfacts. In Memorial Hall, a classroom building erected in memory of Bowdoin's men in the Civil War, I discovered a lone Confederate cavalryman, a Louisiana cavalryman at that, among the hundreds of names inscribed in bronze. A Bowdoin man, Senator Fessenden, had stood like a granite wall against the Reconstruction radicals who clamored for the conviction of President Andrew Johnson and so turned the raging tide. Bowdoin, I learned, had given an honorary degree to Jefferson Davis in the 1850's when he was Secretary of War, and had refused to rescind it despite the hysteria and hatreds of the Civil War. When the college gave me such a degree twenty years after my graduation, President Sills warned me that the last Mississippian so honored had gone on to be president of the seceded South.

When I left Bowdoin, it was with the certainty that all of its graduates would go out into a world of enduring peace and richness, make their way in a short time to whatever summit they selected, and, happily married and comfortably well off, would spend their summers in Maine. Bowdoin's teachers no more had the power of divination than did our financiers and men-in-the-street, and the young men of the late twenties were ill-prepared for the slings and arrows that the next generation would endure as normal.

In the fall of 1944 I again faced the frightening prospect of entering Walter Reed Hospital where Army doctors were discussing whether to remove my right eye and even warned me that I might lose the other eye as well. It was that fall, too, that the loss of the *Democrat-Times* seemed all but inevitable. It was not a pleasant period. We rented a dictaphone, so that I could practice dictating, and for a while I tried typing with my eyes blindfolded, but that was too depressing. Betty bought a shorthand book, which she tried to master after work. We tried to plan for the two eventualities of blindness and being forced out of newspaper publishing. If we lost the paper, we knew we couldn't stand to return to Greenville. We decided that if the worst happened, we would settle down somewhere, live as best we could on the Army retirement pay that would come, and I would dictate imperishable prose either to Betty or the dictaphone. After all, she said, if Milton didn't need his eyes, why should I?

And then, another of those near miracles which have blessed us in every dark time! Jack Stanley, who had been my commanding officer in the Middle East and again in the Pentagon, had some overseas leave coming to him and didn't know where to spend it; so I told him about Camden on

Penobscot Bay, and Hamilton Hall, my favorite cousin, and Emmy, his English wife, and after a telephone call or two, Jack and Georgie, his wife, went to Camden.

Within a week I had a telephone call from Jack who sounded delirious. He had bought for a song, he said, a nearly new cottage in Rockport village, which indistinguishably adjoins Camden, and near by was another and larger old home, once a sea captain's, which was still for sale. It was the last, or almost the last, of a group of houses which had been acquired during the past several years by Mrs. Efrem Zimbalist, who had been Mrs. Edward Bok, the daughter of Cyrus H. K. Curtis, the publisher. Mrs. Zimbalist had restored and furnished several village and coastal homes in Camden and Rockport and had made them available to musicians in whose careers she was interested. But that year she had decided to sell most of these houses to people who passed her scrutiny. Jack and Georgie had. Excitedly, Jack, abetted on the telephone by my cousin Ham, said that I should rush immediately to Camden and sell ourselves to Mrs. Zimbalist as a prospective purchaser of this dream house which was named the Boat Barn. I had more than one hundred days of ordinary leave coming to me, but few ordinary leaves were being granted by the War Department that fall; so, when Jack returned, I duly put in an application for an emergency leave "to settle an estate," which was true enough, and in three days I was back in Maine for the first time in nearly five years.

Mrs. Zimbalist, a gracious lady, escorted me through the Boat Barn, which was lovely beyond expectation, and when we went into what she called the sordid details, her terms were so generous that I all but genuflected. And so we fell heir to the Boat Barn, all of one hundred and thirty years old and furnished in keeping with its age, with a great studio-barn attached to the green-shuttered house, and an orchard and a deep wide lawn, a perfect place for writing and, if necessary, for going blind.

From the day we bought the Boat Barn we didn't much care what else happened, and that gave us assurance and a long-absent peace of mind. The following May after several unpleasant and inconclusive months in Walter Reed, I walked out of those sad confines with one relatively good eye and the no-account one still in place, a fistful of disability-retirement papers, one hundred and six days' accumulated leave, the recovery of our newspaper assured and, ahead of us, the first free and relatively unworried months we had known since marriage.

And they were also the most fruitful. The editorials I wrote in the Boat Barn were the ones which won a Pulitzer prize for the *Democrat-Times* the next year. A letter of application written there brought a Guggenheim fellowship. I finished a poor novel and turned out a half-dozen magazine articles. I flew to Greenville and stayed a couple of weeks to take back the *Democrat-Times* and indulge in some gloating and fence mending; but it was almost entirely a holiday summer, and our first such. The Maine writing regimen was established then, and we have seldom departed from it; at the typewriter from eight to noon or one, and then the rest of the day and night to ourselves.

If I had loved Maine before, I was all but idolatrous then. No one can ever convince us that New Englanders are reserved and uncommunicative. Betty organized a square-dancing group, the first in the Camden-Rockport area in many years; and impatient with the traditional division of the friends we were making into "summer people" and "natives"—the most condescending and resented of descriptions—she and her cohorts divided the square-dance group membership of some sixty between the Maine people and the visitors.

We danced every Friday night in the Boat Barn, and the next summer, costumed in authentic pre-Civil War garb, three Rockport couples and Betty and I won on the Camden green the first Lobster Festival folk-dancing championship. I got a plaque and lumbago.

We were Rockporters from the beginning. Betty found herself on just about every town-club committee. The selectmen invited me to make the address at the village's celebration of V-J day, which I did, standing on a dais before the Rockport roll of honor, a Southerner reminded again that the perpetuation of regional divisiveness is so much our own doing in the South.

We acquired a tiny, unseaworthy boat, which we dubbed the *Smidgin;* and in time the *Smidgin* gave way to the *Channel Cat,* an auxiliary sloop which was built to sleep four, but on most cruises somehow accommodated six. We came to know the green, rocky islands and the bays and the harbors of the Maine Coast, each with its champions who proclaimed that here and not elsewhere on that coast was the one true heaven. We climbed the little mountains that were high enough for out-of-breath folk from the flat Delta, and camped on them overnight, building fires before the three-sided Adirondacks huts and bedding down on fragrantly uncomfortable couches of fir and pine and balsam boughs. We swam in the bay when we could stand its tingling, salty iciness, and when we couldn't, we swam in the lakes.

We played and tried to adapt ourselves to the unending round of parties which had started with the great-grandparents of the rarely changing hosts, for most of the summer families had been coming to Maine for at least three generations, and most of the later comers learned first of Camden and Rockport from those old-timers. Because of Mrs. Zimbalist, Camden and Rockport had attracted an unusual number of musicians; and, if not a colony there was a considerable number of writers and artists; and later, an unusual summer-theater group, made up of college students, who intended to go on as drama teachers and directors. The Boat Barn was jammed with guests all summer long, and sometimes we fled the house and went visiting elsewhere. We were revelling in a strange heaven of freedom from Army restraint, of confidence and productiveness and fun; and it has been that way ever since, summer after summer, two to three months of writing and playing and looking at ourselves and our world. We now consider ourselves as Maine old-timers, in our own minds indistinguishable from the Maine people who are year-round tenth generation and longer, and who are so like Mississippians, even to their political single-mindedness; so like in their origins and the friendliness that so readily replaces suspicion if the stranger is friendly too and not a damned fool; so like in the going out of their sons and daughters because there is not enough at home to satisfy their ambition and even the needs of everyone; so like in their past days of glory, when in Maine the China trade and the pine forests and the quarries and the shipyards created the stately white houses with their widow's walks, while in Mississippi, the cotton bales built the mansions of Natchez and a stubborn legend that is somehow still believable.

And then at Little Round Top, Chamberlain and his Maine farmers and loggers and clerks and seafarers turned back the Mississippians and the Virginians and the others, the planters and sharecroppers, mountaineers and rivermen, and nothing since has been as it was, in either state, and nothing since has been as it should be. For Maine and Mississippi came to share an undeserved destiny and to be shunted from the main current and to bob too long in the directionless backwaters, so that Maine and Mississippi did not grow, and are poor in dollars, and watch their children depart. And Robert P. Tristam Coffin, the poet of Maine's soul, mourns that Maine's old houses are now too large.

But Maine and Mississippi have not quit. Our farmers are persevering in new directions, the Maine men on rock-strewn land that makes the Southerner wonder at the strength and the persistence of its tillers; the Mississippians on the mistreated fields that were richer far than the fields of Maine to begin with, and are becoming rich again through a new wisdom. Our workers may not always have to seek the distant looms assembly lines, for our states are fighting now for new industry, though I hope we in Mississippi never lure an old one from Maine. And I cannot believe that either state will forever surrender its children to the distant cities and its stubborn heritage to an urban society which mocks it. If the surrender is permanent, something will be lost besides population and income. Maine and Mississippi, at the near extremes of geographical north and south, are small beleaguered forts of American individualism, rural and small-town, like-minded, clusterings of the children of the tenacious first ones. And it seems to me that the more dynamic and central and conglomerate our American society becomes, the more it needs as a transitional balance these units which are independently individual and more slowly geared and spread thinly, with space between, across the hills and the valleys of home.

And meanwhile we Mississippians could probably learn one prime lesson from our Yankee cousins. Maine people are purposeful putterers, with no mind to let man's handiwork fall before nature's assaults. I wish they could teach us the usefulness of paint on house and outbuilding, the joy of the home craftsman who won't let the back porch decay in peace, or leave the cracked pane in place or the pantry shelf in winter bare of the summer garden's provender. I wish they could and would.

24

First Hunt

Time was, and not so long ago, when a man could do right well if he had learned as a boy to sit a horse and aim a rifle and swim a river and steer a course and bait a hook and find his way. My father thought these abilities essential enough to see to it that my brother and I had ponies to ride and guns to shoot and enough coaching in swimming and camp-making to cause a minimum of parental worry and a modicum of parental pride. When my own three sons came along, I harked back to those days and promised that I would teach them what my father taught me, even though the reliance of the individual upon himself and the old, personal skills does not have the same outward meaning in our day of the guided missile and the atomic mushroom.

I have tried to help them learn what I learned, and if I

could find no other vindication or pleasure in the eventime of a last American frontier, there would be enough satisfaction and joy to spare in these things; for I have seen seven-year-old Tommy, our youngest, fall from his pony the first time up and cry and mount again, and I have watched him blow a moccasin out of the water with a .410 shotgun blast. I remember the day Hodding, the oldest, caught his first fat bream when he was as young as Tommy is now, and how the sailing dinghy skidded when he took the tiller. And I want to tell of Phil's first hunt. Perhaps it had happened to me, thirty-odd years ago, with the same unplanned suddenness.

Just beyond the telephone table Phil crouched for a last stand, throat and tongue producing the machine-gun chattering which is the direct descendant of my own boyhood's cap-pistol bang-bang. Hand over the telephone, I told him to quiet down, and listened while my friend Wade said that unexpected business would keep him from the duck hunt.

I protested to Wade that at this late hour—we were setting out downriver the next morning on the *Mistuh Charley*—we wouldn't be able to find a substitute, and that he'd have to reconsider.

Phil was listening too. Even as Wade insisted that he really couldn't go, the machine-gun battle ended, and a more intelligible but no less staccato clamor filled the hall.

"Lemme go, Daddy, lemme go, lemme go," Phil pleaded with a tousle-headed ten-year-old's repetitious insistence. "You promised, you promised." He raced away, pounding up the stairs, and he was back by the time I had hung up the receiver.

In his hands was the .22 rifle and .410 shotgun over-and-under combination that, despite his mother's misgivings, we had given him for his tenth birthday two months earlier. Since then his bag had included three moccasins, surprised n early-autumn sluggishness, a few blackbirds, and a turtle isted as probable but unproved. But no real game. Now it vas duck season and Christmas holidays as well.

"It's too cold," I temporized. "You don't have any real huntng clothes, and we'll be leaving too early to get any." But I vas arguing only halfheartedly. Ten years old was young, out it wasn't too young for a hunting trip. My dad had taken ne out for quail when I was nine, and I still insist that I nocked down three with only minor assists.

Now my own son was fidgeting like a penned-up squirrel, his eyes as imploring as his words, and it was easy to go back hrough the years, remembering; but surely my father could not have been as inwardly delighted then as I was now. This vas ancient and tribal and ritualistic, a never-to-be-dupliated experience for us both. I sought to prolong the prelimiaries, telling him he didn't have any long underwear and it vould be freezing cold.

"Mom can fix some of yours," he came back. "And I got boots and a wool shirt. I got your old cap——"

And Mom did cut down the underwear, all of us laughing an hour later as the try-on proved the impossibility of doing a tailor-made job of cutting down a two-hundred-pound nan's long drawers to fit a ten-year-old.

But fit was no obstacle. Phil was up at dawn, though we vere not leaving till eight; and at that hour he was helping oad *Mistuh Charley* with a zealousness he had never shown before.

Mistuh Charley is a Greenville-built river boat, a forty-foot win-screw cabin cruiser, powered with Chrysler Crowns, her broad-beamed hull of double-planked cypress, butane gas or heating and cooking, and accommodations for eight. Four ears old at that time, she had been designed and her contruction supervised by Mistuh Charley Williams, the mightiest Nimrod of the river. We had bought her from Mistuh Charley, and rechristened her in his honor, just a few months before his untimely death. She carried one dinghy topside, and on hunting trips towed an eighteen-foot army landing boat, both of them outboard powered.

So six of us were going on the three-day hunt. Five men and one small, excited boy, shiny-eyed and eager and weighed down with gun and hunting knife, and a duffle bag crammed with the most ill-assorted improvisation of hunting clothes that ever startled hunter or hunted.

Phil had spent many hours on the *Mistuh Charley,* but he had rarely lingered ten minutes in one place. Now, as soon as we got under way, he asked if he could sit out on the bow with his gun to look for ducks. I explained that it was illegal to hunt ducks that way, but that he might improve his target eye by shooting at driftwood. I wouldn't have wanted to sit on the exposed bow, in the face of a whistling wind, for long. But Phil remained there for more than an hour, banging away at enemy submarines, before he gave up. It was just as well. He had used up two boxes of .410's.

We had figured that by early afternoon we would be far up the hairpin-curved, abandoned old channel of the river, unused except by hunters and fishermen since the cutoffs shortened the Mississippi for a total of one hundred and sixty miles between Cairo and the Gulf. There, somewhere north of Spanish Moss Bend, we would tie up among the willows on shore, and set out in the small boats for a likely hunting area in the watery wilderness of the Luna Bar area. We could build our blinds, if all went well, in time for a couple of hours of afternoon shooting, and on the next day's dawn we would return to where thousands of obliging mallard would doubtless await our pleasure.

There were plenty of ducks on the river. We saw them dark

against the slaty sky and riding unconcernedly in the inlets of the old river, and we pointed out to Phil the differences between and relative desirability of green head and teal, and told him how not to be fooled by water turkey.

But afternoon shooting didn't materialize. We were about five miles up the old river, and Phil and I were in the galley—I'm one of those oddities who enjoys playing both captain and cook—when beneath us we felt the hull scrape and grind to a full stop. Whoever was at the wheel had cut across a sandbar and had run aground. It had happened before. *Mistuh Charley* was an old hand at getting off sandbars. We bragged that when we couldn't back off, we just ploughed through them.

But this sandbar was different. It took nearly two hours, and the combined pulling power of both small boats with their outboard motors, to get us off. Nobody minded too much. The soup and sandwiches and fruit were good.

Bundled up more warmly, Phil practiced .22 shooting, having been warned to save his remaining two boxes of .410's. We knew we'd get off in time to blind. Tomorrow we'd make up for what we might have lost this afternoon.

It was about three when we came ashore from the dinghy and landing craft, and there was not too much working time before sunset. Here a high-water chute of Old River lazed past the shifting, inlet-sliced shoreline, crinkling around the slim willow and cottonwood, the late evening sunlight turning the rusty cane to bronze and sparkling reds. The sand was firm for fifteen feet back, and the slope into the chute so gradual that the shallow feeding grounds extended fifty feet or more beyond the bank.

Phil and I picked our spot between Johnny and Roy, who were blinding a couple of hundred feet below, and Rod and Jimmy, who had found what they wanted farther upstream.

For an hour we cut willow and cane and rolled two small driftlogs to our site, angling them so that we could straddle them without interfering with each other and yet be close together. As the sun plummeted, we built our blind around the long seats. It was the most workmanlike one I have ever put together. It had to be, for with a small boy's eyes on you and small boy's belief that his dad can do anything better than anyone else, that blind could be no ordinary hiding place. Everything I remembered from my Boy Scout days went into its construction. We sank stout corner saplings, buttressing them with smaller stakes, and wove the willows and reeds together with almost basketlike precision. Phil worked like a beaver, his cheeks pink, his eyes surveying the handiwork like a veteran, asking and telling me in the same breath just how good our blind was.

"Ol' ducks won't see us," he panted time and again. And he'd make the machine-gun noise again while imaginary game tumbled into the chute.

I didn't know until bedtime how great was his excitement, and how completely the events of the day and the thought of the morning held his imagination. Never had he been so eager at home to do any assigned chore as he was to assist in getting supper ready; never had he eaten any food as ravenously and uncritically as the amateurish steaks, fried potatoes and sliced tomatoes, coffee and canned fruit salad. And, miracle of miracles, he insisted on helping Johnny with the dishes after supper when I exercised a chef's prerogative and turned the dish-washing over to that reluctant assistant.

Afterwards, before bedtime, he sat spellbound and quiet while five grown men, their phrases more carefully weeded out than might otherwise have been the case, joked with him as an equal and spun tall hunting tales which he punctuated with reverent "gosh durns" and "gees" and "cripes." By eight he was heavy-eyed, and I herded him into the forward cabin which we were to share.

But untroubled sleep was not to be Phil's that night. The triple portions of potatoes and steak, the excitement of the afternoon, the thoughts of tomorrow combined to produce a not-unnatural result. I was awakened about ten thirty by the sounds of a violent nightmare. Phil's face was feverish, and even after I woke him, he whimpered over some dreadful dream. I was afraid that he might be sick by morning, so I made him drink bicarbonate of soda, and then, when that kitchen remedy seemed inadequate, we went to the stern where he availed himself of the more primitive cure for a troubled stomach. After that he slept soundly, but I didn't. I worked myself round to blaming his mother for letting him come. Maybe he had food poisoning or a virus or the Lord knew what. I felt helpless and guilty. I listened to his breathing, felt his forehead from time to time and waited miserably for the next dire symptom to appear. And it seemed as if I had just dozed off when the alarm sounded at four thirty.

A completely whole Phil leaped out of his bunk like a rookie fireman, his teeth chattering in the sub-freezing cold. In the darkness he tore up the little companionway, past the galley, into the main cabin, with me close behind him with his shirt and socks. I needn't have been concerned. The long underwear was still long and it enclosed feet and hands. He had turned on the lights and, putting a match to the built-in butane heater, he yelled in proud imitation of a reveille a summons that I had brought home long before from training camp:

"Daylight in the swamp," he howled. "Get your cotton-picking butts out of bed."

It was almost the unexpurgated version, and I made a

mental note to be more careful when and where I used it in the future.

He was tearing around like a souped-up jalopy despite the protesting groans of his elders, making sure that this would be one hunt that was going to start on time.

"Let's get breakfast, let's get going, gotta get those old ducks, hurry up, Daddy," he shouted. Frying pans and coffeepot rattled in the galley, and together we began cooking breakfast. When the aroma of coffee rose tantalizingly from the stove, he looked wistfully at me. "Can I have a cup of coffee?" he asked, man to man. He never had drunk coffee before. But this was different, and so I said yes. It was a tactical error, as we were to discover.

Phil lingered over the unfamiliar, hot brew, and we were all waiting on the stern, ready to board the small boats, when he finally emerged. On his head, settled down around the lobes of his ears, one of my old hunting caps bestrode a knitted wool helmet. He wore a sweater over a wool shirt, topped by a British field jacket which I had brought from North Africa in my thinner days seven years before, but which could have accommodated two Phils. On his feet were fairly water-tight, three-quarter leather boots, over wool socks. Around his neck hung a small haversack, so filled with shells and assorted paraphernalia that his head was bowed as if in prayer. But he carried his over-and-under with as much aplomb as a Texas ranger.

One of the fellows, already in the dinghy, chuckled at the apparition. "We'll use you for a decoy, Phil," he laughed.

But the little fellow was equal to the situation. He didn't answer the gibe. Instead, shifting his gun so that it nestled in his crooked arm in the best Daniel Boone tradition, and straightening his shoulders against the loaded haversack, he questioned me as a veteran if forgetful huntsman.

"Say, Dad," he asked with supreme indifference, "what's the limit?"

I would have hugged him, had not four outsiders been looking on. Gravely advising that the limit was five, I strapped on his lifebelt and warned him that we were about to travel in a little boat and that Old River's current and general trickery were not to be taken lightly. He nodded, wide-eyed, and when I helped him over the side I believe that he clung to my arm a little tighter than the maneuver itself warranted.

We still had nearly an hour to sunrise, but the first blue-gray fingers of dawn were already beginning to reach toward the Delta sky. Phil crouched in the bow, I just behind him, while Johnny steered us through the tricky current. Behind us, the second boat chattered in the darkness, as we headed upriver toward our hunting grounds, some two miles away.

It was bitter cold, and I questioned inwardly the wisdom of bringing my small son out on such a day. Right now, I thought, he may be so uncomfortable that the experience will ruin hunting for him. And then came the familiar sound of mortal tommy-gun combat. Phil was going ashore with the first Marine wave to hit the beach at Tarawa. Something stuck in my throat, and I prayed to the God of hunters and Marines and all good folk that this would be as close to such bloody reality as he would ever get. We turned from Old River into the chute that rippled across the overflowed bar. The wilderness closed in upon us in the narrow channel, and it grew darker again. Somewhere close to us in the tangle of tree and water, a branch crackled like a gunshot.

"What's that, Dad?" Phil whispered; and then aware that I must have recognized the fright in his voice, he added with bravado, "Better load this ol' gun. If that's a deer or something, better be ready." But he was easily dissuaded with the advice that we didn't load guns in the boat. And then, in a few minutes, the dinghy swerved toward shore. As he always did, Johnny had somehow picked out the tree that marked our place as different from the rest of the hazy, unending forest.

Now, at five thirty, there was a thin coating of ice among the willows on the shoreline, and the wind from the northwest had no kinship to the sunny South. Phil was shivering more than the rest of us, but the only complaint he made was, "My feet are kinda cold." And then we were ashore, a few hundred feet from the blinds. We dragged the boats onto the high grounds and covered them with the branches that we had cut and set aside the afternoon before.

Because his boots were not waders, Phil had to be contented with tossing out the decoys from shore. While I arranged them in wily disarray, he kept up a running fire of low-voiced questions. Did they really look like ducks to ducks? Did decoys ever get shot by mistake? Why couldn't you use real ducks for decoys? What if a real duck lit behind a decoy and wouldn't get up?

Then the decoys were all bobbing on the water. We entered our blind, glad that it was so close knit, and sat down on the logs to wait the coming of daybreak and ducks. On his log Phil set up a box full of .410's in an orderly row. I fished out the small packet of sandwiches, candy bars and apples and a thermos jug of coffee that would taste good about ten in the morning, and began a low-voiced final instruction in the art of duck mayhem. Phil listened intently for a few minutes, then tensed, and grabbed his gun.

"I hear something," he whispered, hoarse with excitement. He had. Behind us, a crow was laughing. Phil relaxed. In the grayness, a long line of water turkeys lanced low over the river. Phil raised his gun. His eyes were better than mine, and I stopped him just in time.

"It has to be daybreak anyway," I admonished. We looked at my watch. Another twenty minutes. We settled back to shivery whispering. Ten minutes, five. It was official daylight. Below us, Johnny called persuasively, and looking up to the south we saw a small flock, maybe six, hesitate and then begin streaking toward us.

"Heads down," I whispered. Phil ducked. "Ready . . . ready."

Phil would have first shot. Three inquisitive little teal braked themselves twenty feet in front of us and settled down among the decoys. "Now," I said.

Phil stood up in the blind. The teal rose in quick alarm. I heard a harmless click. I might have shot, but I was determined to watch my son's first encounter with a duck. His face was contorted in shame and rage; he continued to pull desperately on the trigger, and as the teal reached safety he screamed in frustration. He had forgotten to adjust from the .22 barrel to the .410. If I had laughed then, I believe he would have started swimming home.

"Happens to everybody one time or another," I comforted him. "Besides, those little teal count against the limit just like a big fat mallard. We didn't want them."

He grinned in appreciation, but there were angry tears in his eyes. "I'll get the next ones," he vowed. "And say, Dad"—he hesitated—"don't tell the other fellows about this, will you?"

Within the next fifteen minutes I learned the unwisdom of giving a ten-year-old a mug of strong coffee. It was good daylight now, and no ducks had come near since our first visitors, although several flights had arrowed tantalizing high. The hot coffee and cold weather made the demand of nature imperative for Phil.

"I got to go," he said.

"Hurry, boy," I told him. He slid through the blind, and stood up outside, fumbling his clothing with numbed hands. Behind and above us, I heard the familiar, heart-stopping rustle and twisted around. There, almost above Phil's head, flared two startled mallards, who had doubtless flown on a leisurely inspection trip from the feeding grounds on the other side of our landspit, and who had seen the friendly decoys before they saw Phil. We had looked every way except just behind us.

His mission still only midway of completion, Phil dove for the blind and his gun. This time I couldn't help myself. I did more than laugh. I howled. And after his first black moments, so did Phil. Now we have a slightly unprintable poem about it.

The sun came up, warming us and inviting our tongues to speech. The sky was now disappointingly empty of ducks. Our necks craned skyward, as I told Phil in snatches the hunting tales I remembered best. About the incredible time that two snipe, arising from separate ditches fifty feet apart, crossed in flight just as I fired and so fell at the one shot. About dove hunting at his age, when the bean fields were so thick with game that boys sometimes killed doves with air rifles. About how we used to try unsuccessfully to emulate Daniel Boone and bark squirrels. About my dad's setters, and last year's woeful attempt to find bear, boar or deer in the Great Smokies. My father had talked so to me and, remembering my own disbelief, I wondered how much Phil believed.

The morning wore on. It was nearly eight, and Phil was munching his second sandwich, when we heard the fellows below us quacking in insistent invitation. This time the ducks were really coming in. And this time Phil and I would be ready.

In beautiful, unafraid flight, the flock of mallard descended, perhaps twenty of them, glinting green and brown in the dubious light. Just ahead of us they divided, half of them swerving to the north, where our companions waited, the rest settling comfortably in front of us, riding the wind waves and chuckling happy among themselves. Phil was trembling, and I could hear his breath come shudderingly. The first shot roared from the other blind, then another and another.

"Now," I said. We rose. Phil was ready. He fired at a rising mallard, and struck him fair with the small .410 load. The fat male was dead when he hit the water. I emptied my pump gun at the rest and two fell, one dead and the other wounded and swimming. Even as I fired, Phil was yelling like a Comanche. He took away half of the blind in his wild rush to the water, and it was no use to call him back. The cold water closed in above his boot tops, but he reached the mallard, and holding it high began a whooping victory dance. My wounded duck was swimming hard, so I shot again, and crawled through the badly disarranged blind. Phil quieted then, and slipped another shell into his single barrel while I trudged for the two ducks that were floating slowly downstream. Intent only on recovering them, I paid no attention to Phil's suddenly low-voiced warning. And then, as if in proof that some ducks can be as idiotic as others are wise, two unconcerned pintails came in fast, hesitated and with me in plain sight, began to come down. In one hand I held a mallard. In the other was my still unloaded gun.

"Shoot," I yelled to Phil. I didn't have to. The .410 popped again, and a wounded pintail hit the water within fifteen feet of me. And once more in violation of all rules of hunting decorum the warshout of a young and mighty Leatherstocking smote the morning air. But Phil and I didn't care. And this time I didn't laugh when he laid his gun carefully down and headed for the water's edge in response to another urgent summons of nature.

"That ol' coffee sure is something," he said, taking a different kind of aim. And then with the offhand wisdom that marks the veteran hunter, he commented, "Say, Dad, those crazy ducks coming in that way over your head—that wouldn't happen again in a thousand years, would it?" No, I agreed, not in a thousand years. Happily we headed back to the blind and began repairing it. Before the morning was over other ducks were going to come our way. We knew it.

Not in a thousand years, said Phil, would two crazy ducks show such contempt of man. And never again would Phil and I recapture this morning of man and boy and guns; of father and son repeating the tribal rite of the first hunt together, a rite that surely goes back to the day of the club and slingshot. There would be other hunting trips together, I knew; trips more exciting and more productive than this. But never again could a first hunt be. We had shared it, and it belonged to the treasured past of no repeats. And maybe this is proper; for just as there must be limits on ducks, there must be a limit to the treasures which memory stores.

25

On Venal Scribbling

Among my odder keepsakes is a letter from Mister Ed Crump, who has been bossing Memphis since before I was born. It is not a love letter. Mister Ed had taken exception to a remark which I had ascribed to him in a *Holiday* magazine profile of the state of Tennessee. The offending comment, which had been printed several times before was: "Negroes don't vote in Memphis; they are voted." Which has been so, whether he said it just that way or not.

Mister Ed declared he hadn't said it. He added about four hundred more sulphurous words to tell me exactly where I stood with him. I was, he said, nothing but a venal scribbler who would sell my soul for a mess of pottage and that he had lasted and would last a lot longer in Memphis than ever I would in the Mississippi Delta.

I answered that I was sure he had a greater first hand knowledge of man's venality than I did, and then I tore up the letter, because he was an old man and a cousin of Brodie Crump, and Brodie and Louise liked him. Instead, I tucked Mister Ed's letter away in a special file, which includes a scatological denunciation of the *Daily Courier* by Gerald

Smith, who was Huey Long's senior jackal; an assortment of letters and press clippings in which Bilbo put me in my place; sundry comments made about me by John Rankin in and out of Congress; a manifesto regarding the *Courier* by Huey Long himself, which is probably the choicest item; and an assortment of other withering messages including editorials in the *Daily Worker* and unfriendly comment by Lillian Smith and Walter White. It is very satisfactory to be told off from left to right.

But Mister Ed was the only one who said my scribbling was venal, and his comment set me to thinking then and afterwards about the times I have been tempted, and of the opportunity for journalistic venality in general.

So I might as well come clean.

We had been publishing the *Daily Courier* for maybe two weeks when a hotel gambling game was raided. The hotel proprietor had some political power. Why his dice game was raided, I don't know, but it was, and since the *Courier's* office was just a block from the hotel, we knew all about the raid within a very few minutes. The police gave us the names of the house men and the gamblers, and we prepared to give Hammond a very local headline.

We had not even set the story in type before one of the house men turned up. We had played together as boys. He was diffident to begin with, but finally he told me that his boss didn't want that story in the paper, and that he was willing to make it worth my while to keep the story out. My first impulse was to hit him, but I realized that he was just an emissary, and why bother; so I told him that the story would be in the next morning's *Courier*, and then asked him, as a friend, how high the hotel man had been willing to go to keep the story out of the paper. He grinned and said, "Ten dollars." Remember, those were depressed days.

The next cash offer came soon afterwards. Dudley LeBlanc, who much later was to gain notoriety as the producer of Hadacol, had announced his yearning for the governorship of Louisiana. The only thing I knew to his credit was his opposition to Long, but that wasn't enough. During his campaign, when he came to Hammond, he paid a visit to Sidney, our foreman, whom he had known. I was out at the time. He had departed before I returned later, but he had left me a message which Sidney sheepishly relayed. Dudley had said, so Sidney told me, that he would cherish our support, and if it were forthcoming, he would be proud to contribute fifty dollars to our general welfare.

Printer's ink in Louisiana wasn't always considered so cheap, even in those impoverished days. We had not been in business a year when a spotted sheep of a family to whom our own had been close for three generations dropped in and suggested that we have coffee. Over coffee he made a proposal which still inflates my ego, because I hadn't thought then, nor do I think now, that we were worth so much to Long. My tempter said that if we would just keep our mouths shut, as he delicately put it, we could have a completely equipped plant which figured out then at about twenty-five thousand dollars, a big slice of the state printing, which was considerable, and a lot of fairly legitimate advertising that went where the boys wanted it to go.

Bribes are not usually offered so baldly as were these, and we have had others that were less directly proffered. But all of them save one have had a common denominator. Except for that one, they came from politicians. Once, in 1940, it was my privilege to talk to a gracious lady, who was the wife of the President of the United States. Mrs. Roosevelt was the guest at a Nieman Fellowship dinner at the home of President Conant of Harvard, and during the evening we fell into conversation about the morals of newspapers, for which she had little love. Mrs. Roosevelt said that newspapers were fettered by their advertisers. I answered that to the contrary, almost the only threats or bribe offers which I had encountered had come from politicians.

The one variant is now a friendly memory. In the first year of our competitive fight in Greenville, I had written some critical editorial, the target of which I can't remember. In its wake came a telephone call from a merchant who had just begun to give us a half share or more of his advertising. He told me that he didn't like what I had written. I said I was sorry but that opinions were bound to be varied and that I'd be glad to discuss this issue with him. Never mind, he countered, he was a good advertiser, but he didn't see why he should advertise with us if we had such wrong ideas. I asked him if he was trying to frighten us, and when he made a noncommittal answer, I told him that we would give him one final advertisement, free, which would be on the front page, and which would reproduce our exact conversation. I hung up. An hour or so later, we met at a club luncheon. He clapped me on the back and told me I was too hot-tempered, and we have been friends and he has been a good advertiser ever since.

There are more rewarding venalities than scribbling, I am sure. For twenty years I have been trading words for groceries and rent and vacations and a newspaper monopoly and a lot of other necessities and luxuries. We can tally more than a hundred magazine articles and a half-dozen books, and editorials and news stories by the thousands. Most of them have provoked readers to bespeak their approval or anger, which is a reward in itself.

Before our marriage necessity caused me to turn out a

couple of true confessions, and, in collaboration with Hart Bynum, a future godfather of our first son, a Haitian adventure story, but either I couldn't or didn't want to master the pulp story technique, and we never sold another. Then, after the *Daily Courier* had started making loud and uncomplimentary noises in Huey Long's direction, somebody must have heard an echo in New York, and I received the first request for an article. That made us professionals. It also gave us stage-fright. Our inquirer was the *New Republic,* and it offered all of thirty dollars, which to us was a lot of money, for an article on Huey Long. After the letter lay on my desk for nearly a month, and was joined by a follow-up inquiry, Betty took charge. On Sunday morning, when we were about to drive out to my parents for the customary Sunday dinner, she announced that I was going to stay at home until I had at least begun the article. As a gesture, she locked me in, and by the time she brought me a platter of fried chicken from the farm, I had written my first political analysis for a magazine.

The *New Republic* asked for other articles and each one paid a month's rent. In the meanwhile I wrote verses. One poem was published, complete with art, in the *Ladies' Home Journal,* which paid twenty-five dollars. The *Atlantic Monthly* took another, for fifteen dollars, but printed it in a back-of-the-book-department, without identifying the author, which was apparently the way that magazine then broke in minor poetic apprentices; but hard as times were, I protested to the editor that I would have rather had my name appended to that deathless lyric without pay than to have received pay without the world's recognition. We did not, however, return the fifteen dollars.

What happened soon afterward might be considered poetic justice. Out of the blue came a letter from what was then a major magazine, and which, for reasons that will be understandable, will go unidentified. I had been highly recommended, the editor wrote, to do a cover story, a definitive study of Huey Long, his life and works. Would I be so kind as to oblige, and when could they expect the piece? Would I? Here was a chance to say what I thought of Long to a wider audience than the *New Republic* or the *Daily Courier* commanded; and here too, was a sale to a big-time magazine which would most certainly pay for the accouchement, about five months away, of our first-born.

I put my heart into that piece. So did the cover illustrator who turned out a magnificent caricature. The article was enthusiastically accepted. In due time, the proofs arrived. After another month, the publishers wrote that the article would appear in the March issue which would be out in mid-February. Our progeny was due to appear in late March or early April, and we were counting on a check. We were confident that we would receive three hundred dollars though how we fixed on that wondrous amount, I don't know. The check didn't come in January, or even by mid-February, so I wrote a think-nothing-of-it letter, casually mentioning that my records showed that we hadn't been paid for the article, an inconsequential matter really, and no doubt an oversight, but . . .

A week later we received an answer, together with a check. The letter said that in accordance with its new method of reimbursement, the magazine was happy to enclose its check as part payment, and in payment of the balance was giving me five hundred free copies of the issue containing my article, which the circulation department would gladly send to any five hundred friends whose names I would send in. The magazine sold for fifty cents, so I guess I made three hundred dollars for that piece after all, because the check was for fifty dollars; but it is impossible to pay an obstetrician with magazines.

I don't have any illusions about what I write, whether editorials or articles or books. It is mostly opinionated, personalized stuff, having in common only my belief in the rightness of what I am putting down, and the capability of bringing forth a lot of letters, angry or otherwise, from all manner of people. What I have tried to do in my writing is to show my fellow Southerners what is still wrong about us and tell our fellow Americans elsewhere what is right about us, and a great deal is right, even if the professional South-baiters take it as a personal insult every time I say so. Will Percy told me that I was a pamphleteer, and thinking it made me feel bad to have him say so, he reminded me that Tom Paine also was a pamphleteer. Harry Ashmore, who is editor of the Arkansas *Gazette* and the most discerning and unimpressed of my friends, says I have a one-idea mind and that I've got more mileage out of that one idea than has any newspaperman in all history.

I like to get letters that are provoked by something I've written. We get thousands every year. Except for those that patently come from crackpots and worse, we try to answer them all and not perfunctorily, or with cheek-turning response to savage denunciation and plain meanness.

One letter, an alarming one, informed me that the writer was a disabled veteran, and that when the proper time came, he and thousands of red-blooded Americans were going to make the streets run red with the blood of niggers, nigger lovers, Jews and Catholics, including me. I answered that to judge from his letter his disability must be a mental one. To my surprise, I received in return a bewildered communication from the man, professing not to remember having written the previous letter, explaining that he was actually mentally disabled and unable to do more than piece work because of his recurrent attacks, and apologizing for having annoyed me as he had annoyed others during his seizures. We sent him a little money along with a note of sympathy. . . . Maybe it was a racket at that.

These letters generally fall into four categories. The greatest number come from those who disagree violently and emotionally with you, the second greatest from those who agree because what you have said strengthens previously held convictions, the third greatest from friendly, open-hearted people, many of them persons of great ability and achievement, who take time out to give you a figurative handshake and a helpful suggestion, or to share an experience which your words have recalled. The least but most annoying number come from the cranks who lie close to one side or the other of sanity's borderline.

We answer all but the worst crank mail, and I have made some good friends that way, and have met up with a number of them. I don't know why it is, but young Catholic priests make up the largest occupational group of those who write us, and all of these seem to be concerned, spiritually and sociologically, with the American racial dilemma.

But the biggest pile of mail I ever received from any group came from more than a thousand irate Northerners who failed to take lightly a heavy-handed satire which I wrote for *Look*, and which neither the editors nor I thought would be accepted as anything but a bit of fun-poking with a moral. It was written not long after an enterprising but none-too-careful reporter from Pittsburgh cropped his hair and acquired a sunburn, and then spent a few weeks touring the South as a Negro with a representative of the N.A.A.C.P. as his guide. His distorted, prejudiced and frequently erroneous stories were widely syndicated.

I wrote an answering series, which was a little less widely circulated, since four of the metropolitan Northern newspapers which had printed his accounts couldn't be bothered with anything from the other side. Then I thought of caricaturing his series which he had titled "In the Land of Jim Crow" with an article which I named "In the Land of Grim Snow." In it, I sent north a nonexistent reporter, dubbed Ol' Fearless, disguised as a New Yorker, to find out what went on in that benighted region. Ol' Fearless, I reported, acquired his New Yorker disguise by divorcing his wife and going on a diet of dry Martinis and barbiturates. The whole thing was practically slapstick, and neither *Look* nor I was angry with anyone. But a thousand Northern readers of that magazine took us seriously, and wrote, indignantly and even viciously, that I had my nerve, that the picture I had drawn was completely unfair, and who won the war anyway? Some five hundred Southerners wrote sic 'em. But the first prize for regional naïveté went to Jimmy Wechsler, the editor of the New York *Post*, whom I had known on *PM*, and who is a humorless, dedicated man. When Jimmy was through with me, editorially speaking, it was hard to tell me from Simon Legree or the Imperial Wizard. *Time* delightedly picked up a part of his blast and asked me for an answer, but didn't run it, explaining that my comment, whatever it was, was too flippant.

And I guess it was. It isn't often that we have chance down thisaway to tell our neighbors up thataway to stop acting like they say we do.

26

The Great Mule-Train Race

Whenever newspaper editors convene, it is all but inevitable that one subject on the program will relate to the propriety or wisdom of an editor's active participation in community affairs. Similarly, whenever we run out of targets on the *Democrat-Times,* it is all but inevitable that we complain about the poor service Greenville gets from the Illinois Central Railroad, which elsewhere is a good railroad for passengers, but which isn't along the river. So, as introduction to my own views about the editor's proper role in the life of the community, I think I ought to tell the story of the great race between a string of plantation mules and the Illinois Central's once-a-day Memphis-to-Greenville train which we know but do not love by the name of Old Reluctant.

The two most irrepressible members of the staff planned the race. They were Tom Karsell, our managing editor, who is now in Korea, and Edwin Vincent, the city editor, a girl with a boy's name and a man's heart, who died last winter before she was thirty, with twelve years on the *Democrat-Times* behind her. Tom, a lanky, sardonic Indianian, was a caricaturist before he found with us his first newspaper job when he came out of the army in 1945 with three medals and four wounds. I think he and Edwin had both been frightened by locomotives when they were very young, for they were anti-railroad, and especially anti-Illinois Central. This made them, at the time, popular with the Board of Directors of the Greenville Chamber of Commerce, which had just emitted the loudest and most anguished of its many protests at the way the Illinois Central was treating Mississippi's fastest-growing city.

As far back as I can remember, the Greenville Chamber of Commerce has been objecting with uninterrupted lack of success to the Illinois Central's behavior. In what I am told were the good old days, that railroad and the predecessor which it purchased, the Yazoo and Mississippi Valley, ran three passenger trains each way daily between Memphis and New Orleans, five hundred miles down the river. This was the river route, serving such intermediate communities as Greenville, Vicksburg, Natchez, after a fashion, and Baton Rouge. When the I.C. took over, it began cutting off one passenger train after another, making the river route primarily a freight line, and concentrating its passenger service on its original Memphis–New Orleans route, sixty and more miles inland from our river towns. I am sure the railroad had, or thought it had, sound economic reasons, among them the discovery that buses and automobiles could do anything the railroad could do better than the railroad was willing to do it. Whenever the C. of C. protested, the Illinois Central further reduced the service, which would lead to more protests which would lead to more reductions, which led finally to the great race.

By 1949 one lone passenger train, Old Reluctant, puffed its way from Memphis to only as far south as Vicksburg. Old Reluctant required about six hours to go between Memphis and Greenville, a hundred and fifty mile stretch, and it backed ignominiously into Greenville on a spur line, for we lie ten miles west of Leland on the river route's so-called main line. The slow service was more than any self-respecting Chamber of Commerce could tolerate, even though none of its members would be caught dead in one of those dingy, creaking, ancient items of rolling stock.

So the directors had protested again. We were laughing about the duly reported protest one afternoon, and Tom said, "Hell, I could outrun Old Reluctant from Leland to Greenville." Edwin made some scoffing remark about Tom's ability to outrun a balky mule, and Tom's face lit up with inspiration. "Let's race mules, against Old Reluctant," he said, "plantation mules. The First Annual Mule-Train race," he exulted. "A national classic, and what will the I.C. think about that?"

We found out what the Illinois Central thought just a few days after we put out the first advance stories written in deadpan seriousness. The stories, which the press associations carried, related that in remonstrance against poor and slow passenger service, the *Delta Democrat-Times* would race relays of fast plantation mules against the lone passenger train, from Cleveland, Mississippi, to Greenville, a forty-mile course. Our first story and the later ones, told of the enthusiastic approval the proposed race was getting—which was true enough—from mayors of all the little towns on the way, and from civic clubs, and mule fanciers and—not surprisingly—from the Chamber of Commerce.

Because newspapers always look for odd stories to lighten the daily grist, our pre-race dispatches were used all over the country. We improvised new sidelights as we went along. One rider would hand over a cotton-picker's sack of alleged mail to the next mule-express man in the relay. In each town, where change would be made from mule to mule, the mayor would give the mule a key to the city, and a bunch of hay and carrots to the rider. Miss Mule of Mississippi, a beautiful Delta girl, would greet the victor in Greenville. So would a band, the Legion, the mayor and other officials. We promised that the mules would win, but we didn't tell how.

The angry Illinois Central sent down a delegation to talk everyone out of the stunt, for the publicity wasn't good. We laughed at the protesters. So did our mayor and the other mayors along the right of way. Newspapers everywhere wanted more details. We supplied them. *Time* and *Life* and Paramount newsreel decided to cover the event. The Southern director of the Society for the Prevention of Cruelty to Animals telephoned me from Florida, and warned that the society would be forced to seek an injunction if we persisted in our callous program, since it was well known that a mule's constitution would be seriously damaged if it raced a locomotive. Only when I swore him to secrecy and told how the race would be run and won, did he withdraw his threat and hang up the receiver laughing.

The Illinois Central didn't know what we were up to, and I am sure that they were fearful that if we used enough mules, one after another, they could beat Old Reluctant, because a properly trained mule can run fast for a short distance. We had the railroaders either way, for what good would it be to them to answer our predictions with a denial that mules could beat their train?

Our mules won that race, all right, but like so many races, it was fixed. The first mule and rider got off to a fast start in Cleveland, after fitting ceremonies. They galloped a few blocks and then pulled off to a little side road where a cattle truck and one of the Greenville police cars were waiting. The panting mule was pushed into the truck, to be taken back home, and the rider, in Wild West attire, was sped by police car to the outskirts of Boyle, a few miles away, where another mule was waiting. There he mounted the fresh mule and galloped into Boyle; and since mules look pretty much alike anyhow, the train crew and passengers on Old Reluctant were baffled when they saw the same rider and presumably the same mule receiving at the station the accolade of mayor and citizens. Then a new mule and rider took off again, and the fraud was practiced all the way to Greenville. There the last mule and Larry Pryor, the state legislator who rode the final lap in a Southern colonel's frockcoat, broad-brimmed hat, string tie and horse pistols, almost lost the race. The mule was trotting to the finish-line ribbon which stretched across the track at the station, when it became frightened of the bands, the crowd and the little boys who were tagging alongside. Larry had wanted to make a photo-finish, so the hind end of Old Reluctant was close to the hind end of the mule when the mule balked. Old Reluctant might have won the race had not several desperate citizens pulled and pushed the mule to the finish line.

The story, with the inside account of how the race was won, was published the next day on the front pages of hundreds of Sunday-morning papers. But we didn't get better passenger service. In fact, the service got so much worse that most of Greenville pretends that we don't have any passenger service at all, a make-believe which I am sure the Greyhound people and the Southern Airways enjoy; and we aren't really angry any more at the Illinois Central, which had to choose between spending a lot of money to give us decent passenger service or all but cutting out the service altogether. We don't miss each other. Only our mules our lonely.

Some people, and not just those who were friends of the railroad, criticized the stunt. They said it wasn't dignified on the part of the paper or myself, and that we should simply report news and not make it with such prejudiced stunts as the mule race. And some of my fellow editors say that we daily pundits should maintain a sort of Jovian detachment, encouraging the good and denouncing the bad, but not taking personal part in the good or the bad of civic life.

I disagree. That may be proper in a very large city, where the editor and the newspaper are alike impersonal, and where there exists no longer the frontier urge to grow and the frontier pride in growing. I don't see how I can stand apart in Greenville, praising and deriding and warning, and expect to be taken as anything but a town scold. I don't think a newspaper editor should run for public office and remain an editor, nor would I accept such an obviously political pat as a colonelcy on a governor's staff, in case a Mississippi governor would ever be weak-minded enough to offer me that dubious honor. I probably should not have served even on our school board, though I think that is debatable. I believe I should serve on our Library Board, as I do. I ask myself one question. Will such activity, and such acceptance of quasi-political or other public service help Greenville, or Mississippi or the South, or conceivable, even my country? I don't ask whether such participation will make me biased, because I am already biased about these things.

And so it is that the *Democrat-Times*—and individually Betty and the staff and I—participate in a great many enterprises which add up to an expression of a community's drive to economic and political and even spiritual betterment. I hope this doesn't sound fatuous for it isn't meant that way.

On my newspaper's balance sheet appears a tabulation of investments in such non-journalistic ventures as a rice farm, a land-improvement association, a county fair, civic softball and basketball leagues, Greenville's professional baseball association, an industry-locating service and an air line. Having invested in them as civic enterprises, I want them to succeed, and am therefore prejudiced in their behalf. The rice-planting scheme, in which the investors—or contributors—non-farmers all, were told they wouldn't get their money back, and didn't, has led to the large-scale culture of an entirely new crop in the Delta. The non-profit land improvement association investment represented the diversion of the grounds and clubhouse of the old country club—now surrounded by the growing city—to sites for three new churches, a new high school, a public swimming pool, a youth recreation center, and public parks. The stock in the fair will never reach par, but we do have a fair and cattle and livestock show in a land where a generation ago nothing but six-cent cotton and hungry tenants and bankrupt farmers would have been exhibited. The baseball and softball enterprises make money for no one, but they add to a town's recreational outlets. And the industry-locating service has brought us a factory and will probably find more industry for us, so that was a few hundred newspaper dollars well invested.

In such activity we find a principal reason for being. The cadets at the Greenville Air Base swim in a beautiful outdoor pool because the *Democrat-Times,* when I was in the Army, thought that it would be a good idea for the people of Greenville to build a pool for the cadets. The citizens contributed the money. The paper was the catalyst. Each year the *Democrat-Times* gives one hundred dollars each to the outstanding graduates of the Greenville white high school, the Negro high school, and one of the county high schools. It's not much, but all of the white recipients and all but one of the Negro recipients have gone to college, and more than half of them—including all of the Negroes—have told me that they might not otherwise have gone to college. One of them, who is in medical school now, is going to find it easier to put himself through college because our old foemen and friends of the Illinois Central are giving him a summer job as a dining-car waiter. Betty was a pioneer and an original member of the Park Commission, the first in Mississippi to put through an over-all recreational program for white and Negro children and adults, with a full-time director, supervised playgrounds and a fine budget of twenty-five thousand dollars a year.

Every year I give commencement talks in a myriad of white and Negro high schools in the Delta and to college and university graduating classes, as many as I can schedule, because I think that too is important; and in the years since the war I have spoken in forty-four states, not trying to shield or gloss over the manifest ills of the South, but to bring the people I love best, those of the South, and those of this nation as a whole, closer together in understanding.

While I was putting together some random notes in the summer of 1952, before I began writing this book, I came across the May issue of *The Reporter*—not the admirable and partisan national magazine but the equally partisan mimeographed monthly publication of the Greenville Chamber of Commerce. Our *Reporter* that month tabulated the outstanding events of the past several weeks; and I was struck by the fullness of the paper's participation in them. Here are the principal headlines:

CHAMBER HONORS OFFICIALS OF U.S. AIR FORCE AT PARTY

DIXIE 31ST DIVISION CONVOY BIVOUACS IN GREENVILLE

INDUSTRIAL PROSPECTS CONTINUE LOOKING AT GREENVILLE

CHAMBER COMPLETES EXHIBITS FOR SOUTHERN AIRWAYS HEARING

CHAMBER HONORS U.S. GYPSUM COMPANY ON 50TH ANNIVERARY

DELTA FAIR AND LIVESTOCK SHOW HOLDS MEETING

LION OIL NEWS FEATURES MISSISSIPPI DELTA RECREATION NEEDS FOR AIR CADETS

Eight stories of efforts to build one little city in one of the least-developed states: stories to be laughed at in places that are larger and entrenched, but important to Greenville, Mississippi, and therefore to Mississippi, the state, and in turn to that slow-churning region, the South, and ultimately to the parent land.

Chamber Honors Air Force. . . .

Two three-star generals and a dazzling array of lesser brass converged upon Greenville that day. They and a selection of companionable Greenvillians spent the afternoon on the river on our *Mistuh Charley* and Gervys Lusk's *Delphine*, and that night I was toastmaster at the dinner at which some two hundred Greenvillians honored our guests. Since generals are also human, I doubt that the boat party or the party as a whole had any adverse effect, some months later, upon the decision to make the Greenville base, then under civilian contract, a permanent jet-training base; and while I wish there were no need for any military training facilities anywhere, I am glad that as long as we need them, the Air Force has placed one permanently in Greenville.

Dixie 31st Division. . . .

We weren't going to let the boys of the National Guard's 31st Division, whose commanding officer and many of whose headquarters staff officers live in Greenville, spend a couple of nights on the edge of town without making them welcome. So five men were appointed as a committee to give them a good time, and our first decision was to distribute without charge the necessary several thousand copies of the *Democrat-Times* which would list for them on the front page each day the dances, the free movies, and the other entertainment which would be provided. They were just five thousand or so youngsters in uniform, most of them not from Mississippi at all, or even from the South since the original division had been augmented by draftees; but a Mississippi town's Chamber of Commerce and its newspaper combined, as they should have, to give them a good time; and it couldn't have been managed without those free papers that told the soldiers where to go and when.

Industrial Prospects Continue. . . .

Hardly a month goes by without the arrival in Greenville of a scouting party from some industry or another looking for a Southern site. We can't get them all, and we wouldn't want all of those who come looking, but we'd like a few more if only to keep our carpet and wall-board plants from feeling too lonely. And so, whenever such visitors arrive, the *Mistuh Charley* becomes Greenville's official cruiser, and no matter whether it is morning, noon or even night, John Gibson and I forget about running a newspaper and become captain, crew and commentators for the sight-seeing jaunt which always ends with a lunch or dinner ashore; and afterwards, we foregather with our fellow industry-snarers, compare notes on our guests' reactions and lay traps for the next ones; and all this too is an editor's business.

Chamber Completes Exhibits. . . .

Dark was the despair when the Illinois Central all but abolished its passenger service along the river; but our hearts grew light again when after many disappointments, Greenville was included in the extension of the Southern Airways system. At last we were linked closely with the outside world, for whatever that was worth. Dinners, celebrations, a gala opening day, even local buying of not a little stock in the growing company greeted the opening of airlines service in Greenville. And then, only a year later, came the unpleasant report that the Civil Aeronautics Board was undecided as to whether to make the service permanent. Once again, with something less than a newspaperman's impartiality, I joined my fellow citizens in pleading the case for Southern Airways, both in editorials and in a rhapsodic letter which became part of the exhibit for the Board. We still have our airline, and all of us believe those letters from Greenvillians helped.

And so, on and on. A delegation from little neighboring Indianola calls on us to see how we handled the publicity which ensured the one-sided vote in favor of the carpet-factory bond election, for the State Agricultural and Industrial Board director has told them that the *Democrat-Times*'s selling job for that election was the best in the history of the Balance Agriculture With Industry Program. . . . Johnny and I take the morning off to tour again the Gypsum Plant, to eat a commemorative dinner at the club—my fifth dinner out that week—and to join in the chorus of praise for Greenville's first sizable industry. . . . The Delta Fair and Livestock Association is shaky, and we agree at the called meeting of directors and creditors—since the *Democrat-Times* is a creditor to the tune of two thousand dollars and Johnny is a director—to take stock in payment and to devote news and editorial columns for the next month to keep the fair going. . . . A writer from the *Lion Oil News* comes to Greenville, close behind another from Standard Oil, by coincidence, in quest of a new angle on the Delta and cotton, and we spend the evening together while I rack my brains for some new way to sing praises. . . . The commander at the Air Base is worried about recreation for the cadets on weekends, so Betty and I are included in the score of our fellow townsmen who meet with the commanding officer and the city fathers. Before we know it we are on the entertainment committee as official dance chaperones; and after the first dance we bring home six foreign cadets, the advance guard of the host of impeccably polite, bewildered and so-young boys from Scandinavia and France and Belgium and England and Holland and Italy, who learn that they can drop in on Saturdays and Sundays anytime, and without advance warning, to ride or read or eat or nap or court the girls they have brought along.

I suppose that if we were not so engaged in Greenville's business we could do a better job with our own. Our newspaper would be better, professionally, perhaps, if Betty and I stuck to watching the make-up and the over-all news play and to writing Olympian editorials; if Johnny Gibson only watched cost figures instead of serving on C. of C. committees; if Lou Crump left her charities alone and the boys in the shop quit spraining fingers playing softball, and if the men and women in news and advertising and circulation didn't take individual parts in the hundred and one civic activities and controversies that engross the people of any community.

A better newspaper, probably. Better citizens in a better town, no. I trust myself and the folks around me on the *Democrat-Times* to be open-minded and fair, which is something else again from being impartial, when partisan issues arise. I insist upon partisanship. I would be worried about taking sides only if we always took the same side. If there is any controversial or even non-controversial public figure in Greenville whom we haven't patted on one occasion only to slap at a later time, I don't know who he is. Our paper has been called a lot of names, but no one has ever said that it was the creature of any clique, and no one has ever nominated me for a popularity contest, so I think we're safe.

Meanwhile, we're also very busy.

27

It's How We Like It

Just about the silliest remark that was ever made to me came from an intelligent New York woman. She said, in a tone of pity and admiration, "I think it's splendid the way you've dedicated yourself to that little place in Mississippi," as if I were another Dr. Livingston, deep in a Southern jungle. It wouldn't have occurred to her that I thought she also lived in a jungle and that I preferred the leafy kind; but there was no use to try to explain it to her because she knew too much about Mississippi and small towns and had got all of it from books. So I just said, "Well, down home I can always take a nap after lunch before going back to work."

As runner-up for the grand prize for condescending ignorance, I would select a letter written to me by an editor of a national magazine in answer to my suggestion that I do an interpretive piece about Mississippi. I am not going to name the magazine because I still want to sell him that article and some others. He wrote, "I don't think Mississippi is ready for an article yet," just as a knowing mother would tell a small son that he's not big enough for a cap pistol.

There are forty-seven states which are richer than Mississippi; and, according to scenic preferences there are forty-seven which may be more beautiful. Most of them are cooler than Mississippi in the summertime and not as damp in the early spring. As for our Delta, its landscape is not varied enough for some, for it is simply an unbelievably flat alluvial plain. The only elevations for miles around Greenville are the levees, and an assortment of earthen mounds built many centuries ago, and the eleven-foot rise on which we built our house. Water moccasins thrive in our swamps and sloughs and rivers, but I can't remember ever publishing a story of a death from a moccasin bite. The Mississippi River which runs by our communal door is hidden from view unless one is on it or drives on top of the guardian levees to look at it; and it is a tawny, dangerous main stream of the American continent about which no tin-pan-alley composer ever wrote a love song that I know of. Our seasonal cycles of rain and drought are made to order for cotton, and cotton was until only yesterday the Delta's sole economic reason for being. Our countryside is blotched by more unpainted shacks than I have seen anywhere else to the square rural mile, and we Deltans share a persistent and bi-racial disinclination to mend a fence or repair a door or patch a roof or sharpen a plow or take farm equipment in out of the rain, and this may be fairly attributed to a long unawareness that cheap labor is the most expensive. Our fertile soil produces feed and food stuffs and cotton and pasturage as lavishly as any place in the world, but it does equally well by weeds, and weeds and inertia sometimes combine to choke out much of the Delta's natural beauty and more of its potential wealth. Only a quarter century ago our great river was an unceasing threat to field and town, and sometimes overran them, wetly devouring and destroying and nurturing the land. Two thirds of our population is Negro, and among our white citizenry are many who, while protesting today that their laborers will not do an honest day's work for an exorbitant day's pay, forget our own historic indisposition to give an honest day's pay for a full day's work.

Having set down these failings and handicaps and disadvantages, by no means a complete list, I can say also that they are dwarfed by the aspects that we find dear and challenging and beautiful in a frontier land of ferment and persistence and unexplored vistas. If the Delta is overly hot or dusty or wet or barren for a time each year, it is also green and cool and fecund and bright, and who would want perfection without the intervening contrast that makes perfection recognizable?

And what we like about this land most of all is the sense of togetherness it gives.

This togetherness is not altogether unique for it can be discovered in most communities which are small and homogeneous and agricultural in background. But the togetherness of the Delta and to a lesser degree, of Mississippi, has an especial quality, for it is the legacy of a people who have endured much and lost much and won a little against a variety of foemen. It is a togetherness born of the struggle of man against river, man against conquering man, man against plague, man against prejudice, man against his own fool's dream of easy gold, man against a dead deadly past, and man against the questioning Cain who is his worser self.

I would rather be a part of the togetherness of the Delta than to share in the making of any other chapter in the great story of America; for here Betty and I have found adventure, contentment, purposefulness and a measure of success. We are provincial newspaper people, happy in a little city which is large enough for challenge and small enough for us to know the challenged and the challengers by their first names. An enlightened provincialism was important a century ago when our nation was more provincial than enlightened; and certainly it is just as important in our own bedeviled age, for the rise of the great cities and the general dominance of urban society has not yet been accompanied by any appreciable decline in man's suspicion of his nameless and all but faceless fellows.

To us the small town's threads appear as strong, as beautiful, as variegated, as needful and as stimulating as any in the enduring American tapestry. I believe that in the towns and in the small cities of our nation can be found the answer to the dilemma which haunts man as he moves further and further toward collective security, and in so moving detaches himself from individual responsibility toward the neighbor, the town, the state, the nation and God.

I am afraid that this detachment directly threatens the proper conduct of newspapers, and so my primary concern is a selfish one. But whatever endangers freedom of speech and of the press directly endangers every other advantage of a free society. Our democratic freedoms cannot be disassociated and they should not be separately scrutinized or defended. Even so, I cannot help but look from a newspaperman's vantage point at the decline of the individual sense of responsibility. It seems to me that so many of my neighbors and fellow citizens have grown too indifferent because the more we rely on the central whole, the less we are inclined to help animate its parts; and this retreat from personal responsibility has an ominous meaning to a newspaper editor. I am saying nothing new, and certainly more knowing men than I have cried out against every aspect of the threats to the free press and to all our freedoms; but another voice may also properly be lifted. I know that the freedom of information is endangered even here in a remote little city in the lower Mississippi because of the exclusion of newspapermen from more than two thirds of the distant world. I know that the free press is confused and thereby endangered by the very bigness of government which we have created out of our need for security. The small newspaper is the most helpless victim of information by handout and carefully edited official releases and the withholding or distortion of information through political censorship, because we cannot keep our own men in Washington and so must frequently fall down in our handling of the biggest American story, the story of self-government at the federal and state levels. And the small newspaper is also especially threatened by economic pressures, by the costs of publication and the growth of competing media, all of which can be deterrents to its freedom.

Even the best-meaning patriotic citizens in my town and everywhere contribute to this insecurity. They want the over-simplification of the comic strip by which the corruption that festers in the body politic today is simplified into proof that Democrats and bureaucrats are all bad while private-enterprise Republicans are all good, forgetting that the briber of the little federal job holder is almost always some representative of private enterprise who seeks special illegal favor.

Here in Greenville we know the danger of extremism, against which no free institution can forever prevail. The man who agrees with us is a patriot, and he who disagrees is a Red. Mississippi's politicians denounce the national tieup between racketeers and politicians, and refuse to admit that prohibition is a cynical farce in our state. Within Mississippi a national bus company goes into the slot-machine business in racket-ridden Biloxi for 60% of the take, and those slot machines which symbolize political immorality still whirl merrily in the country clubs and veterans' huts of my state and most others for the pleasure of the select.

Greenville has prided itself on a tradition of tolerance for the dissimilar. But here no less than elsewhere I sense now the danger to freedom of the press and the freedom of the human mind that arises from insistence upon the strait jacket of conformity. It is harder and harder for a man or a newspaper to differ from the majority, especially when he takes the unpopular side against a large and frightened majority. We Americans are a frightened people today. In our fear we may forget that a democracy has more moral validity as a shield for the minority of race and religion and political and economic opinion than as a bludgeon for the majority.

Loyalty to their free institutions and to a government which preserves them is the first temporal obligation of Americans. But the editors and teachers of America in particular know that today the risks of the loyal non-conformists are so dangerously great as to circumscribe their very intellectual freedom, for the man is branded a suspect traitor who says "I doubt it" or "Prove it" or "He is a liar" when histrionic heroes and political heels seek to turn themselves into latter-day saints. And the fact that all this has been said many times before does not make it less important to say it again.

I can see it all from here. As I sit at my desk to talk over with my small news staff the best way to get a story which the persons involved do not want us to have, I know that a free press and all our freedoms will be endangered if I become afraid to print every story that has meaning for my town or to comment upon the controversial happening. And I know that when my fellow citizens begrudge me the obligation or seek to punish me for fulfilling it, they likewise endanger the freedoms which they so glibly praise.

As I walk across the street to cover a city-court session, I know that my freedom and all our freedoms are imperiled whenever any defendant or complainant in any court in the land is dealt with unjustly or too generously because of his color or his religion or his financial status, because of his political connections or lack of them or because good and intelligent men refuse to seek judicial office or serve on juries or concern themselves with the conduct of officers of the law.

When I attend a library-board meeting, I know that our freedoms are in danger when complete and equal access to the collective mind of mankind is denied any of our citizens. As a library-board member I know the peril of the self-appointed censor, the indifferent city councilman and the inequality of opportunity for learning to which our Southern dual library system and our unequal schools attest.

When I go to the City Hall to talk with the mayor or pay my taxes or cast a ballot or attend a council meeting, I know that therein all of our freedoms are ultimately tested, and that they remain unsafe as long as 75 per cent of the people of my state are either dissuaded from voting or can't be bothered to vote, and when the average national participation in self-government is less than 60 per cent of all Americans over twenty-one.

When on Sundays I kneel in church with my wife and my sons, I know that all freedoms, the freedom of the press and of political determination and of the very soul, are endangered when the worshipers in our temples look with contempt upon each other's faith or the skin color of any of the children of God; for the political democracy of the Western world, inspired by the Christian and Hebraic faiths, rests upon the concept of the dignity of man, so that freedom of faith and self-government and human dignity cannot long outlast each other.

And when each morning and afternoon I pass the decaying homes of an older and for some a more gracious and leisurely day, I know that our society, our freedoms and our purposefulness on this earth are endangered when the parent runs alley-cat free and the guidance of the child is left to school and church and juvenile court. The first man had the freedom of the alley-cat.

A wise woman once said to me that there are only two lasting bequests we can hope to give our children. One of these she said is roots, the other, wings. And they can only be grown, these roots and these wings, in the home. We want our sons' roots to go deep into the soil beneath them and into the past, not in arrogance but in confidence.

One Saturday afternoon my three boys and I went down to the little cypress-speared lake which fronts our home to hunt for moccasins. The southern end of the lake is thick with bramble growth and bushes and a multitude of great and small trees which afford a home and haven for many creatures. As we approached, a frightened procession of water fowl streaked toward the small dike which separates our lake from the next and more heavily wooded one. In the van, swam nine or ten tiny wood ducks, not six weeks out of their shells. Behind them in anxious protective haste, scurried the mother duck. The four of us and Toppy and Piglet, who are dogs, reached the dike just as they flashed across it. The excited dogs ran toward them. The baby ducks were already in the water again before our curious pets came near. We were close too. The mother, not twenty feet from us, her children safely afloat again and headed toward the underbrush, braked herself to a water-sloshing stop. She turned to face us and swam in a wide semi-circle, beating the lake with her wings and coming within a few feet of the now completely bewildered dogs. Before her maneuver was completed, the little wood ducks had disappeared. She followed them to safety.

The boys were delighted. They would not have let the dogs harm the wood ducks anyway, but they were pleased that the mother duck had attended to the situation herself. Tommy, who is seven, summed up the event. "Shows what you can do when you have to," he said.

We can still do what we have to. America is yet the land of miracles, and the South is performing its own share today. The Southern performance is regional, but I do not consider healthy regionalism a vice or a threat to anyone's security; for the part is of the whole and when our first pride is in the part, does not that ensure strengthening of the sense of personal relationship and responsibility? I am prouder that the South, including Mississippi, has, for instance, all but wiped out lynching than I would be if the United States government itself had been compelled to act. I am prouder that my fellow townsmen have been so greatly tolerant of our opinions which differed from theirs and that we have lived happily among them despite these differences than I would be if we had survived by federal order and federal guarantees of our constitutional liberty to disagree.

And there are less tangible reasons why we don't despair. If I have gained anything in life, it is a belief in the soul and the destiny of man. Out of the sea floated life. It will not return to the sea. Out of the jungle shambled a hairy man-animal and his mate whose sons would sketch the bison on the wall of the cave. Never can the jungle contain their inheritors. Out of the tribe rose the city state and the feudal village, the Magna Carta and a gathering of resolute colonials in Philadelphia. The monstrous ambitions of a Russian murderer cannot erase Thomas Jefferson's illimitable freedoms. Out of the blood sacrifice and the fear of fire and thunder came final recognition of the one merciful God and the blessedness of man's brotherhood. Man will not again embrace demonology.